PORTRAIT OF AN AMERICAN CITY

Kennikat Press
National University Publications
Interdisciplinary Urban Studies Series

General Editor
Raymond A. Mohl
Florida Atlantic University

Acquisitions Editor
Joe T. Darden
Michigan State University

PORTRAIT OF AN AMERICAN CITY

The
Novelists'
NEW YORK

Joan Zlotnick

National University Publications
KENNIKAT PRESS // 1982
Port Washington, N.Y. // London

5/1982
Soc.

For my husband, Jack,
and for our children,
Ira and Carrie

Manufactured in the United States of America

Published by
Kennikat Press Corp.
Port Washington, N.Y. / London

Library of Congress Cataloging in Publication Data

Zlotnick, Joan, 1942–
    Portrait of an American city.

    (Interdisciplinary urban studies series)
(National university publications)
    Bibliography: p.
    Includes index.
    1. American fiction—History and criticism.
2. New York (N.Y.) in literature. I. Title.
II. Series.
PS374.N43Z55   810'.9'327471   81-18660
ISBN 0-8046-9310-2   AACR2

CONTENTS

Joan Zlotnick, born and raised in New York City, a product of its schools —culminating with a doctorate from New York University—presently an associate professor of English (American Literature) at Brooklyn College, is qualified as few others to write about her (our) beloved city. She is well represented in many scholarly journals through numerous articles on American literary topics.

PORTRAIT OF AN AMERICAN CITY

ACKNOWLEDGMENTS

Much gratitude is owed to those who helped in various ways with this project. Special thanks goes to my husband, Dr. Jack Zlotnick, who was an active participant from beginning to end. His assistance with the research, his reading of the manuscript, his advice, patience, and sustained belief in the enterprise were invaluable to me.

I am also indebted to my mother, Bertha L. Nevins, who has always encouraged me in my academic pursuits and who gave unstintingly of her time to care for my children while I worked on the book.

Finally, I should like to thank Ira and Carrie, who learned to live with my deadlines; the wonderful library staff at Brooklyn College, in particular William Gargan, Andrew Garoogian, and Tesse Santoro; and Sylvia Rothberg, who typed the manuscript.

INTRODUCTION

When we think of the great cities of the Western world, London, Rome, Paris, and, of course, New York come to mind. While these European cities are many centuries old, New York, so young by contrast, has achieved stature and fame far beyond its years, and like these cities has frequently been imaginatively re-created in literature.

Chicago, Los Angeles, Boston, and other American urban centers have also served as the setting for novels and short stories, but no city has played a more important role in American fiction than New York. Indeed, the novelists and short-story writers of the past three hundred years have provided us with a record of the city that may sometimes be less accurate or objective factually than that of the historian but one that is almost always more fascinating to read. Filtered through the imagination of authors of different times, social classes, and political persuasions, described by romantics, realists, naturalists, and other categories of writers too numerous to mention, New York has seldom been just a backdrop to fiction. Whether the locale of a particular work is the southern tip of Manhattan when it was still called New Amsterdam, patrician Washington Square in the 1830s, or the Lower East Side at the turn of the century, the city itself is often an integral part of the novel's action and is frequently portrayed symbolically. What is most often felt is the importance of the city as a shaper of destinies and lives.

The importance of New York City in fiction is underscored by the large number of works about young men and women who come there in search of wealth or fame, by the many novels written about particular groups of New Yorkers whose life styles are shaped by the environment in which they have been born and raised, and, last but not least, by such novels as John Dos Passos's *Manhattan Transfer,* in which the protagonist is nothing less than the city itself.

It is surprising that the subject of New York City in fiction has received so little critical attention. Of the few books that have dealt with the subject, all but one are hopelessly outdated, and each and every one of them focuses on those places where famous authors lived and worked rather than on the city as it has been portrayed in their fiction.

While it is interesting to read about the boardinghouses and barrooms frequented by O. Henry or about the location of William Dean Howells's first New York residence, it is far more compelling to explore the ways in which writers used, portrayed, and ultimately judged New York City, which more often than not was depicted as a place of callous commercialism, of despair, corruption, and degradation. Yet there also have been many positive literary images of New York, and some of them have shown the city to be a vibrant and exciting metropolis, offering opportunity, adventure, and glamour to be found nowhere else in the nation.

At present, the increasing momentum of the "I Love New York" campaign and the proliferation of New York courses in colleges and universities has created an unprecedented interest and need for such a book as *Portrait of an American City: The Novelists' New York.* While it is hoped that the book will be useful to students enrolled in New York courses as well as to those interested in related fields such as American literature, or urban, ethnic, and American studies, it is also a work for the general public —for young people in search of a city they have never known, for old people who remember "the good old days" with nostalgia, for those whose ethnic pride may be intensified as a result of reading about any one of New York's many immigrant neighborhoods at the turn of the century, for native New Yorkers living far from the city that they still call home, and for Americans everywhere who wish to know more about America's greatest city and its literature.

Portrait of an American City, then, is a study of New York in fiction over a period of some three hundred years, an attempt to relate literary developments to historical events, and an examination of dominant themes in urban fiction. As is only appropriate, it begins at a time when what was to become New York City had yet to be settled as New Amsterdam.

1

THE COLONY AND THE EARLY REPUBLIC

Although the visit in 1524 of the Italian explorer Giovanni da Verrazano to New York Bay may have marked the beginning of the period of discovery and exploration by Europeans of what was to become New York City, it was not until a century later that any permanent settlement was established there. In 1625, some fourteen years after Henry Hudson's historic expedition up the river that now bears his name, the Dutch West India Company founded New Amsterdam as the capital of New Netherland. At its inception, the capital was little more than a trading post in the midst of a wilderness inhabited by various Indian tribes, among them the Reckagawawancs, or Manhattans.

New Amsterdam's governors included Peter Minuit, Wouter van Twiller, and Wilhelm Kieft, but the best-known of them was the last—Peter Stuyvesant. Unlike his predecessors, Peter Stuyvesant, who served as governor from 1647 to 1664, was committed not only to increasing the fur trade—the raison d'être of the colony—but also to improving the appearance of the settlement and transforming it from a trading post into a town.

With its typical dwelling of one and a half stories, with red tile roof, steeped gable, wooden shutters, and front door divided in two horizontally, New Amsterdam, which by mid-century had a population of about one thousand, soon came to resemble a Dutch village. Although Fort Amsterdam, the center of government activity, contained the governor's residence, barracks for the soldiers, and the Church of St. Nicholas, it did not afford great protection against invasion by either the Indians or the English. A wall was consequently built from river to river on the northern border of the settlement in 1653, but it was frequently in disrepair and did little to ward off attack.

In 1653, New Amsterdam became the first American city to receive a charter granting it the right of self-government, and a *Stadt Huys* (city hall) was established on Pearl Street. Trade and commerce were flourishing; a canal had been constructed on Broad Street; the cobblestones laid on all major thoroughfares and other municipal improvements had transformed New Amsterdam from a small trading post into a burgeoning town when in 1664 the British, at war with the Netherlands, seized control of the colony and renamed it New York after James, Duke of York, the brother of King Charles II.

Under British rule the town grew to a population of 25,000 and extended for more than a mile northward from the southern tip of Manhattan. The architectural flavor of the settlement also changed as more and more buildings were constructed in Georgian style. Commerce increased; seaport facilities were expanded; and amusements were many and diverse in New York under British rule. There were coffeehouses and taverns, and the arrival of Lewis Hallam's repertory company in 1753 did much to upgrade the quality of theatrical performances in the city. Although New York was more noted for its commerce and its amusements than its academic pursuits, King's College—the city's first institution of higher learning, which thirty years later was to be renamed Columbia—was established on Barclay and Murray streets in 1754.

Despite much growth and progress under British rule, obviously all was not well in New York, or for that matter, in the twelve other colonies, during the latter half of the eighteenth century. The Sugar Act (1764), the Stamp Act (1765), and other abhorrent legislation increased the friction between the colonists and the British, which finally resulted in the outbreak of the American Revolution. Soon after hostilities began, it became obvious that military action would shift from Boston to New York. Fortifications were erected throughout the city, and troops of the Continental Army filled the streets. After a number of decisive battles, the British retook New York, which remained under military occupation from 1776 to 1783.

Hardships were commonplace during the British occupation. There was severe overcrowding in the city, and the housing shortage was exacerbated by the great fire of 1776, which destroyed about a quarter of the city, leaving thousands homeless and countless buildings in ruin. There were food and fuel shortages, causing prices to soar, and many necessities could be obtained only on the black market. In sharp contrast to the misery and privation suffered by the colonists, the British military lived a lively and extravagant life.

Following the evacuation of the British in 1783, reconstruction was swift; and in January 1785, New York became the capital of the new nation. It was to remain the capital until 1790 and was to be the site of Washington's inauguration as president of the United States in 1789.

In the next decades, New York made significant gains both in population and prestige. Recognized by the turn of the century as the commercial capital of the new nation, New York could boast a population of 100,000 in 1815. By 1845, the population was 371,000, and the city, expanding northward at a rapid rate, was on its way to becoming a modern metropolis.

The fiction depicting New York in its early years is relatively scarce, and a significant portion is in the form of either fictional history or historical fiction. While fictional history is a fanciful account of historical events, historical fiction is fiction set in the distant past.

A History of New York from the Beginning of the World to the End of the Dutch Dynasty by Washington Irving, who was born and raised on William Street, belongs to the first category. It is among the finest satires ever written. With a blend of humor, irony, sentimentality, mockery, and legend, Irving, through the persona of the scholarly and eccentric Diedrich Knickerbocker, provides a delightful account of Henry Hudson's voyage, the establishment of New Amsterdam, and the British capture of the colony. He also describes life under Dutch rule, border wars, and the foibles and follies of politicians, lawyers, businessmen, and other denizens of the colony. Most important for purposes of this discussion are his descriptions of the city.

Following his account of Henry Hudson's expedition, there is a particularly memorable description of Manhattan as seen by Dutch sailors arriving in New York Harbor several years later:

Wherever the voyagers turned their eyes, a new creation seemed to bloom around. No signs of human thrift appeared to check the delicious wildness of nature, who here reveled in all her luxuriant variety. . . . Where now are seen the gay retreats of luxury,—villas half buried in twilight bowers, whence the amorous flute oft breathes the sighings of some city swain,—there the fish hawk built his solitary nest on some dry tree that overlooked his watery domain. The timid deer fed undisturbed along those shores now hallowed by the lover's moonlight walk and printed by the slender foot of beauty; and a savage solitude extended over those happy regions where now are reared the stately towers of the Joneses, the Schermerhornes [sic] and the Rhinelanders.

Included in the early part of the book are several attempts by Irving to trace the origins of particular place names. Kip's Bay, he claims, was named for the Dutch sailor Hendrick Kip, whose gun "recoiled and gave the valiant Kip an ignominious kick, which laid him prostrate with uplifted heels in the bottom of the boat" and so frightened the Indians that they quickly paddled away in their canoes. He writes also about Hell's Gate, "a narrow straight in the Sound at the distance of six miles above New York ... [which] is dangerous to shipping unless under the care of skilfull pilots, by reason of numerous rocks, shelves and whirlpools," where Commodore Van Kortlandt claimed to have seen "spectres flying in the air and heard the yelling of hobgoblins."

Most interesting is Irving's speculation about the origin of the name Manhattan. He explains that the squaws wore men's hats, and that the name may have been derived from the phrase "man-hat-on." He offers several other possibilities, including the idea that the name Manna-Hatta is derived from the word "manna," Manhattan being a land of manna, or from Manetho, a great Indian spirit who made the island his favorite abode.

Irving writes too about the landmarks of New Amsterdam such as Fort Amsterdam, "which stood on that eminence at present occupied by the custom house."[1] It was surrounded by "a progeny of little Dutch-built houses with tiled roofs and weathercocks" that nestled

under its walls for protection, as a brood of half-fledged chickens nestle under the wings of the mother hen. The whole was surrounded by an enclosure of strong palisadoes, to guard against any sudden irruption of the savages. Outside of these extended the cornfields and cabbage-gardens of the community . . . covering those tracts of country at present called Broadway, Wall Street, William Street, and Pearl Street.

There are references to other streets as well, including Dey Street, once the site of the "Peach War" that errupted in September 1655 after Hendrick Van Dyck killed a squaw attempting to steal fruit from his orchard. About two thousand Indians ran through town, looting, destroying property, and terrifying the settlers. Many injuries and a number of fatalities resulted.

The contrasts between nineteenth-century New York and New Amsterdam are vivid, particularly as seen in Irving's description of Broadway:

The busy hum of multitudes, the shouts of revelry, the rumbling equipages of fashion, the rattling of accursed carts, and all the spirit-grieving sounds of brawling commerce, were unknown in the settlement of New Amsterdam. The grass grew quietly in the highways; the bleating sheep and frolicsome calves sported about the verdant ridge, where now the Broadway loungers take their morning stroll; the cunning fox or ravenous wolf skulked in the woods, where are now to be seen the dens of . . . moneybrokers. . . .

A similar contrast is found in Irving's account of a walk in Battery Park, named for the battery of cannon once mounted along what is now the sidewalk opposite the Custom House:

Where the government house by name, but the custom-house by occupation, proudly reared its brick walls and wooden pillars, there whilome stood the low but substantial red-tiled mansion of the renowned Wouter Van Twiller. Around it the mighty bulwarks of Fort Amsterdam frowned defiance to every absent foe; but like many a whiskered warrior and gallant militia captain, confined their martial deeds to frowns alone. The mud breastworks had long been levelled with the earth, and their site converted into the green lawns and leafy alleys of the battery; where the gay apprentice sported his Sunday coat, and the laborious mechanic, relieved from the dirt and drudgery of the week, poured his weekly tale of love into the half-averted ear of the sentimental chambermaid.

Elsewhere Irving writes that the Battery, "though ostensibly devoted to the stern purposes of war, has ever been consecrated to the sweet delights of peace," and describes it as the scene of the child's gambol, the lover's assignation, the merchant's Sunday refreshment, and the elderly's healthful stroll: in short, "the ornament and delight of New York—and the pride of the lovely island of Manna-hatta."

Whether he is describing the Bowery or Broadway, mocking the Dutch Governors Wilhelm Kieft (William the Testy) or Peter Stuyvesant (Peter the Headstrong), recounting tales of border wars or describing "how the town of New Amsterdam arose out of mud, and came to be marvelously polished and polite," Irving's wildly imaginative history of Knickerbocker New York is a delight to read and well deserving of its designation as a classic in American literature.

Manhattan Acres by Virginia Watson is scarcely a classic, yet this chronicle of the Van Kampen family from 1647 to 1933 provides a fascinating picture of the city in its infancy. There is, early in the book, a long and vivid description of New Amsterdam in 1647, when it was a tiny settlement on the southern tip of Manhattan Island:

Fort Amsterdam was the center whorl from which the three unpaved streets curved northward, De Herre Straet to the west; De Herre Graft—which was in truth a water street, or canal; and De Perel Straet that bordered the river on the east. A few smaller streets and lanes crossed these and ran approximately east and west. . . .

The houses of the burghers served two purposes, as homes and as stores and offices. Some of them had notched rooflines or stepped gables, and the use of wood was giving way to brick, so that more and more of the streets were beginning to resemble Haarlem, Amsterdam, Leyden, and other cities of the Netherlands. There was a ferry which . . . transported passengers to Breucklyn for a few strings of wampum. There was a grist mill in the Fort and [there were] several taverns. . . . The northern end of the town was undefined. . . .[2]

In the second chapter, dated 1664, Watson writes about "the wall at the north end of town," which had been constructed in New Amsterdam more than a decade earlier to protect against Indian and English invasions, and describes other developments in New Amsterdam, boasting that there were now 296 houses in the town, "not to speak of the bouweries and farms beyond the Wall."

Further growth is recorded in the next chapter, dated 1697. With a population of almost five thousand, the town was flourishing. Food was plentiful; housing, comfortable; and the fur trade, brisk, with trappers selling their pelts on Browers Straet and Het Cingle.[3] Centrally located between New England, New Jersey, Pennsylvania, and Maryland, New York could be likened to "a merchant with a counter at both ends of his shop, passing goods from the customers who entered his northern door to trade to those who laid their money on the counter at the southern end," and New Yorkers, proud of their expanding shipping facilities and ever-growing transatlantic trade, could boast that "forty square-rigged vessels, sixty-two sloops, and as many boats were entered at the New York Custom House in one year."

By 1747, a "century and a quarter since Minuit's little colony dug their cellars and built up their palisades very much like beavers, which the city commemorated when it chose that creature for its totem," the village had undergone many changes. Its population having steadily increased until "more than ten thousand names stood on the city records," New York was expanding not only to the north but also to the east and west. In 1730, Greenwich and Washington streets were laid out on the west, and houses were built where "once eels and lobsters had been washed up by the tide." Several years later, Pearl Street, also known as Great Queen Street, was built out along the East River.[4]

Other changes had taken place as well. In addition to the steeple of the Dutch Reformed Church of St. Nicholas, the steeples "of Trinity, the Lutheran church, the New Dutch Church, the French Eglise du Saint Esprit, and the Old Dutch church" could be seen, and "the gabled and corbeled rooflines of the old burgher houses were now broken by the flatter, squarer, simpler lines of English builders." The number of inns had increased, and

the dark Tenier-like interiors of the older taverns competed unsuccessfully with the fresher aspect and larger windows of the Blue Boar, the Three

Pigeons in Smith Street, Dog's Head-in-the-Porridge Pot, and, in particular, the Merchants' Coffee House at the corner of Wall and Water Streets.[5]

Watson also depicts the fashions and amusements of the period as well as markets such as the Oswego Market[6] on Broadway that "was the largest and the favorite for Dutch housewives, keepers of ordinaries, and slaves" who did the marketing for such distinguished families as the Livingstons and the De Lanceys.

Watson treats the American Revolution in some depth and in chapter five writes about the statue of George III on Bowling Green, dedicated in August 1770 and "melted down for "bullets for patriot guns" when the Declaration of Independence was proclaimed,[7] as well as about the fire of 1776 that destroyed Trinity Church and many other landmarks in downtown Manhattan.[8] Watson's portrait of New York during the revolutionary period includes descriptions of Bloomingdale Road,[9] Hanover Square,[10] Harlem Heights,[11] the Theatre Royal on John Street, where during the British occupation General Howe's officers often took part in the productions, and Black Sam's Tavern,[12] which is still in operation today as Fraunces Tavern.

Throughout the chronicle the history of the Van Kampen family is foremost in the author's mind. In chapter six, 1831, the Van Kampens live on State Street, facing St. John's Park,[13] in what was then considered "the best spot of the city." The marriage of John Van Kampen to an Irish immigrant introduces a new dimension into the book, and Watson now writes about St. Peter's, "the oldest and largest Roman Catholic church in the city," which was erected shortly after the Revolutionary War, and about St. Paul's, where Washington worshipped on his Inaugural Day. There are also descriptions of Cherry Street, once the exceedingly fashionable address of President Washington and John Hancock, but now badly deteriorated and inhabited by poor Irish immigrants.

Subsequent chapters describe, among other things, changing neighborhoods, the northward expansion of the city, the establishment of elegant hotels and restaurants uptown, Tammany politics, the draft riots of 1863, the marble mansions that lined Fifth Avenue in the 1890s, the Jazz Age in New York, and in the final chapter Adrian Van Kampen views the city from the top of the newly erected Empire State Building. Since our concern here, however, is not with the modern metropolis but with New York in its early days, let us turn to Louis Zara's *Blessed Is The Land,* a fascinating novel about the first Jewish settlers in New Amsterdam.

Based on a true story, *Blessed Is The Land* is about a group of thirty-six Jews expelled from Brazil by the Portuguese, brutalized by Spanish pirates, and barely tolerated by Peter Stuyvesant, who did not wish to have Jews in New Amsterdam. Zara's novel is a moving story of the perseverance of these Jews, in particular of Ashur Levy, and of their eventual acceptance by the Dutch.

The novel, which opens in 1654 and closes in 1681, not only is the story of this small band of beleagured Jews, but also is a record of life in New Amsterdam, for while Zara describes trapping and trading expeditions and visits to settlements like Breuckelen, Midwout, Amersfoort, and Gravesend,[14] most of the action is set on the southern tip of Manhattan.

First impressions are disappointing:

Beyond a crude dock, on the narrow island at the head of the bay, rose a settlement so minute we could take it all in at a glance: the poor fort with its few brass cannon planted on the sod ramparts, a wooden belfry, the gallows, the whipping post, stonehouses with gables and corbie-steps, barns, open sheds, streets, orchards, tilled fields, and pasture lands with sheep and cattle.

The tiny, primitive settlement is not Amsterdam and it is not Recife, yet after their terrible ordeal the Jews are grateful to be there. They recite the Kaddish—the Jewish memorial prayer—for relatives and friends who did not survive the journey, implore God to bless the land, and without delay began their long and arduous struggle to find acceptance among the Dutch.

Zara depicts the arrogant and despotic Stuyvesant, so hostile to the Jews, and the rule of Colonel Richard Nicholls, who was more sympathetic to their cause, but his portrayal of New Amsterdam is not limited to the Jewish community and its concerns; it includes descriptions of the slave auctions at Schroeyer's Hook;[15] the Indian uprising of 1655, also known as the Peach War, and one of the numerous Indian insurrections that occurred between 1643 and 1655; and of the Marckveldt, or Market Place. Here at the cattle bridge crossing the Herre Graft (a drainage and shipping canal), which today is the site of Tiny Marketfield Street, the settlers gathered every Friday morning to buy and sell goods. Zara also writes about the Stadt Huys, the Dutch seat of colonial government, established in 1653 in the City Tavern, New Amsterdam's first hotel; Het Maagde Paatje, or Maiden Lane, where young girls washed clothes on the bank of a stream; and Bowling Green, located just around the corner from the Battery, which was a cattle market under the Dutch, a parade ground for troops under the British, and the city's first park.

In short, Ashur Levy's diary provides the reader with a vivid account of the city's expansion and prosperity over a period of almost thirty years. In an entry dated 1678, Ashur marvels at the rapid growth that has taken place in the fourteen years since the British conquest. With its population of three thousand, "excluding New Harlem, which is north of us and under its own charter," he predicts that soon "New York may become as populous as Recife" and anticipates further commercial development now that the canal has been filled in and the streets are being paved:

The *graft* has been filled in. The land thus recovered is more valuable than the foul ditch in the side of the island. To supply water against fires, six wells are being dug. The English are not as clean as the Dutch. Where we older families dwell, the housewives still wash the outer walls, and scrub the corbie-steps.

In '58 Brewer Street (formerly Brouwer), was paved with stones, but for many years thereafter not another street was improved. Now there is an eagerness to pave, though this requires increased taxes. . . .

If the changes are useful to trade, as surely they are, then all must give before them good-naturedly, including the dead. The Christian burial-ground on Heerstreat—or Broad Way now—has been removed; the remains were carefully taken up, and laid down again in the new cemetery. The lots were sold by public outcry. In three or four years, if the city continues to expand, our Beth Haim [the Jewish cemetery] will have to be moved.

By this time Ashur Levy is no longer an impoverished outcast but a wealthy and respected burgher, and the Jewish settlers have gone far in their struggle to eradicate prejudice and discrimination from New Amsterdam. The varieties of prejudice, however, are many, and its roots run deep. In *With Cradle and Clock* Knud Stowman depicts the struggle of a young physician to conquer another, quite different form of prejudice found in New York during the early eighteenth century.

With Cradle and Clock deals with Jonathan Kent's struggle against those who believed that only midwives should deliver babies. An outcast from society because of his unconventional views, he lives in an abandoned cottage in the northward reaches of the city behind the site of what is the present City Hall Park, at that time a swampy and undeveloped no-man's-land:

A few pushing landowners apart, all New Yorkers agreed . . . that the swampy area in the fork between the two budding highways [Broadway and the Boston Post Road] was no man's land and every man's land. West of Broadway, which ended blind in a rope walk, were the King's farms and east of the Boston Road the fashionable boweries of wealthy Dutch families clustered around the Stuyvesant manor. But on the Common grazed the cattle of those who had no bowery, and beyond, along the eastern shore of the central Fresh Water Pond, huddled the tanneries, fulsome outcasts from a redolent city. Expanding northward, the city had pushed into this mire, once an idyllic marsh, elements obnoxious for their fetor, poverty, or ill-repute, among them the gallows, the whipping post, the poorhouse, the Negro cemetery, and the powder house.[16]

Stowman describes other New York locations as well, including Dock Street, which had been transformed from a fashionable residential street to a commercial one, and the new City Hall on Wall Street, erected when the old Stadt Huys on Pearl Street became too dangerous to occupy. He writes too about the poor medical facilities in the city in the early eighteenth century, the outbreak of a yellow-fever epidemic in 1702 that caused many residents to flee to Jamaica,[17] and the disgrace of Governor Cornbury, who was dismissed from office and put in debtor's prison in 1708.

Above all, the city is portrayed by Stowman as growing in size, numbers, and sophistication. At one point in the novel, Jonathan describes the city as "happy because it is young and growing. . . . It has space, broad rivers and virgin forests all around." The Reverend Vesey worries that they have built Trinity Church too small, and the last sentence in the book—which is as much about the birth and growth of a city as it is about the delivery of babies—reads, "One by one, New York is mounting to its ordained growth."

Another historical novel of some interest is *Anna Zenger: Mother of Freedom* by Kent Cooper. The book, which opens in 1721, is about the founding of the first "free" newspaper in New York.[18] Although it was Anna Zenger's husband, John, who was imprisoned, tried, and finally acquitted for his "illegal" acts, the book makes it clear that it was Anna who fought most vigorously for freedom of the press in the New World.

The book opens with a description of the city on a spring morning in 1721, when the sun "sent its warm slanting rays over His Britannic Majesty's little city of New York" and a bugle sounded reveille in Fort Amsterdam, now renamed Fort George:

In the narrow winding streets that led down to the East River, all lined with little white cottages, life commenced to stir. In the mansions of Broad Street and the Broad Way African slaves began their menial labors. Dogs barked at the carts that rattled over streets rudely paved with stone.

Accurate in his descriptions of Broad Street and Broadway, which in the early eighteenth century were fashionable residential streets, Cooper goes on to write about Broadway at night when it was "dimly lighted by the new ordinance . . . that every sixth house be granted a small payment to maintain a light on a six foot pole extending from an upper story out into the street."[19] Elsewhere he records the impressions of Harrison, an Englishman who had recently arrived in New York:

He truly believed that no other city in the world had been born as quickly and had drawn into itself such a variety of inhabitants. It had been a melting pot from its discovery a hundred years before. The Dutch predominated through the nineteenth century, and their descendants still formed one-third of the inhabitants of the island. Next in numbers were the English, followed by Palatine Germans sent over by Queen Anne at the beginning of the eighteenth century. Then there were Danes, Portuguese, French, and Spanish, with various religious faiths—Catholic, Protestant, and Jewish.

He was finding the place at once interesting and indescribable. . . . Here in New York he had heard in one day as many as eight languages, a babel as confused as the tangle of the little byways or streets that intersected the great Broad Street which he was traversing: Garden Street, Princess Street, Duke Street, and Mill Street.[20]

While Harrison recognized the importance of trade to New York, he also believed that it was

something more than a mere frontier trading community. With a singular mixture of peoples from so many European nations, the class distinctions were many but the incentive of all was wealth! Because of this, the port had become a great mart and clearing house the like of which, for a city of six thousand white inhabitants, did not exist anywhere else in the world.

Anna Zenger contains many more interesting passages about life in colonial New York, but like Virginia Watson, Louis Zara, and Knud Stowman, Kent Cooper is not a major writer. Perhaps the most fascinating treatment of New York City prior to the nineteenth century by an important American novelist is found in *Satanstoe,* the first volume of the Littlepage trilogy by James Fenimore Cooper, a gentleman farmer from Scarsdale who lived in New York City from 1822 to 1826.

An author whose fame is based more on his Leatherstocking series than on the relatively unknown Littlepage novels, Cooper nevertheless achieved an unusual effect in *Satanstoe.* Because Cornelius Littlepage, the first-person narrator, is writing in 1775 about events that took place in the 1750s and because the author, writing a century later, adds footnotes to describe changes that have occurred since the Revolution, the novel presents a particularly rich and multilayered portrait of the city at three different times in its history.

Littlepage describes, for example, a trip he took to New York City in 1751 when he was a college student:

New York was certainly not the place in 1751 it is to-day; nevertheless it was a large and important town even, when I went to college, containing not less than twelve thousand souls, blacks included. The Town Hall is a magnificent structure, standing at the head of Broad Street. . . . I could hardly admire that fine edifice sufficiently; which, for size, architecture and position, has scarcely now an equal in all the colonies. It is true, that the town has much improved within the last twenty years; but York was a noble place, even in the middle of this century.[21]

Littlepage can barely contain his enthusiasm for Broadway, which then extended for a full quarter of a mile, beginning at Bowling Green and continuing north to Wall Street, and is full of praise for Trinity Church, which, located at the head of Wall Street, appears to him "a monument of pious zeal and cultivated taste."

In a footnote, Cooper brings the reader up to date on the history of Trinity Church and also comments on Littlepage's "provincial admiration" of the edifice:

The intelligent reader will, of course, properly appreciate the admiration of Mr. Littlepage, who naturally fancied his own best was other people's best. The Trinity of that day was burned in the great fire of 1776. The edifice that succeeded it at the peace of 1783, has already given place to a successor, that has more claim to be placed on a level with modern English town church-architecture, than any other building in the Union. When another shall succeed this, which shall be as much larger and more elaborated than this is, compared to its predecessor, and still another shall succeed, which shall bear the same relation to that, then the country will possess an edifice that is on a level with the first-rate Gothic cathedral-architecture of Europe.[22]

The provincial youth is also impressed by "the magnificence of the shops, particularly the silversmiths'; some of which must have had a thousand dollars worth of plate in their windows," and by the taverns, especially the popular Burns' City Arms, situated "at the head of Broadway" in the former town house of Stephen DeLancey.

Writing about a visit to New York City several years later, Littlepage describes the journey from Westchester, explaining that

we might have gone into town by the way of Bloomingdale, Greenwich, the [Lispenard] meadows, and the Collect, and so down past the common upon the head of Broadway; but my mother had particularly desired we would fall into the Bowery Lane, passing the seats that are to be found in that quarter, and getting into Queen Street as soon as possible. By taking this course she thought we should be less likely to miss our way within the town itself, which is certainly full of narrow and intricate passages. . . . Queen Street, indeed, is the great artery of New York, through which most of its blood circulates.

Arriving in town, he found that

New York was certainly, even in 1757, a wonderful place for commerce! Vessels began to be seen some distance east of the Fly Market, and there could not have been fewer than twenty ships, brigs, and schooners, lying in the East River, as we walked down Queen Street.

As for other forms of transportation,

carriages, certainly, were not as common in 1757 as they have since become; but most of our distinguished people rode in their coaches, chariots, or phaetons, or conveyances of some sort or another, when there was occasion to go so far out of the town as the Common, which is the site of the present [city hall] "Park."

Beyond the Common were many country estates, and Cooper refers to several of these, including one belonging to Mr. Speaker Nicolls, the patentee of Islip and a relative of Richard Nicolls, the first English governor of the colony. Cooper describes the house, located "a short distance above the present Union Square, and not far from that of the present Gramercy,"[23] and speculates that if still standing, it "must now be one of the oldest buildings of any sort, in a town of 400,000 souls!"

Satanstoe also contains an extensive account of New York theatre in the mid-eighteenth century. Littlepage writes about Lewis Hallam's celebrated company, the liveried servants who retained choice seats until their masters arrived at the theatre, and "the ornaments, and the lights, and the curtain, the pit, the boxes, the gallery . . . [and] the musicians, [among whom] were amateurs from the army and the drawing rooms of the town."

The procession to the theatre—for it was the custom to walk to dinners and to the theatre because the narrow streets were inconvenient for carriages—is also described:

Instead of going directly down Crown street, into Maiden Lane . . . we went out into Broadway, and round by Wall street, the walking being better, and the gutters farther from the ladies; the centre of the street being at no great distance from the houses, in the narrower passages of the town. We found a great many well-dressed people moving in the same direction with ourselves.

The procession to the theatre, however colorful, did not impress Littlepage as much as the promenade of fashionably dressed young people that took place twice each day—morning and evening—on Trinity Church Mall:

The bands of different regiments were stationed in the churchyard, and the company were often treated to much fine martial music. Some few of the more scrupulous objected to this desecration of the church-yard, but the army had everything pretty much in its own way. . . .

I dare say there were fifty young ladies promenading the church-walk when I reached it, and nearly as many young men in attendance on them; no small portion of the last being scarlet-coats. . . . As no one presumed to promenade the Mall who was not of a certain stamp of respectability, the company were all gayly dressed.

From the Mall, Littlepage had an overview of the city, beginning with Broadway, which he claims will one day "be the pride of the western world." He describes its increasing width as it opened into Bowling Green, as well as the fort and bay that lie beyond, and then goes on to describe the view in the other direction, which he admits "was not so remarkable, the houses being principally of wood, and of a somewhat ignoble appearance." There, beyond the Common,

all was inland, and rural. It is true, the new Bridewell had been erected in that quarter, and there was also a new jail, both facing the Common; and the king's troops had barracks in their rear; but high, abrupt, conical hills, with low marshy lands, orchards and meadows, gave to all that portion of the island a peculiarly novel and somewhat picturesque character. Many of the hills in that quarter, and indeed all over the widest part of the island, are now surmounted by country-houses, as some were then, including . . . that farm which, by being called after the old Dutch govern-nor's [Stuyvesant's] retreat, has given the name of Bowery, or Bouerie, to the road that led to it. . . .

But the reader can imagine for himself the effect produced by such a street as Broadway, reaching very nearly half a mile in length, terminating at one end, in an elevated, commanding fort, with its background of batteries, rocks, and bay, and at the other with the Common, on which troops were now constantly parading, the Bridewell and jail, and the novel scene I have just mentioned.[24]

While *Satanstoe* depicts the city in greatest detail and at several different periods in its history, other works by Cooper are also set, at least in part, in New York. Among them are *Homeward Bound* and its sequel, *Home as Found,* both of which deal with the contrasts between Europe and New York in the first half of the nineteenth century.

Toward the end of *Homeward Bound* Madamoiselle Viefville, a French visitor to the city, and her companions, who are returning home after a long absence, view Manhattan from their ship. While Madamoiselle Viefville expects little of this provincial city and is pleasantly surprised by what she sees, her companions are clearly disappointed.

As their ship passes through the Narrows, Mr. Effingham comments on the "meanness and poverty in the view," and we learn that his daughter is "too fresh from the gorgeous coast of Italy to be in ecstacies with the meagre villages and villas that more or less lined the bay of New York." Later, Mr. Effingham says that the city is "mean in appearance rather than imposing and so decidedly provincial as not to possess a single feature of a capital." Fault is also found with the Battery, "for it had neither the extent and magnificence of a park nor the embellishment and luxurious shade of a garden," and with Broadway, deserted and disappointing, despite its worldwide fame.

Some defense of New York is offered. It is argued, for example, that

thirty years since it was meaner and more provincial than it is today. A century hence it will begin to resemble an English town. . . . This town today contains near three hundred thousand souls, two-thirds of whom are in truth emigrants from the interior of our own or of some foreign country; and such a collection of people cannot in a day give a town any other character than that which belongs to themselves. It is not a crime to be provincial and rustic; it is only ridiculous to fancy yourselves other-wise, when the fact is apparent.

Contrasts between Europe and New York are also discussed at length in *Home as Found,* in which the characters analyze differences in social forms, customs, and even architecture. Particular streets and neighbor-hoods are described, among them Hudson Square, which

the lovers of the grandiose are endeavoring to call St. John's Park; for it is rather an amusing peculiarity among a certain portion of the emigrants who have flocked into the Middle States within the last thirty years, that they are not satisfied with permitting any family or thing to possess the name it originally enjoyed, if there exists the least opportunity to change it.

In this novel Cooper writes about Wall Street, one of the first fashion-able downtown residential streets to give way to commerce, the Merchants' Exchange, one of its most prominent buildings, and the great fire of December 1835 that began in a warehouse at Pearl and Hanover streets and destroyed hundreds of buildings on seventeen blocks, including the Merchants' Exchange and many other important commercial establish-ments. Although he does at times depict New York as socially and aesthetically inferior to Europe, Cooper does not fail to acknowledge its importance as a thriving commercial center.

While Cooper's contrast is between wealthy New Yorkers and their European counterparts, the two remaining books to be discussed in this chapter deal with contrasts between New York's affluent and impoverished classes. *Charlotte: A Tale of Truth* by Susanna Haswell Rowson is about a fifteen-year-old English girl, Charlotte Temple, who elopes to New York with a British army officer and is left pregnant and penniless to fend for herself in the heartless city, and George Lippard's *New York: Its Upper Ten and Lower Million* is, as its title implies, a book about the city's haves and have-nots.

Much critical attention has been centered about the claim that Rowson's novel, published in 1791, is based on the true story of Charlotte Stanley, the daughter of an English clergyman, who eloped with John Montrésor in 1774. Already married, Montrésor is said to have lived with his family on Montrésor's Island, today known as Randall's Island.

Whether or not the story is based on fact, there is a tombstone in Trinity churchyard bearing the name of Charlotte Temple. Charlotte's father is said to have arrived in New York in time to bury his daughter there, and when Rowson came to America in 1793 and visited the grave-site, the tombstone supposedly still bore the name of Charlotte Stanley. Because parish records were destroyed in the fire of 1776 and because the inscription plate on the tomb long ago disappeared, questions remain about the authenticity of the inscription, which at the time of the construction of the new building in 1846 was changed to Charlotte Temple.

The novel itself offers very little description of the city. We learn that upon their arrival in New York, Montraville, unmarried but in other respects presumably modeled after John Montrésor, established Charlotte "in a small house a few miles from New York"—thought to be located on what is now the corner of Pell and Doyers streets—and there is a description of Charlotte's arduous journey by foot to the city to have her baby. She meets her end there, having been taken in by the servant of a wealthy and influential "friend" who has rejected her pleas for help.

George Lippard, a self-styled social critic, would appear to have been concerned with the likes of Charlotte Temple. Despite the surfeit of melodrama in his novel about heirs who in their contention for a fortune are involved in kidnapping, murder, suicide, orgies, and abortions, he claims to be a realist, explaining that the horrors that occur in the book are "horrors, not born of romance, but of that under-current of real-life, which rolls on evermore, beneath the glare and uproar of the Empire City."

Lippard writes at length about the city's downtrodden, among them a seamstress who, after having been cheated out of her wages by the proprietor of a Canal Street shirt store, makes her way home to a tenement apartment:

Poor girl! Down Broadway, until the Park is passed, and the huge Astor House glares out upon the darkness from its hundred windows. Down Broadway, until you reach the unfinished pile of Trinity Church, where heaps of lumber and rubbish appear among white tombstones. Turn from Broadway and stride this narrow street which leads to the dark river: your home is here.

Back of Trinity Church, in Greenwich Street, we believe, there stands on this December night a four storied edifice, tenanted only a few years ago, by a wealthy family. . . .

The cellar is [now] the home of ten families.

The first floor is occupied as a beer "saloon;" you can hear men getting drunk in three or four languages, if you will stand by the window for a moment.

Twenty persons live on the second floor.

Fifteen make their home on the third floor.

The fourth floor is tenanted by nineteen human beings.

The garret is divided into four apartments, one of these has a garret-window to itself, and this is the home of the poor girl.[25]

Living in "that palace of rags and wretchedness," her plight is only slightly less desperate than that of the streetwalker Lippard writes about later, who is

a tenant of one of the houses owned by Trinity Church. She is out in the cold, dark night—the poor blasted thing you see her,—seeking, out of the hire of her pollution, to swell the revenues of Trinity Church.

He also describes the Five Points, one of the city's most notorious slums, where strollers are

confronted at every step by a desperate or abandoned wretch, their ears filled with the cries of blasphemy, starvation and mirth,—mirth that was very much like the joy of nethermost hell.

Whether he is describing Broadway or the Battery, the Astor House or the warehouses along the East River, a brothel or the infamous den of Madame Reismer the abortionist,[26] Lippard's theme is the indifference and heartlessness of the rich and the abuses of the clergy in a city he describes as a battlefield "in which millions are battling every moment of the hour . . . for fame, for wealth, for bread, for life."

This image of New York City as a battlefield is one that recurs any number of times in the fiction of the next one hundred and twenty-five years.

2

THE EMERGING METROPOLIS

Readers familiar with nineteenth-century fiction who may have been expecting to read about the great American writers Poe, Hawthorne, and Melville either in the previous chapter or in this one will be surprised to find that none of the fiction by Poe or Hawthorne and only a few of Melville's minor works are discussed. Poe's stories rarely took place in identifiable American cities, and the setting for Hawthorne's tales and novels was frequently Italy or New England, but almost always, what counted far more than the exterior setting was the inner landscape, the world of the imagination, the dream or hallucination that was so compelling in their works. Melville's great fiction was of course set on the mighty, symbolic sea. Clearly, the city at mid-century was not the most fertile soil for the dark and brooding romantic imagination.

The New York fiction of this period is for the most part realistic rather than romantic. Unlike the romantics, the realists, who by the sixties, seventies, and eighties were part of the dominant literary tradition, found in New York City a rich vein of material, and their fiction portrays in great detail a growing, thriving, and vital city pushing its way northward at a rapid rate.

In 1840 the population of New York City was three hundred thousand; by 1860 it was eight hundred thousand, the tremendous growth due in large measure to the Irish and German immigrations which occurred as a result of the potato famine in Ireland and of political eruptions in Europe. To accommodate its growing numbers, the city expanded northward, and by mid-century was already built up past Union Square. Fifth Avenue, which as late as the eighteen forties had been a deserted, muddy road, was now the most fashionable residential street in the city, and soon Gramercy

Park would also become a prime residential area. Farther uptown there were country estates and farmland, but that region, too, would soon change, for the plans to develop Central Park—work on the park began in 1857—encouraged real-estate speculation as far uptown as the forties and fifties. Business in the city had also greatly increased, and Broadway was the city's most developed commercial avenue. The city's first department store—Stewart's—was erected on Broadway in 1846, and many other fashionable shops, hotels, and restaurants were located there. Broadway had become such a prominent street that by mid century, there were few unbuilt lots left below Union Square.

The educational, cultural, and transportation facilities of New York were also growing, and many luxuries, such as indoor plumbing and central heating, were beginning to be found in its wealthier residences. The city, however, was to undergo even more rapid and dramatic changes within the next few decades. The Civil War and its aftermath, the completion of Central Park, the growth and development of the railroads, the advent of Tammany Hall politics, the growth of unions, and the great migrations of Jews from Eastern Europe are only a few of the factors that would greatly alter New York as it continued to expand northward.

The fiction of the period provides an excellent record of the growth of the city, which began in the lower part of Manhattan and gradually pushed northward. This is especially true of four works, all of which are set—at least in their opening pages—before mid-century, but which trace the development of New York over several decades. These books are H.C. Bunner's *The Story of a New York House,* Edgar Fawcett's *A New York Family,* Edith Wharton's *Old New York,* and Henry James's *Washington Square.*

Bunner's novel is quite literally the story of a house that was purchased in 1807 and demolished to make way for a factory some seventy years later. The history of the house is no less than the history of the city, and it begins with Jacob Dolph's desire to buy a house in which his descendents can someday live, for he has become convinced that the house he is now living in on State Street[1] will not be suitable for that purpose:

He had watched the growth of trade; he knew the room for further growth; he had noticed the long converging lines of river-front with their unbounded accommodation for wharves and slips. He believed that the day would come—and his own boy might see it—when the business of the city would crowd the dwelling-houses from the river side, east and west, as far, maybe, as Chambers street.

And he had felt appalled that the back of the new City hall had been built of cheap red sandstone rather than of marble, because it was believed that few "would ever look down on it from above Chambers street."[2]

There is a wonderful sequence of scenes describing Dolph's walk to the country, where he intends to build his new house. He passes "the poplar-studded Battery," where he "kept on bowing, for half the town was out, taking the fresh morning for marketing and all manner of shopping." Continuing his stroll northward, he

went across the hill where Grand Street crosses Broadway, and up past what . . . today is Houston Street, and then turned down a straggling road that ran east and west. He walked toward the Hudson and passed a farmhouse or two, and came to a place where there were no trees, and only a few tangled bushes and ground-vines.

Upon his return to the city, Dolph meets up with Abram Van Riper. The conservative Dutch merchant, who lives on Pine Street, taunts him, "What's this I hear about you building a preposterous tomfool of a town-house out by Greenwich? . . . You haven't got this crazy notion that New York's going to turn into London while you smoke your pipe, have you?"

In spite of Van Riper's scorn, the house is built, and the Dolphs maintain two residences until 1822, when the outbreak of a severe yellow-fever epidemic in the city forces them to close the State Street house. That epidemic was to have a great impact on the development of the "uptown" area, turning Washington Square and its environs into a highly desirable residential neighborhood by the mid-thirties. The movement uptown had already begun before the outbreak of the epidemic, and even the conservative Van Riper now realizes that his Pine Street address is no longer fashionable.

Commercial development had changed the downtown area, and some wealthy families had begun to build farther uptown. The outbreak of the epidemic in lower New York merely hastened the inevitable process. As people fled the city in ever-increasing numbers, hastily constructed wooden houses to accommodate the newcomers sprang up in the Greenwich area. A number of families moved back downtown after the epidemic was over, but enough remained so that what had been country soon became citified.

Bunner describes in detail the exodus from the city during the epidemic of 1822:

In every house, in every office and shop, there was hasty packing, mad confusion, and wild flight. . . . Wagons and carts creaked and rambled and rattled through every street, piled high with household chattels, up-heaped in blind haste. Women rode on the swaying loads, or walked beside with the smaller children in their arms. Men bore heavy burdens, and children helped according to their strength. . . . To most of these poor creatures the only haven seemed Greenwich Village. . . .

The panic was not only among the poor and the ignorant. Merchants were moving their offices, and even the Post Office and the Custom House were to be transferred to Greenwich.

Years later, after old Jacob Dolph is dead and his son and namesake must sell some of the "uptown" property, he is advised by Van Riper's son to wait if he can, because the price of land in Greenwich is still rising. Indeed, by the 1850s, Bleecker Street had become the dividing line between the fashionable and the unfashionable:

Above Bleecker Street, the cream of the cream rose to the surface; below, you were ranked as skim milk. The social world was spreading up into the wastes sacred to the circus and the market-garden. . . . But the old families still fought the tide of trade, many of them neck-deep and very uncomfortable. They would not go from St. John's Park, nor from North Moore and Grand Streets. . . . They resented the up-town movement, and resisted it. So that when they did have to buy lots in the high-numbered streets, they had to pay a fine price for them.

Jacob Dolph is able to hold on to his father's house only until the panic of 1873, caused by the manipulation of the gold market by multimillionaires Jim Fisk and Jay Gould. He manages, however, to visit the property from time to time thereafter and is witness to its deterioration:

First it was rented, by its new owner, to the Jewish pawnbroker, with his numerous family. Good, honest folk they were, who tried to make the house look fine. . . . Then it was a cheap boarding house, and vulgar and flashy men and women swarmed out in the morning and in at eventide. Then it was a lodging house, and shabby people let themselves in at all hours of the day and night. And last of all it had become a tenement house, and had fallen into line with its neighbors to left and right, and the window-panes were broken, and the curse of misery and poverty and utter degradation had fallen upon it.

At last the house is demolished to make room for an eight-story factory, and the story of a house, a neighborhood, and a city's growth over some seventy years is completed.

Although its title focuses on a family rather than on a house, *A New York Family* by Edgar Fawcett is as much a history of the city's growth and its changing neighborhoods as is Bunner's novel. The book traces the economic rise and decline of the Everards, and the houses and neighborhoods to which they move are emblems of their changing status. Frederick Everard is a German immigrant who starting out as a grocer in Hoboken, eventually becomes a wealthy and respected merchant with a flourishing business on Grand Street, which at that time was "a popular and fashionable center" noted for its dry-goods and clothing stores. He also owns a small house on nearby Henry Street:

> The Everards were now living . . . with a mode and tone that neighbors who put rights of caste well above theirs did not more than just appreciably excel. A few of the Amsterdam or Van Corelaar stock, doubtless, dwelt nearby, but clad their contiguity with no patrician signs. . . . People in Montgomery, Frankfort, and other streets close at hand, got to know and exchange visits with them. Even the aristocratic realm of East Broadway did not withhold at least a partial heed. . . . The whole being said, no family held its head higher than the Everards. If the sneer was passed upon them that they were retail grocers, they did not know it; and, perhaps, it was rarely passed.

Some years later, however, the neighborhood uptown property became increasingly desirable:

> Some of the best shops were quitting Grand Street and the lower Bowery and were ranging their windows along Broadway. Frankfort, Montgomery, Henry, and other near streets were swiftly losing vogue. . . . Second Avenue had failed as the life-teeming thoroughfare prophecy named it. Bond Street was held more attractive, and Prince, Broome, Bleecker, Amity, and Houston Streets were each full of spacious private abodes. Grace Church . . . rose a stately sentinel at the upper end of Broadway; but already Union Square, so brief a distance beyond it, was flanked with buildings that roofed citizens of wealth and worth. From the centre of University Place you could still see both Hudson and East Rivers flash between the infrequent structures on either side, but every month was lending a new impediment to these delightful outlooks.

Everard, like Jacob Dolph, realizes that the city is rapidly moving northward and decides to buy a house in the country—on Seventeenth Street, between Fifth and Sixth avenues. He is firmly convinced that the area "won't be country long." He tells his dubious partner that there are many "big merchants from Water Street" who live as far uptown as Astor Place and that his property "isn't more than half a mile further up." He goes on to explain, "It *is* pretty rustic in those parts, I allow; but they've got street lamps along the empty lots, and they've promised soon to pave Fifth Avenue all the way to Twenty-third Street." While his partner concedes that some portions of Fifth Avenue are already habitable—and indeed, from Washington Parade Ground (as Washington Square was then called) to Ninth or Tenth streets, Fifth Avenue was a tree-lined boulevard with many fine houses—he still refers to "Everard's corner" as a "mudhole."

After the move uptown, the Everard children enjoy living in the country, romping on wide, grassy fields, and playing in Union Square, which at that time was a park enclosed by a high iron fence that was removed in the 1870s. Soon, however, the countrified atmosphere would disappear. Union Square would become a residential area for many well-born and wealthy families including the Roosevelts, and later, theatres, restaurants, hotels, and fine shops like Tiffany's and Brentano's Literary Emporium would open there. By the eighteen eighties, it would be a busy, noisy area, and well on its way to becoming a theatrical and shopping district, as families moved out of the elegant homes that lined the four sides of the park. Many of these mansions would eventually be turned into rooms and studios for the bohemians who congregated in Greenwich Village during the nineties. Because he wrote *A New York Family* late in the century, Fawcett was able to move ahead of his narrative and describe "the invasion of Union Square by commerce":

Ah, yes, we remember; here was the old Van Wagenen mansion, with a Knickerbocker austerity on the part of its inmates that seemed to affect the very ring of its doorbell. It is now an upholsterer's, with a blaze of rich-dyed Orient fabrics to lure us past its portals.... And here again, as we recall, dwelt that godly old church deacon, Jacob Van Suntvoord.... A fashionable photographer supplants him now, and flaunts pictures of the last popular actress (he did so abominate theatres!) where the shaded blinds of his drawing rooms once rose sedately above the tranquil streets.

The next move of the increasingly prosperous Everard family is to Fifth Avenue. They live well, on what is by this time the best street in New York City, until Everard's financial ruin at the hands of Boss Tweed forces them to move to a narrow brick house on Thirty-ninth Street.

For almost twenty years, William Marcy Tweed was the undisputed political boss of New York, and it is not surprising that Tammany politics is a subject treated in many stories and novels set during this period. Fawcett's depiction of this corrupt politician is, however, more thorough than most, and Tweed actually appears as a character in *A New York Family*. Furthermore, Fawcett devotes many pages to the history of Tweed's rise and decline,[3] and his invective against him is—to say the least —memorable as he describes his "knaveries," which "had been for some time breeding like a knot of prolific vipers," and writes of "the audacities of Tweed and . . . his confederates [that] almost transcend credence."

Although unconcerned with Tammany politics and writing about a class of New Yorkers far different from the prominent and respected merchants described by Fawcett, Edith Wharton also writes about Manhattan's northward expansion in *Old New York,* a collection of four novellas encompassing several decades in the city's social history. In *False Dawn* (set in the eighteen forties), the socially prominent Halston Raycies lived on Canal Street, reluctant no doubt, like the old families described by Fawcett, to move uptown. In *The Old Maid* (set in the eighteen fifties), there is a reference to a doctor who is "versed in the secret history of every household from the Battery to Union Square," which comprised, in fact, just about the whole area of New York City at mid-century. The older generation still lived downtown, although not as far down as Canal Street. Old Mrs. Lowell, like the author's own grandparents, lived on Mercer Street, and there is a reference to the Waverly Place branch of the family. The younger generation, however, has started to move uptown. Like the author's parents, the newly married James Ralstons have moved into "one of the new houses in Gramercy Park, which the pioneers of the younger set were just beginning to affect." To reach there, one must drive "through spreading suburbs and untidy elm-shaded streets." Farther uptown, it is, of course, even more countrified. Wharton writes about a country home on Ninety-first Street, but comments, towards the end of the story, that the area "was already overspread with a network of mean streets . . . [and that] the growth of the city made it certain that the place must eventually be sold."

Perhaps the most vivid sense of the city's growth is portrayed in *New Year's Day.* The novella takes place in the eighteen seventies, but the narrator looks back to his (yes, *his*) childhood, when his grandmother lived in a house on West Twenty-third Street—the street on which Wharton herself was born in 1862—

which grandpapa had built in his pioneering youth, in days when people shuddered at the perils of living north of Union Square—days that grandmama and my parents looked back to with a joking incredulity as the years passed and the new houses advanced steadily Park-ward . . . leaving us in what, in my schooldays, was already a dullish back-water between Aristocracy to the South and Money to the North.

The story centers around a fire that takes place in the "no longer fashionable" Fifth Avenue Hotel,[4] and there are colorful descriptions of the fire-brigades of the seventies, but what is most valuable in this story—and in the rest of the *Old New York* series—is the way in which it traces the growth of the city and describes the dwelling places of its finest families over a period of four decades. Indeed, Wharton's writings about prominent families living in nineteenth-century New York are by no means limited to these little-known novellas, as will be demonstrated later in this chapter in a discussion of *The Age of Innocence.*

Henry James, too, writes about the homes of New York's well-born families, and in *Washington Square,* the story of a father's ruthless domination of his daughter, he relates the history of what at one time was New York's most patrician neighborhood. Early in the novel there is a reference to Dr. Sloper's marriage in 1820 to "one of the pretty girls of the small but promising capital which clustered about the Battery and overlooked the Bay and of which the uppermost boundary was indicated by the grassy wayside of Canal Street."[5] What follows is a description of the northward expansion of the city. Newly married, the Slopers live in a red-brick house near City Hall, on a street that had reached the apex of its prosperity in about 1820.

After this the tide of fashion began to set steadily northward, as, indeed, in New York, thanks to the narrow channel in which it flows, it is obliged to do, and the great hum of traffic roared farther to the right and left of Broadway. By the time the Doctor changed his residence, the murmer of trade had become a mighty uproar. . . . and when most of his neighbors' dwellings (also ornamented with granite copings and large fanlights) had been converted into offices, warehouses, and shipping agencies, and otherwise applied to the base uses of commerce, he determined to look out for a quieter home.

The upshot is that the Slopers purchase a house in Washington Square, "the ideal of quiet and genteel retirement, in 1835." James goes on to describe the square, which contained "a considerable quantity of inexpensive vegetation, enclosed by a wooden paling," and the nearby "august precinct of the Fifth Avenue, taking its origin at this point with a spacious and confident air which already marked it for high destinies." He comments, too, on the contemporary (1880) state of Washington Square, which, with its "established repose which is not of frequent occurrence in other quarters of the long, shrill city," appears "riper, richer, [and] more honorable" than other neighborhoods.

James then describes the house itself, having in mind, no doubt, his grandmother's house at 18 Washington Square North—James was born on nearby Washington Place—which was eventually demolished to make way for an apartment building. The "handsome, modern, wide-fronted" edifice, "with a big balcony before the drawing-room windows, and a flight of white marble steps ascending to a portal which was also faced with white marble," was identical with its neighbors, and when it had been built almost half a century earlier supposedly embodied "the last results of architectural science."

The elegance of Washington Square, whose most prestigious side—the northeast side, extending from Fifth Avenue to University Place—was known as "Old Row," is in marked contrast to other neighborhoods described in the novel. Dr. Sloper's sister, Mrs. Almond, for example, lived

uptown, in an embryonic street . . . where poplars grew beside the pavement (when there was one), and mingled their shade with the steep roofs of the desultory Dutch houses, where pigs and chickens disported themselves in the gutter.

Commenting once again on the contemporary scene, James explains that "these elements of rural picturesqueness" were no longer a part of New York scenery but could still be remembered by certain people of middle age who would now "blush to be reminded of them."

James refers frequently to the northward expansion of the city. A young man about to be married explains that it does not matter which house he has taken because before long he will be moving farther uptown:

"It's because the city is growing so quick—you've got to keep up with it. It's going straight uptown—that's where New York's going. If I wasn't afraid Marian [his fiancée] would be lonely, I'd go up there—right up to the top—and wait for it. Only have to wait ten years—they'll all come up after you."

Catherine Sloper, the doctor's daughter, is, however, more conservative. She continues to live in the Washington Square house for many years after her father's death, undaunted by the fact that it is now considered an old house and unmoved by suggestions that she buy one of the smaller, more conveniently located brownstones which had by then "begun to adorn the transverse thoroughfares in the upper part of town."

The downtown area Dr. Sloper left when it lost its residential character is the setting for most of Herman Melville's New York fiction. Although his reputation scarcely rests on these works, Melville's descriptions of the city at mid-century in such short stories as "Bartleby the Scrivener," "The Fiddler," "Jimmy Rose," and "The Two Temples," as well as in his novel *Pierre; or The Ambiguities,* should not be overlooked.

The best-known of these works is, of course, "Bartleby the Scrivener," the story of an eccentric copyist who refuses first to work and then to leave the downtown law offices of his employer. In this story Melville writes about Trinity Church, City Hall, Broadway, Canal Street, and other downtown locations, but Wall Street is described in the most detail and assumes symbolic significance as the story develops.

Melville, whose two brothers were lawyers with offices at 10 Wall Street, tells us that Bartleby worked at No. —— Wall Street and describes the building, "which of week-days hums with industry and life, at night-fall echoes with sheer vacancy, and all through Sunday is forlorn." He also describes the street itself, crowded and busy on working days, and on Sundays "as deserted as Petra; and every night of every day it is an emptiness."

Emptiness is perhaps the key word here, for Melville implies that Wall Street—which is synonymous to him with commerce and materialism—is the cause of modern man's alienation and despair. This is hinted at early in the story through repeated references to walls, walls that separate and alienate Bartleby from other people, and eventually from life itself. At the end of the story Bartleby is found dead of starvation in the yard of the Tombs, with "his face towards a high wall."

Some critics view "Bartleby" as a parable about the defeat of the artist by the world of commerce. Another of Melville's tales, "The Fiddler," treats this theme. It is the story of Hautboy, once a world-famous violinist, now reduced to teaching music, who is living "in the fifth story of a sort of storehouse, in a lateral street to Broadway." The narrator recounts his meeting with Hautboy and their visit to the famous Taylor's,[6] where they had "stews and punches at one of the small marble tables," and laments the fate of his friend, who is unrecognized as he walks along Broadway: "with you and me, the elbow of the hurrying clerk, and the pole of the remorseless omnibus, shove him."

Like "The Fiddler," "Jimmy Rose" is about the decline of a once-prominent man, and much of the story deals with his house on C——— Street, probably Courtlandt Street,[7] where Melville once lived. Melville writes about the once-fashionable residential street, its parlors

now, for the most part, transformed into counting-rooms and warehouses. There bales and boxes usurp the place of sofas; day-books and ledgers are spread where once the delicious breakfast toast was buttered. In those old wards the glorious old soft-waffle days are over. Nevertheless, in this old house . . . so strangely spared, some monument of departed days survived. Nor was this the only one. Amidst the warehouse ranges some few other dwellings likewise stood. The street's transmutation was not yet complete. Like those old English friars and nuns, long haunting the ruins of their retreats after they had been despoiled, so some few strange old gentlemen and ladies still lingered in the neighborhood, and would not, could not, might not quit it.

"The Two Temples" is set a bit farther uptown—at Tenth Street and Broadway, to be exact, the site of exclusive Grace Church, which opened in 1846. The story, rejected for publication by *Putnam's Monthly* in 1854 on the grounds that it would be considered offensive to the congregation and clergy of Grace Church in particular and to churchgoers in general, is about a would-be church-goer who has walked three miles uptown from the Battery to worship, only to be denied admittance by the warden, who claims that there are no galleries. To the narrator, this is "the same as if he's said they didn't entertain poor folks," and he is convinced that he would have gained entry had his appearance—and his approach—been different:

I'll wager that had my new coat been done last night, as the false tailor promised, and had I, arrayed therein this bright morning, tickled the fat-paunched, beadle-faced man's palm with a bank-note, then, gallery or no gallery, I would have had a fine seat in this marble-buttressed, stainglassed, spic-and-span new temple.

The resourceful narrator manages, however, to gain entry and to climb up in the tower, where he feels as if he were "inside some magic lantern," surrounded as he is on three sides by the "gigantic Gothic windows of richly dyed glass."[8] From his lofty position, he looks down upon the people below "so snug and cozy in their padded pews" and watches as the warden drives "three ragged little boys into the middle of the street." Eventually he is discovered by Warden Brown, who representing him as a "lawless violator and a disturber of the Sunday peace," turns him over to the authorities, and the story ends on an ironic note, the narrator explaining that he was both fined and reprimanded "for having humbly indulged myself in the luxury of public worship."

Pierre is perhaps Melville's most damning picture of New York as an inhospitable and even sinister place. A curious mixture of romanticism and realism, it is a puzzling and uneven novel about the psychological and philosophical problems that beset the young, idealistic Pierre, a writer who comes to the heartless city, where he must do battle not only with his incestuous desires for his half sister Isabel but also with poverty, social hypocrisy, and the literary establishment. Once again, Melville suggests that New York City, where the dollar reigns supreme, is a place in which the artist will surely meet with defeat.

From the moment of Pierre's arrival in New York, the city is portrayed as dark and evil. As they begin to feel the hardness of the pavement beneath the coach, Pierre says that "the buried hearts of some dead citizens have perhaps come to the surface." When Isabel inquires if they are "so hard-hearted here," Pierre replies, "Milk dropped from the milkman's can in December, freezes not more quickly on those stones, than does snow-white innocence, if in poverty it chance to fall in these streets."

While driving through dark and deserted streets in the warehouse section of the city, they must suffer the insolence of their driver. This leads to bitter invective against New York's cabmen, whom Melville calls a "hideous tribe of ogres" feeding on the misery of others and in league with the city's most abhorrent criminals and debauchées. Not long after their arrival in New York, Pierre has occasion to find himself in a watch house, or police precinct, where he witnesses a scene that fills him "with inexpressible horror and fury." He sees "frantic, diseased-looking men and women of all colours, and in all imaginable flaunting, immodest, grotesque, and shattered dresses . . . leaping, yelling, and cursing." It seems to Pierre that "the thieves-quarters, and all the brothels . . . hospitals for incurables, and infirmaries and infernoes of hell seemed to have . . . made one combined sortie, and poured out upon earth through the vile vomitory of some unmentionable cellar." So much for his first impressions of New York.

Eventually Pierre finds cheap lodgings in "the lower old-fashioned part of the city," in a building inhabited mostly by artists of various sorts—painters, sculptors, poets, and the like. The building is located behind a church, which Melville calls the Church of the Apostles, but what he probably had in mind was the South Baptist Church at 82 Nassau Street, behind which he himself had once lived on Dutch Street. Melville tells the history of the church and of the neighborhood itself, explaining that the church had been erected "when that part of the city was devoted to private residences, and not to warehouses and offices as now," but that "the tide of change and progress had rolled clean through its broad-aisle and side-aisles, and swept by far the greater part of its congregation two or three miles uptown." He writes at length about the streets in the area, stressing their seclusion and silence after business hours and on Sundays. He writes about one particular street

full of cheap refectories for clerks, foreign restaurants, and other places of commercial resort; yet the only hum in it was restricted to business hours; by night it was deserted of every occupant but the lamp-posts, and on Sunday, to walk through it, was like walking through an avenue of sphinxes.

Melville's emphasis is once again on the sense of alienation experienced by the city-dweller, who from his window looks out on "a wilderness of tiles, slate, shingles, and tin." This sense of alienation is also apparent in the description of Pierre's evening walks: He walks "through the greatest throughfare of the city . . . [where] the utter isolation of his soul, might feel itself the more intensely from the incessant jogglings of his body against the bodies of the hurrying thousands," through "the night desolation of the obscurest warehousing lanes," and along "dark narrow side-streets, in quest of the more secluded and mysterious tap-rooms," where he can watch "the varied faces of the social castaways, who here had their haunts from the bitterest midnights." An apt conclusion to this novel portraying New York as a heartless and alienating place is the defeat of the sensitive and idealistic Pierre, who in the final chapter is incarcerated in the city prison where, having been found guilty of murder and sentenced to death, he commits suicide.

Not far from the warehouse and financial districts described by Melville lived many of the newly arrived Irish immigrants who had fled their homeland because of the hunger and privation caused by the potato famine. *Men of No Property* by Dorothy Salisbury Davis is a historical novel about these immigrants. She depicts in vivid detail their first glimpses of the city with its dozens of church spires, most of them without crosses; buildings "looking piled on one another and capped with turrets like crowns; a thousand masts on as many ships ... a great green park; a raft ... and a sign on the raft: STOP AT MRS. O'REILLY'S BOARDING HOUSE."

Davis goes on the describe the ship's docking and the runners and hawkers on the pier who peddle their wares:

train tickets they were hawking and lodgings for a shilling a night, a free cart for your baggage and that in their hands already; the girls were tapped for employment, but only the pretty and strong, and men tried to lock arms with the free ones while a black-coated evangelist shouted, "Beware!"

Some of the new arrivals find rooms on Cherry Street, the whole of which "seemed a combination of homes and factories. It had the look of running more to manufacturing although the houses serving both had carried an air of respectability into old age." Others take lodgings on Chrystie Street, and the book contains a detailed account of Mrs. Riordon's respectable boardinghouse for girls, which was located there. For two dollars a week, there are "tiny rooms" and "towels that a good washing would vanish"; the week is made up mostly of fast days, and "if you looked up from the mush seeing the pattern of the plate shining through it when she set it before you, she'd say: 'It's a fast day. You wouldn't want to be violating the regulations of Holy Mother the Church?'"

Davis describes the life of the "great company of laboring men and women ... butchers, dockworkers, mechanics, coachmen ... and the women they courted and married." There are colorful accounts of an employment agency on Bleecker Street and Broadway, of the Catherine and Jefferson Street markets, of Irish saloons, and one scene takes place in a Washington Square mansion, where a young Irishman waits downstairs for his sweetheart, who is a servant girl there. Davis writes about the corner of Broadway and Chambers Street, which with its "tradesmen, mechanics, clerks, bootboys ... hawkers ... garble of talk ... snorting of horses, creak of vans and pulleys ... [and] endless rumble of wheels," she describes as "the busiest corner in America."

As some of the immigrants prosper, or come to have dealings with others more prosperous than themselves, there are scenes in elegant restaurants like Delmonico's[9] and fine hotels like the St. Nicholas,[10] and Davis writes about a visit by one of her characters to the Crystal Palace. Made of glass in the shape of a Greek cross and the site of America's first world's fair, which opened in 1853, the Crystal Palace stood on Sixth Avenue between Fortieth and Forty-second streets, where Bryant Park is now located.

Of particular interest are accounts of the Astor Place Riot of 1849 and the Draft Riots of 1863. During this period in New York's history, riots were by no means uncommon occurrences, as witness the Abolition Riots of 1834 and 1835, the Flour Riots of 1837, the Bread Riot of 1857, and others.

The Astor Place Riot was, however, somewhat unique in that its cause was wholly absurd. It erupted when the English actor William Macready was playing the title role in *Macbeth* at the Astor Place Opera House at the same time that the American actor Edwin Forrest was playing it at the Broadway Theatre.[11] Davis describes the disruptions that occurred inside the Opera House on opening night and how the next day signs were posted throughout the city that read: "Working Men—Shall Americans or English Rule in This City?" All were invited to "express their opinions" that night at what was referred to as the "English Aristocratic Opera House," and large numbers came to shatter windows, break street lamps, and open fire hydrants. The militia was called in to quell the riot, and shots were fired; twenty-two were killed and forty wounded.

Davis writes also of the draft riots that occurred in New York City during the Civil War in protest against the clause in the conscription law that allowed anyone whose number was called to pay three hundred dollars to the government to hire a substitute. This angered the Irish, whose slogan became "Rich man's money, poor man's blood." The relationship between Irish and blacks was already strained, the Irish resentful of competition in the labor force; now there was more anger because the Irish were being made to fight in the Civil War to further the interests of their rivals.

On July thirteenth, looting and rioting, which was to last for three days, broke out in the city. The Irish terrorized the black population, caused over two million dollars worth of damage, and killed eighteen people. Hundreds of rioters were killed by the police. Davis describes some of these happenings:

The ferries were running all night, carrying women and children out of the city. It was, by report, the only transport in motion. The cars and the busses were lined up and abandoned, and the sky was alight with the fires. Two navy gunboats guarded the Battery, their guns trained, should the Treasury come under attack.

Chatham Square filled with drunken men and women and the burning of the Twenty-second Street arsenal and of the Colored Orphan Asylum, located on Fifth Avenue at Forty-third Street, are also included in Davis's grim portrait of the city under siege.

The struggle of the Irish for a political voice in New York City is a dominant theme in the novel, which vividly depicts the increasing power of Tammany Hall politicians, the election of Mayor Fernando Wood, the conflicts of the Irish with the pro-American, anti-Catholic Native American and Know-Nothing parties, and the fierce political conflicts among the Irish themselves.

William Dean Howells, like Dorothy Salisbury Davis, described New York's immigrant population, but he did not limit himself to any one group. He wrote about many immigrant groups and about native-born Americans as well, depicting in much detail the neighborhoods in which they lived. Himself a newcomer to the city,[12] Howells had some prejudices against New York when he came here to live in 1889; nonetheless, he found the city a constant source of fascination and painted a picture of New York City during the last three decades of the nineteenth century that can best be described as panoramic.

Among his novels set in New York are *The World of Chance,* which deals with a young writer who has come to the city in search of fame,[13] and *The Coast of Bohemia,* about aspiring artists who have come to New York to study at the Art Students League, which was then on Twenty-third Street.[14] Also set in New York are *Their Wedding Journey* and *A Hazard of New Fortunes.* These last two works are, in a sense, companion pieces, since Isabel and Basil March, the central characters of *Their Wedding Journey*—which was based on a trip actually taken by the Howells and his wife in 1870—reappear in *A Hazard of New Fortunes.* In the latter, the Marches move to New York—just as the Howellses themselves did in 1889—and they often have occasion to discuss how much the city has changed in the course of nearly two decades.

Soon after disembarking from the train that brought them to New York City, the first stop on their wedding journey, the Marches take a walk, going "down one of the numerical streets" toward Broadway, and Howells writes of its "invasion" by the "bustling deities of business." First had come the doctors with inordinate door-plates; then a milliner filling the parlor window with new bonnets; here even a publisher had hung his sign beside a door, through which the feet of young ladies used to trip, and the feet of little children to patter. Here and there stood groups of dwellings unmolested as yet outwardly; but even these had a certain careworn and guilty air, as if they knew themselves to be cheapish boardinghouses or furnished lodgings for gentlemen, and were trying to hide it.

He also writes about the "eternal building up and pulling down" that went on along Broadway:

Here stood the half-demolished walls of a house, with a sad variety of wall-paper showing in the different rooms; there clinked the trowel upon the brick, yonder the hammer on the stone; overhead swung and threatened the marble block that the derrick was lifting to its place.

Isabel calls Broadway a "shabby street," but Basil thinks that it has "some grandeur of its own" and insists that the world affords no sight more splendid than the view of the roaring, swelling "human rapids" on Broadway from Grace Church.

The Marches continue walking downtown and notice that the streets are growing busier. "About the Astor House, . . . there was already a bustle that nothing but a fire could have created at the same [early morning] hour in Boston." They arrive at the Battery, which Basil describes as "not a very pleasant place, but . . . near . . . and historical . . . and open." Howells writes of the "sickly locust trees" and "mangy-grass plots" found there and concludes that "all places that fashion has once loved and abandoned are very melancholy; but of all places . . . the Battery is the most forlorn."

One of the most interesting aspects of this book—and of *A Hazard of New Fortunes* as well—is that Howells describes not only the city but also the Marches' feelings about it. We learn, for example, that while the Marches agree that parts of the city are "exceedingly handsome" and even grand in some respects, they find it to be

too vast, too coarse, too restless. They could imagine it being liked by a successful young man of business, or by a rich young girl, ignorant of life and with not too nice a taste in her pleasures; but that it should be dear to any poet or scholar, or any woman of wisdom or refinement, that they could not imagine. They could not think of any one's loving New York as Dante loved Florence . . . or as Johnson loved . . . London.

The Marches' negative attitude towards New York is particularly evident in the early part of *A Hazard of New Fortunes,* when Basil is offered a position as editor of *Every Other Week,* a New York magazine with offices on Eleventh Street, between Fifth and Sixth avenues. Isabel tells her husband, "I could go West with you, or into a new country—anywhere; but New York terrifies me." Explaining that the immense city "disheartens and distresses" her, she expresses the fear that she "could never have any inner quiet" there.

Basil, too, has doubts, but the Marches eventually decide to come to New York, the city where "everybody belongs more or less . . . [but] nobody has to belong . . . altogether." The first weeks are taken up with apartment hunting, and no novel describes in more detail the New York real-estate market in the late eighteen eighties. In a preface to the book written some twenty years later, Howells assures his readers that they may trust in his "fidelity and accuracy in the article of New York housing."

Actually, apartment houses were a recent innovation when the Marches went to live in New York City. Although the poor had lived in tenements for many years, more affluent New Yorkers were doubtful about the idea of living under the same roof as strangers, and it was not until 1869 that the first apartment house was built on East Eighteenth Street, west of Third Avenue. In the *Herald* and the *World* Isabel reads about "Elegant, light, large . . . flats . . . with 'All improvements—bath, icebox, etc.'—for twenty five to thirty dollars a month" and about elevator buildings with names like "the Wagram, the Esmeralda, [and] the Jacinth," where apartments with steam heat are available for from forty to sixty dollars.

Notwithstanding such alluring advertisements, the Marches spend many frustrating days, searching in vain for suitable quarters but gaining much knowledge about housing and neighborhoods in New York City:

They came to excel in the sad knowledge of the line at which respectability distinguishes itself from shabbiness. Flattering advertisements took them to numbers of huge apartment-houses chiefly distinguishable from tenement-houses by the absence of fire-escapes on their façades, till Mrs. March refused to stop at any door where there were more than six bell-ratchets and speaking tubes on either hand. . . . She found that there was an east and west line beyond which they could not go if they wished to keep their self-respect, and that within the region to which they had restricted themselves there was a choice of streets. At first all the New York streets looked to them ill-paved, dirty, and repulsive. . . . But they began to notice that some streets were quiet and clean . . . though never so quiet and clean as Boston streets. . . . Whole blocks of these down-town cross streets seemed to have been redeemed from decay, and even in the midst of squalor a dwelling here and there had been seized, painted a dull red as to its brick-work and a glossy black as to its wood-work, and with a bright brass bell-pull and door knob and a large brass plate for its key-hole escutcheon, had been endowed with an effect of purity and pride which removed its shabby neighborhood far from it.

What is made clear in the book is the proximity of New York's "good" and "bad" neighborhoods. The Marches wonder, for example, about

the old-fashioned American respectability which keeps the north side of ... [Washington] Square in vast mansions of red brick, and the international shabbiness which has invaded the southern border, and broken it up into lodging-houses, shops, beer-gardens, and studios.

The novel treats at length the Greenwich Village area, known for most of the nineteenth century as the American Ward because of its lack of immigrant population.[15] In the latter part of the century, however, immigrants began to settle in the western and southern part of the Village, as did many writers and artists. Tenements began to be seen in Greenwich Village, and many of the elegant brick homes on Washington Square South were converted into rooming houses.

Howells describes Basil's walks through the Village, which he continues to take long after he and Isabel have found an apartment:

He liked the streets of small brick houses, and here and there one painted red, and the mortar lines picked out in white, and with now and then a fine wooden portal of fluted pillars and a bowed transom. The rear of the tenement houses showed him the picturesqueness of clothes-lines fluttering aloft, as in Florence; and the new apartment-houses, breaking the old sky-line with their towering stories, implied a life as alien to the American manner as anything in continental Europe. In fact, foreign faces and foreign tongues prevailed in Greenwich Village, but no longer German or even Irish tongues or faces. The eyes and the earrings of Italians twinkled in and out of the alleyways and basements, and they seemed to abound even in the streets.

There are more descriptions of the tenement houses, their doorsteps swarming with children, their windows filled with the faces of women, and their basements given over to "green-grocers' shops abounding in cabbages, and provision stores running chiefly to bacon and sausages, and cobblers' and tinners' shops, and the like, in proportion to the small needs of a poor neighborhood."

Walking seems to have been the major leisure-time activity of the Marches, who strolling along Fifth Avenue noticed that "the line of these comfortable dwellings, once so fashionable, was continually broken by the façades of shops," and who particularly enjoyed returning to places they had visited during their wedding journey in New York, including the Battery, where they imagined how the ghosts of the past "might have met each other in their old haunts," marveling at "the colossal lady on Bedloe's Island, with her lifted torch, and still more [at] the curving tracks and the châlet-stations of the elevated railroad."[16]

The elevated railroad is a constant source of fascination for Basil, who makes a distinction between the two lines, preferring the East Side one to the West because it "offered more nationalities, conditions, and characters to his inspection." While most of the passengers on the Sixth Avenue line were men going to and from work, or their wives going to and from shopping, on the Third Avenue El he can see

the people of Germanic, of Slavonic, of Pelasgic, of Mongolian stock. . . . The small eyes, the high cheeks, the broad noses, the puff lips, the bare, cue-filleted skulls of Russians, Poles, Czechs, Chinese; the furtive glitter of Italians; the blond dullness of Germans; the cold quiet of Scandinavians. . . .

On one occasion Howells describes the Marches' journey to the end of the West Side line and their view of

the city pushing its way by irregular advances into the country. Some spaces, probably held by the owners for that rise in value . . . it left vacant comparatively far down the road, and built up others at remoter points. It was a world of lofty apartment-houses beyond the Park, springing up in isolated blocks, with stretches of invaded rusticity between, and here and there an old country-seat standing dusty in its budding vines with the ground before it in rocky upheaval for city foundations.

The descriptions of the El are seemingly endless: Howells writes about the "superb spectacle" of it at night and about "the track that found and lost itself a thousand times in the flare and tremor of the innumerable lights." He describes the "histrionic decorativeness of the stations . . . the vagaries of the lines that narrowed together or stretched apart according to the width of the avenue, but always in wanton disregard for the life that dwelt . . . around, below, above, and, no doubt thinking of the Thalia Theatre on Canal Street, he mentions "the insolence with which the railway had drawn its erasing line across the Corinthian front of an old theatre, almost grazing its fluted pillars."

Howells also writes about Chatham Square and Mott Street, about the "uptown" streets running in numbers as far as the Forties, and about Castle Garden, the concert hall at the Battery, which was acquired by the city in 1855 and used as an immigrant processing center until the opening of Ellis Island in 1892. *A Hazard of New Fortunes* contains some good descriptions of the city's restaurants, especially the French and Italian ones in Greenwich Village where a complete dinner—sometimes with wine—could be purchased for as little as fifty cents. Howells also writes about Union Square and a riot that occurred there as a result of a streetcar strike reminiscent of the strike of 1882.

In his description of the riot in Union Square and in other aspects of *A Hazard of New Fortunes,* Howells's socialist leanings are keenly felt. The book cannot be accurately described as a political novel, however. For an in-depth look at the local political scene in New York City during the last decades of the nineteenth century it is necessary to turn to Paul Leicester Ford's *The Honorable Peter Stirling.*

Based partly upon the author's unsuccessful attempt to enter politics in Brooklyn's Fourth Ward but erroneously believed by many to have been based on the life of the young Grover Cleveland, the book was extremely popular in its day. In marked contrast to many contemporaneous novels portraying the corrupt Boss Tweed, it is about an honest politician's rise to power and his eventual candidacy for governor of New York.

The young Peter Stirling, who comes to New York City to open a law practice, is advised to "locate on Broadway, anywhere between the Battery and Canal Street" and eventually rents an office near Worth Street. While waiting for his first client, Stirling spends many hours in the small triangular park in the angle formed by the joining of Worth and Park streets, on the site of what was once the notorious Five Points, probably the worst slum in the city's history. The area surrounding the park is described as

one of the most densely crowded tenement districts in New York. It had no right to be there, for the land was wanted for business purposes, but the hollow on which it was built had been a swamp in the old days, and the soft land, and perhaps the unhealthiness, had prevented the erection of great warehouses and stores, which almost surrounded it. It was not a nice district to go through, for there was always a sense of heat, and dirt, and smell, and crowd, and toil and sorrow throughout. It was probably no nicer to live in, and nothing proved it better than the overflow of children from there into the little, hot, paved, airless angle. Here they could be found from five in the morning till twelve at night.

It is through his visits to this park and his friendship with the slum children that Stirling's first case develops, a case against the dealers in contaminated or "swill" milk. Such abuses actually occurred in New York in 1858, but Ford places them in the eighteen seventies and describes at length the cow barns located on Fifty-eighth Street and Eleventh Avenue and the wide-spread corruption in the dairy industry.

Once Stirling has won the case, his career in politics—as well as in the law—is launched. Starting off as chairman of a local political primary, he is soon on his way to becoming a party boss. Ford writes about the local political scene, about torchlight parades and political conventions, about the tenement housing bill and saloon legislation, about blackmail and perjury by corrupt politicians, and—late in the novel—about Stirling's role in the railway strike and anarchist uprising that occurred following the panic of 1893, which triggered off a period of widespread depression, unemployment, bankruptcy, and strikes in New York and elsewhere in the nation.

Perhaps most fascinating of all is Ford's depiction of the evolution of power on the part of the political boss, beginning with votes garnered in Denis Moriarity's Saloon on Centre Street, and his lengthy defense of the political boss at a time when the term seemed to most to be synonymous with graft and corruption. Stirling explains that the bosses

are quite as honest, unselfish, and reasonable as the average of mankind. Now and then there is a bad man, as there is likely to be anywhere. But in my whole political career, I have never known a man who could control a thousand votes for five years, who was not a better man, all in all, than the voters whom he influenced. More one cannot expect.

Although *The Age of Innocence,* written by Edith Wharton in 1920, is set in New York during the seventies, the setting is far different from that of *The Honorable Peter Stirling.* Removed from the arena of New York City politics and unconcerned with the common lot, Wharton continues to write, as she did in *Old New York,* about the refined and genteel ways of New York's well-placed families.

Born into such a family and highly sensitive to the social nuances among upper-class New Yorkers, Wharton uses houses and neighborhoods to characterize their inhabitants and to indicate their social status. Countess Ellen Olensky, whose desire for a divorce and disregard of social forms threatens the respectability of her family and sets her apart from them, lives on West Twenty-third Street, the Chelsea street where, readers may recall, Wharton was born in 1862, a time, no doubt, when the street had been more fashionable. Ellen lives in a "peeling stucco house, with a giant wisteria throttling its feeble cast-iron balcony" in a "strange quarter" inhabited by "small dressmakers, bird-stuffers and 'people who wrote.'" Ellen tells Archer, her cousin May's fiancé, that she will not be permitted to remain there because her family considers it an undesirable neighborhood. She goes on to explain, "I've never been in a city where there seems to be such a feeling against living in *des quartiers excentriques.* What does it matter where one lives? I'm told this street is respectable." Archer, who at this time lives on nearby Twenty-eighth Street, simply replies, "It's not fashionable."

A short time later, Archer moves to East Thirty-ninth Street. Renouncing passion for obligation, he has gone ahead with his plans to marry May Welland, although by this time he is in love with Ellen. Cautious as he is, he nonetheless exhibits some small measure of daring when he moves into a neighborhood that "was thought remote" and a house that "was built in a ghastly greenish-yellow stone that the younger architects were beginning to employ as a protest against the brownstone of which the uniform hue coated New York like a cold chocolate sauce."

Perhaps the most daring of all the characters in *The Age of Innocence* is old Mrs. Mingott. Her social position is secure, and she does not mind living in the most unfashionable area. Her "cream-coloured house" is described as "visible proof of her moral courage," for it is located "in an inaccessible wilderness near the Central Park." Mrs. Mingott, who had had the house built many years before, acts "as if there were nothing peculiar in living above Thirty-fourth Street." Less bold perhaps but equally un-yielding to fashion are the conservative Dagonets, who refuse to leave Washington Square even though the neighborhood is considered very old-fashioned.

Whereas Mrs. Mingott and the Dagonets, whose lineage is impeccable, can live anywhere in the city without loss of status, other families like the Beauforts and the Reggie Chiverses—who have less impeccable back-grounds but more money—live in Fifth Avenue mansions and use both their money and their addresses to help them to ascend the social ladder. Without doubt, Fifth Avenue was New York's most fashionable residential street at this time,[17] and Wharton writes not only about its mansions and their inhabitants but also about the "fashionable [afternoon] hour," when there was a procession of carriages along the avenue, and about the early evening hours, when the Avenue was filled with strollers going to make after-dinner calls.

A particularly interesting glimpse into the pastimes and passions of New York's old patrician families is found on the opening pages of *The Age of Innocence,* where Wharton describes the Academy of Music, located on Fourteenth Street at Irving Place. She writes about its "shabby red and gold boxes," and how it was "cherished . . . for being small and incon-venient, and thus keeping out the 'new people.'" There was, however, "already talk of the erection, in remote distances 'above the Forties,' of a new opera house which should compete in costliness and splendor with those of the great European capitals." Wharton is referring, of course, to the Metropolitan Opera House, which in 1883 opened on Broadway and West Thirty-ninth Street. The enormous opera house, with a seating capacity of over three thousand, was built by a corporation formed by newly wealthy families like the Vanderbilts, the Rockefellers, the Goulds, the Whitneys, and the Morgans, who were not welcomed by the old English and Dutch families who occupied the fifteen boxes in the Academy of Music. Unable to compete with its rival, however, the Academy was forced to close its doors in 1885.

The novel also provides a vivid picture of transportation in New York City during the eighteen seventies. Wharton describes the "private broughams ... the spacious family landau ... [and] the humbler but more convenient 'Brown coupé'" that delivered opera-goers at the academy. Later in the book there is a description of Archer "crawling northward in a crowded horsecar, which he exchanged at Fourteenth Street for one of the high, staggering omnibuses of the Fifth Avenue line."[18] Soon after this, while awaiting the arrival of the Washington express at the Pennsylvania terminus in New Jersey, Archer muses about people who predicted that someday there would be "a tunnel under the Hudson through which the trains of the Pennsylvania railway would run straight into New York" and likens them to the visionaries who "predicted the building of ships that would cross the Atlantic in five days, the invention of a flying machine, lighting by electricity, telephone communication without wires, and other Arabian Night marvels."

There is another glimpse into the future when Archer and Ellen walk through the Metropolitan Museum, which had been incorporated in 1870 and occupied various temporary quarters before moving a decade later to its present Central Park location, facing Fifth Avenue between Eighty-first and Eighty-fifth streets. Archer comments, "Some day I suppose it will be a great museum." This prophecy, by the way, as well as a number of those foreseen by the "visionaries," is shown to have come true in the concluding chapter of the novel, which is set more than a quarter of a century after its opening pages.

Charles Dudley Warner also writes about New York's wealthy denizens. Although his characters possess far less in the way of pedigree and finesse than Wharton's, they own considerably more in the way of cold cash. Warner, now primarily remembered for having collaborated with Mark Twain on *The Gilded Age,* was a successful novelist in his own right. His trilogy consisting of *A Little Journey Into the World, The Golden House,* and *That Fortune* relates the history of Rodney Henderson, a tycoon modeled on such self-made millionaires as Jay Gould and Cornelius Vanderbilt. Henderson has made his fortune in the stock market, and Warner treats in considerable depth the economic history of New York City during the last decades of the nineteenth century, when in a period of postwar prosperity fabulous fortunes were being made on Wall Street.

In *A Little Journey* Warner describes the physical layout and the operation of the stock exchange in some detail. He writes about the high chamber with its elevated gallery and about the

narrow railed-off spaces full of clerks figuring at desks, of telegraph operators clicking their machines, of messenger boys arriving and departing in haste, of unprivileged operators nervously watching the scene and waiting the chance of a word with some one on the floor. . . . On the floor itself are five hundred, perhaps a thousand, men, gathered for the most part in small groups about a little stand upon the summit of which is a rallying legend, talking, laughing, screaming, good-natured, indifferent, excited, running hither and thither in response to changing figures in the checker-board squares on the great wall opposite—calm, cynical one moment, the next violently agitated. . . .

Having taken pains to describe the operation of the newly invented ticker tape (1867) in particular and of the stock exchange in general, where Henderson and others like him made their millions, Warner goes on to write about their extravagent style of life. The book contains, for example, a description of the brilliant scene at the newly built Metropolitan Opera House, where

there was a certain glow of feeling, as the glass swept the circle, to know that there were ten millions in this box, and twenty in the next, and fifty in the next, attested well enough by the flash of jewels and the splendor of attire.

No doubt, Warner had in mind a Monday-night performance at the Metropolitan, since that was the night when society in full regalia turned out to attend the opera. The main attraction for many ticket holders appears to have been the wealthy in their furs and jewels, and the management obligingly passed out diagrams identifying the box owners. And after the opera,

the streets were as light as day. At no other hour were the pavements so thronged, was there such a crush of carriages, such a blockade of cars, such running and shouting, greetings and decorous laughter, such a swirl of pleasurable excitement. Never were the cafés and restaurants so crowded and brilliant.

The same money that financed the Metropolitan Opera House—the money of the Goulds, the Vanderbilts, the Morgans, and other families like them—was also buying uptown property and building palaces "that began to repeat in size, spaciousness of apartments, and decoration the splendor of the Medicean merchant princes." This period in New York history is in fact sometimes referred to as the era of the marble palaces. The first of these elaborate edifices was built on Fifth Avenue and Thirty-fourth Street in 1869 by department store magnate Alexander T. Stewart. Other fabulously wealthy New Yorkers followed suit. While not all the mansions were made of marble, all of them were pretentious, and many were inspired by the châteaus, palazzos, and castles of Europe.

In *A Little Journey,* Henderson, for example, buys "a vast establishment big enough for a royal court," which has

a reception-room, drawing-room, a conservatory, a music-room, a library, a morning-room, a breakfast-room, a small dining-room, and a state dining-room, Mr. Henderson's snuggery, with his own library, a billiard-room, a picture-gallery . . . [Mrs. Henderson's] suite and Mr. Henderson's suite, and the guest-rooms, and the theatre in the attic.

In *The Golden House,* the second Mrs. Henderson wishes to build a palace of gold "to show New York millionaires how to adorn their city." She proposes to have an interior tropical garden and "gorgeous and monumental" façades. "Artists and sculptors are to decorate it, inside and out," and it will have "color on the exterior, gold and painting, like the Fugger palaces in Augsburg, only on a great scale." She is determined to "make the city brilliant" and to use "her wealth for the public benefit."

Other women in Warner's novels have different ways of using their "wealth for the public benefit." Some of them are involved in charity work on the Lower East Side, and interwoven with the story of New York's very rich is the story of its very poor, who make up, as it were, a kind of foreign city:

The shop signs were in foreign tongues; in some streets all Hebrew. On chance news-stands were displayed papers in Russian, Bohemian, Arabic, Italian, Hebrew, Polish, German—none in English. The theatre bills were in Hebrew or other unreadable type. The sidewalks and the streets swarmed with noisy dealers in every sort of second-hand merchandise—vegetables that had seen a better day, fish in shoals. It was not easy to make one's way through the stands and push-carts and the noisy dickering buyers and sellers, who haggled over trifles and chaffed good-naturedly and were strictly intent on their own affairs. . . . The houses seemed bursting with humanity, and in nearly every room of the packed tenements, whether the inmates were sick or hungry, some sort of industry was carried on. In the damp basements were junk-dealers, rag-pickers, goose-pickers.

Warner goes on to write about

the sweaters' dens, and the private rooms . . . where half a dozen pale-faced tailors stitched and pressed fourteen and sometimes sixteen hours a day, stifling rooms, smelling of hot goose and steaming cloth, rooms where they worked, where the cooking was done, where they ate, and late at night, when overpowered with weariness, lay down to sleep.

Indeed, some of Warner's descriptions of the Lower East Side are as good as those of Abraham Cahan and the other writers discussed in Chapter 4, which is a study of the literature by and about Jewish immigrants in New York at the turn of the century.

3

THE GAY NINETIES

By 1890 New York had expanded far from its modest beginnings at the southern tip of the island of Manhattan and contained 90,000 residential and 25,000 commercial buildings. The construction of a mass rapid-transit system and adequate sewage, the building of Central Park and Brooklyn Bridge, the expansion of the Croton Reservoir system, and the introduction of telephone and electric lighting facilities citywide were among the major accomplishments of the past decades. These mammoth tasks behind them, New Yorkers could now concentrate on efforts to beautify the city through the construction of more parks and ornate and monumental buildings.

The richest city in America, New York in the Gay Nineties was a well-functioning and well-populated modern metropolis. When the five boroughs were united into a single city in 1898, the population of Greater New York was 3.4 million. By all measures, New York had grown far more greatly than anyone could have foreseen at the start of the nineteenth century.

The fiction of the period portrays a prosperous city, but it also suggests that both the description of New York as a wealthy city and the appellation the Gay Nineties are in some respects misleading. To be sure, New York in the nineties was a rich city; its millionaires were too numerous to count, and life was, no doubt, gay for them; but it was neither rich nor gay for New York's poor.

Widespread poverty, particularly among the immigrant population, existed in the city, and there were many slums, including those in the Jewish quarter on the Lower East Side, in nearby Little Italy and Chinatown, and further uptown on the West Side, in Hell's Kitchen, with its predominantly Irish and German population.

It would appear that the Bowery, which divided the Jews on the east from the Italians on the west, has received more attention in the literature of this period than any other New York Street. From 1860 to 1875 it was a thriving theatrical center, but in the seventies deterioration began to set in, and by the nineties when Stephen Crane and the other authors discussed in this chapter wrote about it, it had become a dirty, dingy, noisy, vice-ridden street filled with flophouses and saloons, prostitutes, drunkards, and panhandlers.

Probably the best known of all literary works set on the Bowery is Crane's first novel, *Maggie: A Girl of the Streets.* Although the original version was written while he was a student at Syracuse, and before he knew very much about life on the Bowery—which he later was to call "the only interesting street in New York"—Crane did live in New York while he worked on the revisions, and he incorporated many of his first-hand experiences into the book. At once a naturalist concerned with the influence of environment on character and action and an impressionist interested in the act of perception and the perceiver, Crane wrote a story filled with images of a brutal environment that impinged itself on Maggie's consciousness, curtailed her freedom of choice, and finally helped to bring about her downfall.

The story makes specific reference to two streets, Rum Alley and Devil's Row, probably inspired by certain downtown alleys with names like Ragspicker's Row, Battle Alley, and Rat Trap. Maggie lived in an old, decrepit tenement that "creaked from the weight of humanity stamping about in. . . .[its] bowels." Here "gruesome doorways gave up loads of babies to the street and the gutter," and

long streamers of garments fluttered from fire-escapes. In all unhandy places there were buckets, brooms, rags, and bottles. In the street infants played or fought with other infants or sat stupidly in the way of vehicles. Formidable women, with uncombed hair and disordered dress, gossiped, while leaning on railings, or screamed in frantic quarrels. Withered persons, in curious postures of submission to something, sat smoking pipes in obscure quarters.

The above quotation makes reference to quarrels, and indeed fighting is a dominant metaphor in this naturalistic work, which portrays the city as a jungle in which only the fittest can survive. Brawls erupt in the tenement apartments, on the sidewalks, and in the streets. Of the many descriptions of violence, the one of Maggie's brother Jimmie driving his horse-drawn truck through snarled downtown traffic is of particular interest because it provides the reader with a glimpse into the abominable traffic conditions that prevailed in New York during the nineties:

He invaded the turmoil and tumble of the downtown streets, and learned to breathe maledictory defiance at the police, who occasionally used to climb up, drag him from his perch, and punch him. In the lower part of the city he daily involved himself in hideous tangles. . . . [and sometimes] he entered terrifically into the quarrel that was raging to and fro among the drivers on their high seats, and sometimes roared oaths and violently got himself arrested.

Contemptuous of the "strings of street-cars that followed him like intent bugs" and annoyed at pedestrians, whom he viewed as "mere pestering flies," Jimmie respected only fire engines, which could split "a mass of blocked trucks . . . into fragments as a blow annihilates a cake of ice."

While Jimmie was earning his living as a truck driver, Maggie went to work in a collar-and-cuff factory, and with a few deft strokes, Crane re-creates the depressing atmosphere of the sweatshop:

The air in the collar-and-cuff establishment strangled her. She knew she was gradually and surely shrivelling in the hot, stuffy room. . . . The begrimed windows rattled incessantly from the passing of elevated trains. The place was filled with a whirl of noises and odours. . . . the grizzled women . . . [seemed] mere mechanical contrivances sewing seams and grinding out, with heads bent over their work, tales of imagined or real girlhood happiness, or of past drunks, or the baby at home, and unpaid wages.

In an effort to escape from the sweatshop, Maggie takes up with Pete, whom she believes can take care of her, and he does, at least for a while. In describing the beer halls, saloons, and vaudeville shows to which they go, Crane paints a vivid picture of the places of entertainment that catered to New York's working class during the last decade of the nineteenth century. Particularly memorable is his description of a huge hall where singers, dancers, and ventriloquists performed on the stage while the audience—consisting of all "the nationalities of the Bowery"—drank beer and ate fancy cakes purchased from "little boys in the costumes of French chefs [who] paraded up and down the aisles."

But some of Crane's finest descriptions of the city come after Maggie has been abandoned by Pete and rejected by her brutal, alcoholic mother. Crane condenses Maggie's decline into a single night and portrays it as a prostitute's journey from the brilliantly lit theater district, then the Madison Square area, to the darker side streets, and finally to the gloomy waterfront section,

where the tall black factories shut in the street and only occasional broad beams of light fell across the sidewalks from saloons. . . . She went into the blackness of the final block. The shutters of tall buildings were closed like grim lips. The structures seemed to have eyes that looked over them, beyond them, at other things. . . .

At the feet of the tall buildings appeared the deathly black hue of the river. Some hidden factory set up a yellow glare that lit for a moment the waters lapping oilily against the timbers.

It is here in these dark and oily waters that Maggie, defeated by her environment, finds the only solace possible: death.

Another of Crane's slum dwellers who suffers defeat in a brutal environment is George Kelcey. Like *Maggie, George's Mother* contains many glimpses of slum life with its dilapidated apartments, its drunkards hurling bottles out of windows, its children playing with the broken shards as if they were toys. Perhaps its most vividly impressionistic view of the city is found in its opening pages, where Crane describes an unidentified downtown street on a rainy evening:

There were long rows of shops, whose fronts shone with full, golden light. Here and there, from druggists' windows or from the red street-lamps that indicated the positions of fire-alarm boxes, a flare of uncertain, wavering crimson was thrown upon the wet pavements.

The lights made shadows, in which the buildings loomed with a new and tremendous massiveness, like castles and fortresses. There were endless processions of people, mighty hosts, with umbrellas waving, banner-like, over them. Horse-cars, a-glitter with new paint, rumbled in steady array between the pillars that supported the elevated railroad. The whole street resounded with the tinkle of bells, the roar of iron-shod wheels on the cobbles, the ceaseless trample of the hundreds of feet. Above all, too, could be heard the loud screams of the tiny newsboys who scurried in all directions.

It is on this avenue that George, returning home from work, meets up with an old friend who is now an alcoholic. The two stop at a bar, and this marks the beginning of George's own drinking, which eventually leads to his ruination.

Crane writes about others ruined by drink in "The Men in the Storm." This sketch, set in a "dark west-side street," is about a group of men—many of them alcoholics—waiting outside "a charitable house where for five cents the homeless of the city could get a bed at night and, in the morning, coffee and bread." By afternoon the homeless men have already begun to huddle in nearby doorways and to seek shelter from the storm "under the stairs that led to the elevated railway station." As evening approaches, they leave their shelters and begin to mass in front of the building, pressing "close to one another like sheep in a winter's gale, keeping one another warm by the heat of their bodies."

Crane describes their remarkable patience, which eventually gives way to passion as they fight one another for a place in the shelter. Although no particular street is named and no shelter identified, Crane's is a painfully realistic portrait of New York's most desperate inhabitants.

The subject seems to have greatly interested Crane as can be seen in his autobiographical sketch "An Experiment in Misery," where he writes about a visit to a flophouse filled with cots "cold as melting snow" upon which men, who were, for the most part, "statuesque, carven, dead" lay. He describes the terrible odors, which

seemed to be from human bodies closely packed in dens; the exhalations from a hundred pairs of reeking lips; the fumes from a thousand bygone debauches; the expression of a thousand present miseries.

After a sleepless night in the flophouse and a breakfast consisting of "a bowl of coffee for two cents and a roll for one cent," the protagonist walked over to City Hall Park, where he saw

the background of a multitude of buildings, of pitiless hues and sternly high [which] were to him emblematic of a nation forcing its regal head into the clouds, throwing no downward glances; in the sublimity of its aspirations ignoring the wretches who may flounder at its feet.

Not all of Crane's stories are set in the city's poor neighborhoods. He also writes about the glittering Tenderloin,[1] a notorious section further uptown filled with saloons, gambling establishments, and brothels where the more well-to-do enjoyed their pleasures and their drink; and in "The Tenderloin As It Really Is" describes the Haymarket,[2] where

everything [was] wide open. . . . No sneaking in side doors. Everything as plain as day. Reubs from the West used to have their bundles lifted every night before your eyes. Always somebody blowing champagne for the house. Great! Great! Diamonds, girls, lights, music.

Also included in his New York sketches are descriptions of a Park Row restaurant, of Coney Island, which with the opening of the Steeplechase in 1897 had become a world-famous amusement center, and of bicycling on Western Boulevard, which, starting at Fifty-ninth Street and following the course of the old Bloomingdale Road, in later years would be renamed Broadway. It is clear, though, that one of Crane's major interests was the life of the poor in the city.

Another author with similar interests was Brander Matthews, who wrote *Vignettes of Manhattan* and *Vistas of New York,* which contain a number of stories set in New York slums. Among the most interesting of these is "In Search of Local Color," set on Mulberry Bend, the curving portion at the lower end of Mulberry Street, which was one of the city's worst slum areas and located almost on the exact site of the old Five Points. Its earlier inhabitants had been the Irish and the blacks, but by the eighteen nineties they were mostly Italians, and the area had become known as a "Little Italy."

In Matthews's story a settlement worker and his friend go on a tour of Mulberry Bend. They meet on the corner of the Bowery and Rivington Street and walk north on the Bowery. After a while, they turn into a side street and walk west, finding that at most crossings

three of the corners always, and four of them sometimes, were saloons. The broad gilt signs over the open doors of these bar-rooms bore names either German or Irish, until they came to a corner where one of the saloons called itself the Caffé Christoforo Colombo.

They soon reach Mulberry Bend, where the narrow sidewalks are virtually impassable because of various types of "encroachments":

Here, for instance, [was] a stand on which unshelled pease [sic] wilted under the strong rays of the young June sun. There, for example . . . might be a pail with dingy ice packed about a can of alleged ice-cream, or else a board bore half a dozen tough brown loaves, also proffered for sale to the chance customer. Here and there, again, the dwellers in the tall tenements had brought chairs to the common door, and were seated, comfortably conversing with their neighbors, regardless of the fact that they thus blocked the sidewalk. . . .

And the street was as densely packed as the sidewalk, . . . hand-carts there were, from which men, young and old, were vending . . . wares— fruit, more often than not; fruit of a most untempting frowziness. Now and then a huge wagon came lumbering through the street, heaped high with lofty cases of furniture from a rumbling and clattering factory near the corner. . . . There were countless children, and they were forever swarming out of the houses and up from the cellars and over the sidewalks and down the street. . . .

Describing the "incessant clatter and shrill cries of the multitude in the street" and "the rancid odor of ill-kept kitchens [that] mingled with the mitigated effluvium of decaying fruits and vegetables," Matthews also writes about the multipurpose fire escapes, which the Italians, coming as they did from a warm climate where they were accustomed to being outdoors much of the time, used

as an outdoor room added to their scant accommodations. They adorned it with flowers growing in wooden boxes; they used its railings to dry their . . . shirts; they sat out on it as though it were the loggia of a villa in their native land.

"Before the Break of Day" is another of Matthews's stories set in one of the city's poorer neighborhoods. His protagonist, Maggie O'Donnell, lives in a small wooden house surrounded by tenements, and Matthews explains that a number of such buildings are

still left in that part of the city, half a mile east of the Bowery and half a mile south of Tompkins Square, where the architecture is as irregular, as crowded, and as little cared for as the population. Amid the old private houses erected for a single family, and now violently altered to accommodate eight or ten—amid the tall new tenements, stark and ugly—here and there one can still find wooden houses built before the city expanded. . . .

Despite the area's numerous saloons and other signs of deterioration, Maggie considers it a fine neighborhood, for she was raised in "a ramshackle old barrack just at the edge of Hell's Kitchen; and there was never any quiet there, day or night, in the house or in the street." Indeed, few sections of the city were at that time as notorious as Hell's Kitchen, which, located in the waterfront area southwest of Times Square, was ruled by gangs and filled with factories, freight yards, and tenements.

A prolific writer of New York fiction, Matthews set several of his sketches in Central Park, and these provide a welcome relief from the depressing slum stories as well as giving an interesting glimpse into the huge project undertaken by Frederick Law Olmsted and Calvert Vaux, who designed the 180-acre park on which construction began in 1857. "A Vista in Central Park" actually refers to the park as a place where one can escape from the "want and despair of the great city." Here, there are no beggars to be seen, but only rather "well-fed and well-clad" families, and there is "a general air of prosperity gladly displaying itself in the sunshine."

Matthews writes about the Sunday afternoon "carriage parade" along the drive, which is exceedingly crowded because of the bicycling craze that seized New Yorkers in the nineties. Adding to the congestion are "park omnibuses" that circle the lake as well as landaus, hansom cabs, dog carts, coupés, phaetons, and four-in-hand carriages. The lake, too, is crowded with gondolas "propelled adroitly by their standing boatmen," canoes, rowboats, and barges with striped awnings.

Of particular interest is a reference to the "towering apartment house [that] lifted itself aloft over the [western] edge of the park." The allusion is probably to the Dakota, the first apartment house to be built on Central Park West. The elegant eight-story building in the German Renaissance style was named the Dakota Apartments because when construction began in 1880 the Seventy-second Street location was considered as remote as the Dakotas, which were then Indian territory.

Not all Matthews's stories are set in New York's slums or in Central Park. Several, including "In the Midst of Life" and "In a Hansom," depict downtown journeys. In the first of these, which is set on Christmas Eve, the protagonist starts out from the Madison Square area and soon passes the Fifth Avenue Hotel at Twenty-third Street. He goes over to Sixth Avenue, crowded with last-minute shoppers and peddlers of every description, passes Fourteenth Street, with its "chaos of carriages, carts, and streetcars," and continues on his way downtown,

passing the butchers', where carcasses of sheep and of beeves hung in line garlanded with ropes of evergreen; passing the grocers' where the shelves were battlemented with cans of food; passing the bakers', where bread and cakes, pies and crullers, were displayed in trays and baskets.

He reaches the Jefferson Market Courthouse—which when it was built in 1874, adjoining a jail, a firehouse, and a market, was considered one of the ten most beautiful buildings in America and which is still in use today as a branch of the New York Public Library—and a short time later his destination:

a little house, an old two-story building, wan with long use, yet dignified in its decay. The tiny dwelling had a Dutch roof, with two dormer-windows; and it had been built when the Dutch traditions of New Amsterdam were stronger than they are today.

In the second story the journey is not by foot and the destination of the traveler is decidedly unpleasant. A convict is being driven to South Ferry, presumably to board a boat that will take him to the penitentiary on Blackwell's Island, today known as Roosevelt Island.[3] The trip begins on Fifth Avenue, near Central Park, and there is a description of the crowd outside the Plaza, "men and women and children, bicycles and electric-cabs, carriages and cross-town cars, all weltering together." The hansom cab progresses down the avenue, which "is an alluring spectacle late in the afternoon of the first Saturday in June," with its "solid mass of vehicles in ceaseless motion" and its "sidewalks . . . filled with humanity."

The hansom eventually turns into Broadway, going "on down-town past Union Square with its broad trees, and past Grace Church, with its graceful greenery." Further south

Broadway began to seem emptier. . . . When they drew near to the City Hall, the great street, although not so desolate as it is on a Sunday, lacked not a little of its week-day activity. It was as though a truce had been proclaimed in the battle of business; but the forts were guarded, and the fight would begin again on the Monday morning.

After the hansom passed the Post Office, the buildings on the right and the left raised themselves higher and higher, until the cab was at last rolling along what might be the bottom of a canyon.

Continuing on toward the Battery, the hansom is "at last under the ugly frame-work of the Elevated almost at the South Ferry gate," which is, for the prisoner, the end of the line.

Matthews was a great admirer of H.C. Bunner, and in an introduction to a 1925 edition of Bunner's stories, he describes him as a pioneer in New York fiction who"drove a furrow of his own in soil scarcely scratched before he tilled it." This is, of course, the same Bunner who was the author of *The Story of a New York House,* discussed in the previous chapter. He also wrote some excellent short stories and sketches set in New York City at a later period. One of them, "The Bowery and Bohemia," describes some of the same slum areas treated by Matthews.

The sketch begins with a description of the "French Quarter," the name for Bohemian Greenwich Village, where Bunner had lived during the late eighteen seventies and early eighties. He had already written about this area in *The Midge,* whose protagonist, Captain Peters, lives on the south side of Washington Square and frequents places like the Brasserie Pigault, where the patrons drink beer, read newspapers, and play dominoes; and Charlemagne's, which Bunner places on Houston Street and describes as a place frequented by "newspapermen, actors, artists and un-classified Bohemians" where you could get "a grand and wholesome dinner for fifty cents."

Although there is no evidence that the Brasserie Pigault and Charlemagne's ever existed, they are modeled on any number of similar establishments that were to be found in the French Quarter in the late nineteenth century. Among them was Pfaff's, a bistro frequented by Walt Whitman, William Dean Howells, and H.L. Mencken, which Bunner describes in "The Bowery and Bohemia." In the same work he explains how Bohemia

has been moved not only across that river of human intercourse that we call Broadway—a river with a tidal ebb and flow of travel and traffic—but across a wilder, stranger, and more turbulent flood called the Bowery, to a region of which the well-fed and prosperous New Yorker knows very, very little.

What follows is a lengthy discussion of the Bowery, in which Bunner first reminisces about his earliest childhood impressions of the Bowery, including his father's stories about the good shooting there used to be at its upper end, and about the romance and excitement he found there in his own adolescence. Later he describes the Bowery of his adulthood, focusing for the most part on its picturesqueness rather than on its sleazy saloons, brothels, flophouses, prostitutes, pimps, and other unsavory characters. He calls it "the alivest mile on the face of the earth" and explains how it

either bounds or bisects that square mile that the statisticians say is the most densely populated square mile on the face of the globe. This is the heart of the New York tenement district. As the Bowery is the Broadway of the East Side, the street of its pleasure, it would be interesting enough if it opened up only this one densely populated district. But there is much more to contribute to its infinite variety. It serves the same purpose for the Chinese colony in Mott, Pell, and Doyers Streets, and for the Italian swarm in Mulberry Bend, the most picturesque and interesting slum I have ever seen.

There follows a description of Mulberry Bend in which, unlike Matthews, he emphasizes the charm rather than the despair of the region. On its vendors' stands

are displayed more and stranger wares than uptown people ever heard of. . . . Certainly they are the queerest part of the show. There are trays and bins there in the Bend containing dozens and dozens of things that you would never guess were meant to eat if you didn't happen to see a ham or a string of sausages or some other familiar object among them. But the color of the Bend—and its color is its strong point—comes from its display of wearing apparel and candy. . . . The pure arsenical tones are preferred in the Bend, and, by the bye, anybody who remembers the days when ladies wore magenta and solferino, and wants to have those dear old colors set his teeth on edge again, can go to the Bend and find them there.

Bunner then writes about the other—or east—side of the Bowery, which he calls a Babylon, and describes how its houses, "homely, decent, respectable relics" of another era, have been transformed into rooming houses, poor

but proud in their respectability of the past, although the tide of ignorance, poverty, vice, filth, and misery is surging to their doors and their back-yard fences. And here, in hall bedrooms, in third-story backs and fronts, and in half-story attics, live the Bohemians of today, and with them those other strugglers of poverty who are destined to become "successful men" in various branches of art, literature, science, trade or finance.

It is evident from a discussion of "The Bowery and Bohemia" as well as from our earlier consideration of *The Story of A New York Family* that Bunner is a chronicler of change in New York City. In "From Tiemann's to Tubby Hook," he writes about changes in the northern part of the city, from Manhattanville, where ex-Mayor Tiemann's house was located, to Tubby Hook, which today is known as Inwood. He describes the quaint old frame houses with their great gardens that dotted this part of New York's Upper West Side until the advent of the architects and realtors who transformed the rural area from a "fair countryside of upland and plateau, lying between a majestic hill-bordered river and an idle, wandering marshy salt creek" to an area "checkered and gridironed with pavements and electric lights" above which the elevated railroad roared. Bunner describes how "great, cheerless hideously ornate flat buildings reared their zinc-topped fronts toward the grey heaven" as the area fell victim to the city's northward expansion and as streets to the north of 155th Street, the last one marked on the commissioner's map of 1811, were opened.

Bunner expresses bitterness toward the realtors who bought acreage from families once rich but now forced to sell off their paternal estates strip by strip, and who then constructed sleazy and cheap houses for the poor; and he writes with nostalgia about the old Bloomingdale Road, "with its great arching willows, its hospitable old road-houses withdrawn from the street and hidden far down shady lanes that led riverward," which was eventually widened, renamed, and bereft of its rusticity and charm.

Despite the excellence of his sketch "From Tiemann's to Tubby Hook," when we think of Bunner's New York City, we think of downtown Manhattan. Another author who wrote about that area was F. Marion Crawford, but Crawford's characters are not bohemians. The Lauderdales are wealthy and conservative New Yorkers living on Clinton Place, which, Crawford explains, "nowadays is West Eighth Street." It "had never been a fashionable Street; though it lay in what had once been a most fashionable neighborhood."

Although Crawford is not generally identified with New York City and although most of his novels are set in faraway exotic places, both *Katherine Lauderdale* and *The Ralstons* take place in New York. Replete with a dying millionaire, a vast inheritance, greedy and scheming heirs, a cruel father who imprisons his daughter in her room, a secret marriage, and an artist who dies of an overdose of morphine, these melodramatic novels contain some surprisingly realistic descriptions of the city, more particularly of the downtown streets where Katherine Lauderdale wanders, either alone or in the company of her lover, John Ralston, whom she has been forbidden to see.

Crawford writes about University Place, and about the "row of stables leading westward out of University Place which is called Washington

Mews."[4] He describes Waverly Place, with its red-brick houses, and Washington Square, where on a snowy day "all the American boys would be snowballing the Italian and French boys from South Fifth Avenue" and where on a spring day the organ-grinder would be playing while "slim American children, who talked through their noses, and funny little French children with ribbons in their hair, from South Fifth Avenue, and bright-eyed darky children" danced.

Katherine and John have an arrangement that allows them to meet regularly:

John came down to Clinton Place by the Sixth Avenue elevated, and got out at the corner. Thence he walked past the Lauderdale house to Fifth Avenue, and crossed Washington Square to South Fifth Avenue, by which he reached the Bleecker Street Station of the elevated railway. The usual place of meeting was on the south side of the square. If Katherine were coming that morning there would be something red in her window. . . . He, on his part, let fall a few seeds of grains on the well-swept lower step of the house as he passed to show that he had gone by.

Together for a brief time in the early morning hours, they wandered "in the purlieus and slums about South Fifth Avenue and Greene Street," but when John boards the train, Katherine hurries toward Washington Square, for the neighborhood, although "a safe and quiet one . . . is largely inhabited by foreigners."

Seemingly concerned about areas that are and are not safe for young girls, Crawford on another occasion describes the "region between Clinton Place and Fourth Avenue" and says that it is not "best for a young girl to walk about alone there." And he writes about Avenue A and Tompkins Square, "a bad neighborhood at night, and the haunt of the class generally termed dock rats, a place of murder and sudden death . . . but by day as quiet and as safe as anyone could wish."

A street that is described in some detail is Lafayette Place—Lafayette Street was not opened until much later—a cul-de-sac where Katherine's cousin lived in what was known as "Colonnade Row," a line of white marble houses with tall pillars and balconies. These unusual houses, completed in 1838, were originally very fashionable, and their residents included the Astors and the Vanderbilts. By the nineties, however, "Colonnade Row" and Lafayette Place had suffered a decline. Crawford describes the street as "an unfashionable nook, rather quiet and apparently remote from civilization" and calls it "an unfrequented corner—a quiet island, as it were, around which the great rivers of traffic flow in all directions." He also mentions the fact that the Astor Library [5] is located there.

Crawford also writes about some uptown streets: about Uncle Robert's house on "a new block facing Central Park," about Murray Hill, and about Broadway, with its shops, theatres, and hotels, located just

one short block from . . . Sixth Avenue, where there is an important station of the elevated railroad, and there are the usual carts, vans and horse-cars chasing each other up and down, and not leaving even enough road for two carriages to pass one another on either side of the tracks.

Curiously enough some of the most interesting descriptions in Crawford's novels about the passions and problems of a wealthy New York family are of the city's poorer neighborhoods. The same is true of the fiction of Richard Harding Davis, whose best-known stories are about the wealthy Cortland Van Bibber, but who also writes about less affluent New Yorkers.

Although many of the Van Bibber stories are set in elegant restaurants like Delmonico's and at exclusive clubs, some of them portray Van Bibber coming into contact with the seamier side of city life with which he is entirely unfamiliar. One such story is "The Hungry Man Was Fed," in which Van Bibber, who had not been "south of the north side of Washington Square, except as a transient traveller to the ferries on the elevated railroad," visits the downtown area and looks "about him at the new buildings in the air, and the bustle and confusion in the streets, with as much interest as a newly arrived immigrant." He strolls along lower Broadway but soon finds it unpleasant, for pedestrians "bumped against him and carts and drays tried to run him down when he crossed the side streets." Most unsettling of all is his experience with a panhandler.

In "An Experiment in Economy," Van Bibber has lost a considerable sum of money at the races and decides to economize on breakfasts, forgoing "his coffee and rolls and . . . parsley omelet" at Delmonico's on Fifth Avenue and Twenty-sixth Street. "By some rare intuition" he guesses that there are places uptown "where things are cheaper than at his usual haunt." He eventually finds a modestly priced restaurant where he breakfasts on coffee and rolls, but concerned that the waiter thinks him impoverished, gives a thirty-five cent tip on his fifteen cent bill.

At dinnertime, he goes in search of one of the "table d'hôte places on Sixth Avenue" and while eating spaghetti, thinks about the Little Neck clams and other delicacies he might be having at Delmonico's. Soon after this episode, he decides his "experiment in economy" is a failure, and he ends it.

In "Van Bibber and the Swan Boats," Van Bibber, elegantly dressed in his riding clothes, is in Central Park, awaiting the arrival of his horse and groom. Here he has another encounter with an aspect of New York life unfamiliar to him. Much to his dismay, he winds up taking three young girls from Hester Street for a ride in a swan boat. Although he is uncomfortable in their presence and embarrassed at the possibility of being seen in such unfashionable company, he cannot help but be pleased that they "seemed as though they were enjoying it more than he ever enjoyed a trip up the Sound on a yacht or across the ocean on a record-breaking steamer."

The situation is reversed in "Van Bibber's Man-Servant," where instead of Van Bibber mingling with the lower class, his servant mingles with the upper class and actually passes himself off as a gentleman. In the story, Van Bibber is planning to entertain some friends at Delmonico's. While the occasion is not formal enough to be held in a private dining room, he does not wish to keep his guests standing in the hall waiting for a table. He decides, then, to send his servant over to keep a table for him, despite the fact that this practice is not permitted:

As everybody knows, you can hold a table for yourself at Delmonico's for any length of time until the other guests arrive, but the rule is very strict about servants. Because, as the head waiter will tell you, if servants were allowed to reserve a table during the big rush at seven o'clock, why not messengers? And it would certainly never do to have half a dozen large tables securely held by minute messengers while the hungry and impatient waited their turn at the door.

Knowing that his servant looks more like a gentleman than many of the diners, Van Bibber is certain that his breach of conduct will not be discovered. And he is absolutely right, for when his plans are changed and the dinner party is cancelled, his servant ends up dining at the fashionable restaurant, and nobody suspects that he is a servant.

In the Van Bibber stories then, Davis writes not only about the gentleman who gives the series its name but also about his servant, and about the working-class girls and panhandlers with whom he comes in contact. In other stories, Davis focuses on unsavory characters like Hefty Burke and Rags Regan. Hefty, "one of the best swimmers in the East River," works as an assistant to an ice-truck driver, earning ten dollars a week, and is in love with a janitor's daughter, whom he courts in Tompkins Square Park. Rags is a softhearted criminal whose flight from the authorities over the rooftops of a group of tenement houses on East Thirty-third Street gives the reader a glimpse into slum life along the streets near the East River.

Perhaps the most well-known novel set in New York City during the nineties is Theodore Dreiser's *Sister Carrie,* which is the prototype of the modern city novel, dealing as it does with the dream of success in the big city, which entices the newcomer with its dazzling array of riches and pleasures; the high cost of this yearning for success; and the ultimate heartlessness and coldness of the great metropolis.

Like his protagonist, Carrie Meeber, Dreiser was a Midwesterner who came to New York by way of Chicago, but Chicago had prepared neither of them for the splendors of New York, and like Carrie, Dreiser was awed by the spectacle that lay before him. This sense of awe, coupled with a naturalistic theory, which emphasizes environment as a factor in shaping character and determing action, and a style that is at times almost documentary, accounts in no small measure for the enormously detailed picture of New York City that is found in *Sister Carrie*.

Soon after arriving in New York, Carrie and Hurstwood, a tavern manager twice her age who has left a family and a successful career behind him in Chicago, find a third-floor apartment on West Seventy-eighth Street, near Amsterdam Avenue,[6] from which they can hear "the whistles of the hundreds of vessels in the harbor," and, because the area was so sparsely settled, they can see the Hudson River from their west windows and the treetops of Central Park from their eastern ones. Carrie marvels "at ten families living in one building and all remaining strange and indifferent to others," and the theme of alienation in the great metropolis begins to emerge.

She marvels most, though, at the splendors of the city: "the magnificent residences, the splendid equipages, the gilded shops, restaurants, resorts of all kinds." She is impressed by Broadway, which she sees for the first time when a friend takes her to a matinée at the Madison Square Theatre, on Twenty-fourth Street and Fourth Avenue.

The walk down Broadway, then, as now, was one of the remarkable features of the city. . . . It was a very imposing procession of pretty faces and fine clothes. Women appeared in their very best hats, shoes, and gloves, and walked arm in arm on their way to the fine shops or theatres strung along from Fourteenth to Thirty-fourth Streets. Equally the men paraded with the very latest they could afford.

Stating that it was commonplace for a new garment to have "its first airing on Broadway," Dreiser goes on to explain that

several years later a popular song, detailing this and other facts concerning the afternoon parade on matinée days, and entitled "What Right Has He On Broadway?" was published, and had quote a vogue about the music-halls of the city.

Carrie observes the showy parade of made-up women and "men in flawless top-coats, high hats, and silver-headed walking sticks" who stare brazenly at them, and she takes in the atmosphere of elegance that surrounds her on all sides:

Jewellers' windows gleamed along the path with remarkable frequency. Florist shops, furriers, haberdashers, confectioners—all followed in rapid succession. The street was full of coaches. Pompous doormen in immense coats, shiny brass belts and buttons, waited in front of expensive sales-rooms. Coachmen in tan boots, white tights, and blue jackets waited obsequiously for the mistresses of carriages who were shopping inside. The whole street bore the flavor of riches and show.

Carrie has another thrill when she is taken to dinner at Sherry's, located on Fifth Avenue at Forty-fourth Street, which catered to a most affluent clientele and had about it "an almost indescribable atmosphere . . . which convinced the newcomer that this was the proper thing." After ascending the "imposing steps" and being bowed to by a number of uniformed attendants, Carrie enters the dining room, where

incandescent lights, the reflection of their glow in polished glasses, and the shine of gilt upon the walls, combined into one tone of light. . . . The white short fronts of the gentlemen, the bright costumes of the ladies, diamonds, jewels, fine feathers—all were exceedingly noticeable.

Bedazzled as she is by the elaborate decor, the moldings of fruit and flowers on the walls, the gilt ceilings, the bevel-edge mirrors, and the regal apparel of the diners, Carrie does not fail to notice that

the tables were not so remarkable in themselves, and yet the imprint of Sherry upon the napery, the name of Tiffany upon the silverware, the name of Haviland upon the china, and over all, the glow of the small, red-shaded candelabra and the reflected tints of the walls on garments and faces made them seem remarkable. Each waiter added an air of exclusive-ness and elegance by the manner in which he bowed, scraped, touched, and trifled with things.

Dreiser does not neglect to mention the extravagant menu and the equally extravagant prices, including

an order of soup at fifty cents or a dollar, with a dozen to choose from; oysters in forty styles and at sixty cents the half-dozen; entrées, fish and meats at prices which would house one over night in an average hotel.

Carrie has the opportunity to see many other displays of the city's luxury. She comes to know Fifty-ninth Street and Fifth Avenue, where "a blaze of lights from several new hotels which bordered the Plaza Square gave a suggestion of sumptuous hotel life," and she is thrilled by the great park parade of carriages, beginning at the Fifty-ninth Street entrance and winding past the [Metropolitan] Museum of Art to the exit at One Hundred and Tenth Street and Seventh Avenue. Her eye was once more taken by the show of wealth—the elaborate costumes, elegant harnesses, spirited horses, and, above all, the beauty.

Impressed by the elegance and despondent because of her own moderate means, Carrie decides to pursue a theatrical career, and Dreiser writes about her attempt to get a position in the chorus of the Casino and at the Empire Theatre.[7] By the end of the novel, Carrie has become a rich and famous actress. She lives at the Hotel Wellington and at the legendary Waldorf[8] in the kind of splendid surroundings she has always yearned for. Yet happiness eludes her in the cold and alienating city.

Hurstwood fares even worse in New York. While Carrie finds success but not happiness, he finds neither. Middle-aged when he comes to New York, he cannot get suitable work and eventually finds himself unemployed. He begins to spend time in hotel lobbies, going at first to Broadway Central, "which was then one of the most important hotels in the city." Later he visits the Morton House and other hotels in the Madison Square area. He takes to gambling, and having reduced rather than improved his circumstances, eventually seeks a job as a motorman in Brooklyn during the bitter transit strike of 1895.

The trip to Brooklyn is a long and memorable one. Hurstwood takes a horsecar and a ferry,[9] and there is a good deal of walking involved. His impression of Brooklyn is unfavorable, for "after New York, Brooklyn looked actually poor and hard-up," and his employment there is brief, for he is badly beaten by the strikers and their sympathizers. He returns to idleness, and his deterioration is accelerated when Carrie leaves him. In describing Hurstwood's decline, Dreiser, like Crane, writes at length about New York's seamiest side: its cheap hotels, flophouses, soup kitchens, and its tide of wasted humanity.

At first Hurstwood takes lodgings in a third-rate Bleecker Street hotel at fifty cents a day; later he moves to a thirty-five-cent room. When most of his money is gone, he moves to a "fifteen-cent lodging house in the Bowery, where there was a bare lounging-room filled with tables and benches as well as some chairs," and later becomes a regular at a convent mission house on Fifteenth Street. Elaborating on such charities, Dreiser explains that

institutions and charities of this kind are so large and so numerous in New York that such things as this are not often noticed by the more comfortably situated. . . . Unless one were looking up this matter in particular, he could have stood at Sixth Avenue and Fifteenth Street for days around the noon hour and never have noticed that out of the vast crowd that surged along the busy thoroughfare there turned out, every few seconds, some weather-beaten, heavy-footed specimen of humanity, gaunt in coun- tenance and dilapidated in the matter of clothes.

In documentary fashion, he goes on to describe the men who "belonged to the class that sit on the park benches during the endurable days and sleep upon them during the summer months." He also writes about a baker who has been distributing free loaves of bread to the poor from his shop on the corner of Broadway and Tenth Street for nearly a quarter of a century, and in a passage reminiscent of Crane's "The Men in the Storm" he de- scribes the city's homeless waiting to enter a shelter on a side street near the Bowery:

They had on faded derby hats with dents in them. Their misfit coats were heavy with melted snow and turned up at the collars. Their trousers were mere bags, frayed at the bottom and wobbling over big, soppy shoes, torn at the sides and worn almost to shreds. . . . There were old men with grizzled beards and sunken eyes, men who were comparatively young but shrunken by diseases, men who were middle-aged. None were fat. . . . Not a normal, healthy face in the whole mass; not a straight figure; not a straightforward, steady glance.

When the doors are finally opened and the men have pushed their way in, Hurstwood can at last lie down on a cot, turn on the gas, and put an end to his life.

Success and failure in the big city is a common theme in Dreiser's fiction. In *The Genius* he traces the career of Eugene Wilta, a young artist from the Midwest, who at first finds fame and later finds defeat in New York.

Like Carrie Meeber, Eugene is dazzled by his initial impressions of New York. A Midwesterner, he is impressed by both the sea and the skyline:

What a wonderful thing this was, this sea—where ships were and whales and great mysteries. What a wonderful thing New York was, set down by it, surrounded by it, this metropolis of the country. Here was the sea; yonder were the great docks that held the vessels that sailed to the ports of all the world. . . . Here were Jay Gould and Russell Sage and the Vanderbilts and Morgan—all alive and all here. Wall Street, Fifth Avenue, Madison Square, Broadway—he knew of these by reputation.

Soon after his arrival, Eugene finds a room on lower Seventh Avenue for which he pays four dollars a week. Depositing his suitcase there, he immediately goes out to see more of the city. On this, his first, day in New York, he walks "downtown to the City Hall and up Broadway from Fourteenth to Forty-second Street." This is a good beginning, and before long, Eugene comes to know all of "the wonders of metropolitan life."

Repeatedly Dreiser describes the young artist's perception of the city's fabulous wealth, "which took his breath away":

New York presented a spectacle of material display such as he had never known existed. The carriages on Fifth Avenue, the dinners at the great hotels, the constant talk of society functions in the newspapers made his brain dizzy. . . . It was nothing uncommon, he heard, for a man to spend from fifteen to twenty dollars on his dinners at the restaurant.

It is not surprising that Eugene sees displays of wealth wherever he turns, for his arrival in the city coincides with the "opening of a golden age of luxury in New York" when tremendous fortunes were being made, and the upper part of Manhattan

was growing like a weed. Great hotels were being erected in various parts of the so-called "white light" district. There was beginning, just then, the first organized attempt of capital to supply a new need—the modern sumptuous eight, ten and twelve story apartment house, which was to house the world of newly rich middle class folk who were pouring into New York from every direction.[10]

An unending source of fascination, the city becomes the subject of Eugene's drawings and paintings, and he begins to gain a reputation in New York art circles, which Dreiser describes as being "broken up into cliques with scarcely any unity." He writes of the worlds of sculptors, painters, and illustrators—all quite separate entities—and of "studio buildings scattered about various portions of the city: in Washington Square; in Nineth and Tenth streets; in odd places, such as Macdougal Alley and occasional cross streets from Washington Square to Fifty-ninth Street."[11] There are descriptions of such clubs as the Salmagundi, the Lotus, and the Kit-Kat, and of "reception nights where artists could meet and exchange the courtesies and friendship of their world."

During these years of rising fame, Eugene lives for a while in a studio on Waverly Place, and after his marriage moves to 61 Washington Square.[12] After suffering a breakdown, he decides to leave New York; and when he returns, after an absence of two years, he finds that the city has undergone many changes:

A subway was built. The automobile, which only a few years before was having a vague, uncertain beginning, was now attaining a tremendous vogue. Magnificent cars of new design were everywhere. From the ferry-house in Jersey City he could see notable changes in the skyline, and a single walk across Twenty-third Street and up Seventh Avenue showed him a changing world—great hotels, great apartment houses, a tremendous crush of vain-glorious life which was moulding the city to its desires.[13]

Until he can get on his feet again, he and his wife, Angela, live in a cheap room on Twenty-fourth Street near Eleventh Avenue, having chosen the place "because it was near the North River [an earlier name for the Hudson] where the great river traffic could be seen." When success comes to Eugene again, this time in the lucrative advertising field, the Wiltas move to a luxurious apartment on Central Park West, but Eugene is not content to remain there, and they soon move to Riverside Drive near Seventy-ninth Street. With its "park atmosphere, its magnificent and commanding view of the lordly Hudson, its wondrous woods of color and magnificent sunsets," Riverside Drive seems to Eugene "one of the few perfect expressions of the elegance and luxury of metropolitan life."

They find "a very handsome apartment of nine rooms and two baths including a studio room eighteen feet high, forty feet long and twenty-two feet wide," for which they pay the "comparatively modest sum of three thousand two hundred." Despite their wealth and their sumptuous surroundings, the Wiltas are unhappy, and by the end of the book, Eugene appears, like so many of Dreiser's other characters, to have lost all—marriage, mistress, and career—in the alluring but ultimately treacherous city where materialism is shown to erode talent as surely as it corrupts values.

4

FROM SHTETL TO SWEATSHOP

In the last decades of the nineteenth and first decade of the twentieth century, New York City underwent many changes, owing in large
measure to the mass immigration of Eastern European Jews. Like the
German Jews who had preceded them in the forties, they were fleeing
from anti-Semitism. Although the German Jews had been unfairly taxed
and restricted in many ways, they had been permitted to participate in
the life of the community; the Eastern European Jews, however, were
confined to the Pale and severely restricted. Even within their own segregated area, they could not hold government jobs, own land, practice certain crafts, or enter a university. Far worse, many young Jewish males
were abducted, forced into military service for as long as twenty-five
years, and against their wills converted to Christianity.

The eighteen eighties was a particularly difficult period for Eastern
European Jewry. An outbreak of pogroms in 1881 was followed in 1882
by the May Laws, a series of exceedingly harsh anti-Semitic ordinances
that compelled large numbers of Russian Jews to emigrate to America.

Many more came following the terrible pogroms of the nineties, the
massacre in Kishinev in 1903, in which thousands of Jews were slaugh-
tered, and the invasion of Jewish towns and villages in 1905 by anti-
Semitic bands known as "the Black Hundreds." In 1880, there were
250,000 Jews in the United States; between 1881 and 1924, when legislation to limit immigration was passed, 2,300,000 Jews had immigrated to
this country.

Unlike the German Jews, who came here in significantly smaller numbers and who became, for the most part, itinerant peddlers before eventually settling down and establishing businesses in various parts of the nation,

most of the Eastern European Jews settled in New York. Whereas before 1880 there were approximately 50,000 Jews in New York City, by 1919 there were 1,400,000, most of them living on the Lower East Side, which was described at the turn of the century as one of the most severely congested areas in the world. Here they found a sense of security—and when needed, economic aid—from their *landsleit,* who came from the same town or *shtetl.* Unlike their German counterparts, most were skilled laborers who went to work in the sweatshops. Even those who became peddlers stayed for the most part on the Lower East Side, which in a short time became a Jewish ghetto filled with tenements, synagogues, pushcarts, and sweatshops, and boasting its own Yiddish newspapers, theatres, and cafés.

The literature presented in this chapter, written at different times and by authors of different backgrounds and political persuasions, depicts life on the Lower East Side. It also describes the development of the garment industry and trade unionism, the conflict between the Russian and German Jews, and the struggle of the immigrant, who was at once tied to the past and eager to become a part of the present through assimilation.

It would be misleading, of course, to imply that for several decades New York Jewish life was exclusively centered on the Lower East Side. In an attempt to present a balanced picture, I have included two novels set in other areas of the city, but clearly the focus of this chapter is on the Jewish ghetto that Henry James was to describe in *The American Scene* as "the New Jerusalem on earth."

Abraham Cahan, the founder and long-time editor of the *Jewish Daily Forward,* labor organizer, and leader of the Social Democratic party, is probably the best-known of the first-generation Jewish-American authors to write about the Lower East Side, where he himself lived and worked.[1] In his fiction Cahan paints a vividly realistic picture of the whole fabric of life among the immigrants, whose acquaintance with their new country began at Castle Garden.

There is an excellent description of Castle Garden, reeking with carbolic acid and human misery, in "A Providential Match":

Leaning against the railing or sitting on their baggage, there were bevies of unkempt men and women in shabby dress of every cut and color, holding on to ragged, bulging parcels, baskets, or sacks, and staring at space with a look of forlorn, stupefied, and cowed resignation. The cry of children in their mothers' arms, blending in jarring discord with the gruff yells of the uniformed officers, jostling their way through the crowd, and with the general hum and buzz inside and outside the inclosure, made the scene as painful to the ear as it was to the eye and nostrils, and completed the impression of misery and desolation.

And in *Yekl: A Tale of the New York Ghetto,* the story of an immigrant who in the course of time changes his name from Yekl to Jake and divorces his old-fashioned, pious, and bewigged wife, Cahan writes about the streets where the newcomers went to live, streets where one

had to pick and nudge his way through dense swarms of bedraggled half-naked humanity; past garbage barrels rearing their overflowing contents in sickening piles, and lining the streets in malicious suggestion of rows of trees; underneath tiers and tiers of fire escapes, barricaded and festooned with mattresses, pillows, and feather-beds not yet gathered in for the night. The pent-in sultry atmosphere was laden with nausea and pierced with a discordant and, as it were, plaintive buzz.

There follows a particularly vivid description of Suffolk Street:

Suffolk Street is in the very thick of the battle for breath. For it lies in the heart of that part of the East Side which has within the last two or three decades become the Ghetto of the American metropolis, and, indeed, the metropolis of the Ghettos of the world. It is one of the most densely populated spots on the face of the earth—a seething human sea fed by streams, streamlets, and rills of immigration flowing from all the Yiddish-speaking centres of Europe. Hardly a block but shelters Jews from every nook and corner of Russia, Poland, Galicia, Hungary, [and] Roumania. . . .

In *Yekl* Cahan writes about other streets on the Lower East Side, about Pitt Street, where a scribe sold newspapers and cigarettes and wrote letters to relatives still in Europe "for a charge varying, according to the length of the epistle, from five to ten cents" and would "for an extra remuneration of one cent . . . read a letter." And he depicts Grand Street, one of the two main thoroughfares of the area (the other was Delancey Street), with its millinery shops, dance halls, promenaders, peddlers, and the numerous cafés that played such an important part in the social and cultural life of the Lower East Side.[2]

In "The Imported Bridegroom," Cahan describes Norfolk Street, the location of Beth Hamedrash Hagodol (the Great House of Study), once the largest Russian synagogue in America. Now designated as a New York City landmark building, it was built in 1852 and was originally the Norfolk Street Baptist Church before it became a synagogue in 1885. Of particular interest are the descriptions of the classes conducted there. In one room is a *Mishna* class, its participants "poor peddlers or artisans,—a humble, seedy, pitiable lot, come after a hard day's work or freezing, to 'take a holy word into their mouths.'" In the adjoining room the daily *Gemarah* class is in progress, attended by

some fifteen men of all ages and economical conditions from the dodder-
ing apple-vendor, to whom the holy books are the only source of pleasure
in this life as well as in the other, to the well-fed, overdressed young furni-
ture-dealer, with whom the Talmud is a second nature, contracted in the
darker days of his existence in Russia.

The students are enthusiastic and noisy, every so often bursting "into a
bedlam of voices and gesticulations."
    In still a third room are *lomdim,* or learned men, seated at long tables,

each intent upon the good deed of studying "for study's sake" by himself: some humming to their musty folios melodiously; others smiling and
murmuring to them, like a fond mother to her babe; still others wailing or
grumbling or expostulating with their books, or slapping them and yelling
for delight, or roaring like a lion in a cage.

Indeed, those immigrants who clung to their traditions despite the pressures to become Americanized must have found unique spiritual sus-
tenance in their synagogues, where they could escape from the crowded,
squalid tenements in which they lived, the even more-crowded, noisy
streets where they stood behind pushcarts and hawked their wares, or the
sweatshops where they cut out garments or bent over sewing machines
for long, tedious hours.
    Of all Cahan's descriptions of Lower East Side life, those about the
sweatshops are probably the best. In "A Sweat-Shop Romance," he writes
about Leizer Lipman's "cockroach shop." Located in the kitchen of a
cramped three-room tenement apartment on Essex Street, it faced a dingy
courtyard and was littered with bundles of cloth as well as "cooking uten-
sils, dirty linen, . . . hats, shoes, shears, cotton-spools, and what-not. A
red-hot kitchen stove and a blazing grate full of glowing flat-irons . . .
helped to justify its nickname of sweat-shop in the literal sense of the
epithet."
    Cahan writes about sweatshops in many other stories as well, describ-
ing the unsafe and unhealthy working conditions, the long, exhausting
hours, and the competition among the pieceworkers who, fearful that
there would not be enough work to go around, called the fastest workers
"bundle-eaters"; but for a full history of the garment industry in New
York City, and in particular of the cloak-and-suit trade, we must turn
to his novel *The Rise of David Levinsky.*
    Arriving in America in 1885 as a penniless orphan, Levinsky first earns
a living by peddling collar buttons, garters, pins, and the like, on the
Lower East Side, along with approximately twenty-five thousand others
whose pushcarts filled almost the whole Lower East Side area but who

converged in largest numbers on Orchard and Rivington streets, particularly at their intersection. Boarding in private homes—an arrangement exceedingly common at the turn of the century—he at length goes to work in a sweatshop, and endures much poverty and privation before he finally becomes acculturated to his new environment. But his acculturation—and success—exact a high cost in humanity and decency.

In relating Levinsky's story, Cahan has ample opportunity to record both the history of the garment industry and the changes that occurred in it in the late eighteen eighties and early nineties when control passed from the German to the Russian Jews. Explaining that as late as the eighteen seventies most American women wore shawls instead of cloaks, Cahan describes how the demand for cloaks, imported from Germany and worn by only a few affluent women, grew and how

gradually, some German-American merchants and an American shawl firm bethought themselves of manufacturing these garments at home. The industry progressed, the new-born great Russian immigration—a child of the massacres of 1881 and 1882—bringing the needed army of tailors for it.

Cahan goes on to explain how some of the tailors decided to go into business on their own and how the Russian Jews eventually gained control of the industry:

The old cloak-manufacturers, the German Jews, were merely merchants. Our [the Russian] people, on the other hand, were mostly tailors or cloak operators who had learned the mechanical part of the industry, and they were introducing a thousand innovations into it, perfecting, revolutionizing it. We brought to our work a knowledge, a taste, and an ardor which the men of the old firms did not possess. And we were shedding our uncouthness, too. In proportion as we grew we adopted American business ways.

There are many other discussions of the garment industry, which in a single decade—the eighteen nineties—more than doubled its production. Cahan writes about the formation of the Cloak and Suit Makers' Union, the numerous conflicts between labor and management that occurred during those turbulent years when the union was in its infancy, and the strike of 1910 that spread as far as Philadelphia and came to be known as the "uprising of 20,000." Clearly emblematic of his moral turpitude is Levinsky's view that public opinion was on the side of the strikers not because their cause was just but because their neighborhood was considered "exotic," and visiting an East Side café "was regarded as something like spending a few hours at the Louvre."

Even when the strikers' demand for higher wages was won, the scurrilous Levinsky managed to turn the advantage to himself because he was able to recruit employees willing to work on his terms, i.e., every Friday afternoon they "would receive the union pay in full, but on the following Monday each of them would pay . . . back the difference between the official and the actual wage." Thus able to undercut his competitors, Levinsky could boast that "the absolute triumph of the union was practically the making of me."

A Horatio Alger story with a Jewish flavor and an ironic title, *The Rise of David Levinsky* is indeed about the making of a millionaire. It is the story of a penniless orphan who arrives in New York not only with earlocks and tattered clothing but also with moral and spiritual values that will be cast aside along with the other emblems of his past. Cahan, aware of the high cost of Levinsky's worldly success and often nostalgic for the European past, laments the spiritual, moral, and even intellectual decline of his protagonist; he questions the value of Levinsky's achievements, and perceives his economic rise as a moral decline.

It is a matter of historical record that only a few of the Lower East Side's immigrant population attained either the phenomenal success or the moral bankruptcy of a David Levinsky. Most were honest—decent men and women who, working long hours to feed, clothe, and educate their families, looked forward to the time when they could move to a better neighborhood. Of those who achieved extraordinary success, many made significant contributions to American society in such areas as science, medicine, literature, art, music, and politics. In both groups there were those who, despite the pressure to assimilate, held on to their religious beliefs and traditions. But the rise to power or the acquisition of great wealth by a scoundrel who repudiates his heritage, along with its moral code, makes for good reading. Another Lower East Side novel, *Haunch, Paunch, and Jowl* by Samuel Ornitz, tells the same kind of story.

Haunch, Paunch and Jowl is about the rapacious and cynical Meyer Hirsch's rise to wealth and fame as a judge from his impoverished beginnings in Ludlow Street on the Lower East Side, where his family lived in two dark rooms with a toilet in the backyard. A "transient, impatient . . . [alien] in . . .[his] parents' home," ashamed of his shabbiness in "that strict, rarified public school world," and disgusted with what he describes as "the harsh . . . *cheder* life,"[3] Meyer spends most of his youth on the streets, where he quickly becomes learned in the ways of thievery, vice, and corruption.

The author describes how Meyer and the other Ludlow Streeters—arch rivals of the Essex Guerillas—learned to supplement "the scanty home provender" by snatching black bread, smoked fish, fruit, and other foods from the local pushcarts, and he writes about the protection money paid by Lower East Side merchants to stave off such acts of vandalism.

Meyer comes to know the red-light district on the Lower East Side, especially Allen Street. Now famous for its antique shops, at the turn of the century it was notorious for its brothels, and it caused no end of despair to the traditional Orthodox Jews living in the area. Ornitz describes the transformation of the "stodgy home street" into "a thronged, roisterous thoroughfare," commenting that "even for the wide-open town that New York was at the time, the brazen and bare-faced desecration of a home street was shocking."

Meyer's street education is supplemented by studies at City College; and Ornitz, like so many other first-generation Jewish-American authors, writes about the vine-covered "rusty old chapel on Twenty-third Street," which with its "air of scholarly detachment . . . [and] cloister quiet and dignity" provided the young people of the ghetto with a singular opportunity for a free and excellent college education.

But Meyer continues to obtain the bulk of his education on the rapidly growing East Side. There "the small wooden houses with their slanting roofs, the Georgian brick houses with their garrets and the makeshift shopbuildings" are being replaced by tenements, in which "a small area set off by a thin wall of lathe and plaster is a room. And the miracle of paying the rents exacted is accomplished by the number of boarders you can crowd into the so-called rooms."

Here, on the stoops of tenements, on street corners, and in his own kitchen, Meyer listens to the voices of Socialists, anarchists, revolutionaries, and trade unionists, all of whom played an important part in the history of the period, but he clings to his belief in the power of money and the ethic of personal success. In his quest for material wealth he becomes involved in Tammany Hall politics, having decided to become a Democrat because successful lawyers "were those with pull."

Meyer makes his first speech in Big Jim Hollorahan's club. Addressing a group of Irish constituents, he praises "the Big Boss, the peepul's one and only friend," whose good works in actuality "consisted of giving out a few dozen shoes in the winter, free Thanksgiving baskets, and a free picnic for women and children in the summer." Assigned to work on the East Side by a far-sighted Tammany politician who is worried about the Socialist appeal in that neighborhood, Meyer addresses a Jewish audience, praising the Democrats, reviling the Republicans, and lying "atrociously about the Socialists."

Ornitz describes "dough day," when each district captain receives funds for use on Election Day. "The price of a vote in those days was two dollars, and to a poor man . . . this was a lot of money." Those whose votes cannot be bought are beaten with clubs and blackjacks; ballot boxes are stolen—with the help of the police— and others are substituted in their places. Tammany is victorious, of course, and there is a big celebration on Election night.

Knowing that "legal knowledge only, on the part of a lawyer, even plus cleverness and preparation—entitles a lawyer to starve in New York courts," Meyer keeps his hands in " 'the political grab-bag' [in] . . . that hurly-burly time of New York's nineties" when judgeships could be purchased for "a stated sum."

From an apprenticeship in fixing court cases, Meyer grows in stature and wealth as a lawyer with Tammany connections. He gets protection money—and votes—from pushcart vendors, who fear attacks from Irish gangs, and gains control of the pickpocket concession at "the Brooklyn Bridge terminal, where swirling, pushing crowds made pocket-picking easy and lucrative."

These and other equally unsavory activities prove profitable, and soon Meyer is able to move uptown: "Uptown. The apex of prosperity. Fitted snugly in the smug brownstone West Eighties overlooking Central Park. Uptown. On the crest. Uptown." He now has the means to live on Riverside Drive, otherwise known as "Allrightnik's Row," where "the newly rich Russian, Galacian, Polish and Roumanian Jews" are moving into "great elevator apartment houses."

The term "Allrightnik," originally used by the Russian Jews to express scorn for the wealthy uptown German Jews, suggests something of the conflict that existed between the two groups. Hostility between the German manufacturers and the Russians who took over the garment industry has been hinted at earlier in this chapter, but their discord was not restricted to the business area.

Let us recall that by the time the great influx of Russian Jews reached America in the eighteen eighties, the German Jews, who originally came here in small numbers in the forties and settled in many parts of the country, had become assimilated. Many were wealthy and prominent, and were eager to maintain their status.

The huge numbers of Russian Jews who came to live on the Lower East Side presented a real threat to New York's German Jews, who looked with dismay upon these coarse, dirty, and outlandishly garbed Yiddish-speaking immigrants. Fearful that they would be identified with the uncouth newcomers and that their own positions would be imperiled, they remained for the most part aloof and disdainful, although they did sponsor many charitable organizations, such as HIAS and the Educational Alliance, to help their coreligionists.

On their part, the new Jewish immigrants responded with anger. Meyer's uncle Philip "hates the German Jews . . . who look down upon the Russian Jews as an animal apart . . . who are proud, powerful and rich," and when he becomes a manufacturer, says, "I'll climb higher and higher up the road to wealth till I reach the seats of the mighty—the German Jew . . . so good, so respectful, so proud: with their vaunted charities and rich temples."

Like David Levinsky, Philip succeeds at the expense of the German-Jewish manufacturers, and this novel, like Cahan's, depicts the takeover of the garment industry by the newcomers, the antagonism that existed between these two groups, and the economic rise and moral fall of its protagonists.

Comrade Yetta by Arthur Bullard, a non-Jewish settlement worker who edited and wrote for Socialist publications; and *Jews Without Money* by Michael Gold, a well-known radical and spokesman for proletarian literature in the 1930s, are concerned not with the Jewish immigrants or their children who find fame and fortune here, but with those who repudiate the capitalistic system.

Bullard's protagonist is a young women employed in a sweatshop, and like Cahan's fiction, *Comrade Yetta* contains many descriptions of the brutal and dehumanizing conditions in those places. The plight of the workers, however, is nowhere more vividly conveyed than in the following passage describing "the ebb and flow of . . . [the] tide of tenement dwellers." Deserted at five in the morning, except for milk wagons and an occasional truck, the trickle of human activity begins to increase toward six, and

by six the flood is at its height. So dense is the rush that it is hard to make way against it, eastward. So fast the flow that the observer can scarcely note the faces. . . . Then for close to twelve hours these side streets are almost deserted again—till the ebb begins. It is hard to decide which sight is the more awesome: the flow of humanity hurrying to its inhuman labor or the same crowd ebbing, hurrying to their inhuman, bestial homes.

Many young women who despised life in the sweatshops and in their "inhuman, bestial homes" were lured into prostitution, and Bullard describes Yetta's encounter with a pimp who tries to win her over. He also takes the opportunity to write about the underworld in the Lower East Side and about its principal gang, which consisted of "a varied assortment of toughs, 'strong-arm men,' pickpockets, 'panhandlers,' and pimps." Explaining that in 1903 there were no "rigid classes and cliques" in New York's underworld, Bullard describes how many a man who claimed to be a prize-fighter sometimes "stuck up a drunk." The . . . pickpocket did not disdain the income to be derived from the sale of "phony" jewellery. It was no longer possible to distinguish a "yeggman" from a "flopper," and even bank robbers wrote "begging letters." And of all "easy money," the easiest is from prostitution.

There was, of course, a Tammany connection. The "political manifestation" of the gang was the James B. O'Rourke Democratic Club, while its social life was centered about "a 'Raines Law' hotel on lower Second Avenue. It had a very glittering back parlor for 'ladies.' There, and in the Hungarian Restaurant next door . . . [the gang] spent their moments of relaxation."[4]

Their "more professional headquarters" were located on Chrystie Street in a dimly lit pool parlor behind a barber shop:

If you walked in from the brightly lighted shop in front, you could not tell how many people were there, nor how many pistols were pointed at you. From the toilet-room in the back was an inconspicuous door into the alley, which, besides its strategic advantages, led to the back door of . . . [a] pawnship. Much stolen goods followed this route.

Yetta manages to escape from the clutches of her would-be procurer —whose description sounds much like that of Paul Kelly, a notorious Lower East Side gangster who led a group of gunmen, pimps, and pickpockets that controlled gambling joints and brothels and had ties with Tammany Hall—and eventually becomes involved in unionizing the garment industry.

Bullard relates the history of the unionization of the garment workers in even more detail than Cahan, his viewpoint being that of the employees rather than that of the manufacturers. There is a vivid description of the skirt-finishers' ball, where Yetta hears for the first time the cry, "Workers, Unite!" and where her new "career" is launched. Scenes depicting union meetings, strikes, picket lines, police brutality, court corruption, and the workhouse on Blackwell's Island where Yetta is imprisoned follow one upon another in rapid succession, and the book deals at length with the nascent American Federation of Labor and the other competing labor organizations that were on the scene at that time.

Bullard's intent in *Comrade Yetta* is twofold. In the first part of the novel he wants to shock his readers into a realization that capitalism is responsible for the grinding poverty and privation in the Jewish ghetto; in the second he attempts to demonstrate the ways in which trade unionists and Socialists alike can work together to affect changes in the system.

Michael Gold, like Bullard, seeks to shock his readers into an awareness of the abuses of capitalism, but only at the very end of *Jews Without Money* is his protagonist converted—and the conversion is to Communism rather than to Socialism. Throughout, Gold's focus is on the backbreaking work done by the immigrants, on their great faith in a country that he believes betrayed them, and above all on the terrible physical aspects of life on the Lower East Side that they were compelled to endure. He describes, for example, the tenement in which he grew up as "nothing but a junk-heap of rotten lumber and brick" and the street on which he lived as "a tenement canyon hung with fire-escapes, bed-clothing, and faces." Here on the street that "roared like a sea" and "exploded like fireworks,"

people pushed and wrangled. . . . There were armies of howling pushcart peddlers. Women screamed, dogs barked and copulated. Babies cried.
    A parrot cursed. Ragged kids played under truck-horses. Fat housewives fought from stoop to stoop. A beggar sang.

Images of filth abound. Garbage was dropped from tenement windows, and in the warm weather "the East Side heavens rained with potato peelings, coffee grounds, herring heads and dangerous soup bones." Gold writes about the smell of garbage and "the stink of cats [that] filled the tenement halls," and stressing the ugly aspects of ghetto life, he describes how a dead horse on the street became "a plaything in the queer and terrible treasure of East Side childhood."

The Jewish slum children play on the lots of Delancey Street, where their playthings are "twisted junk, rusty baby carriages, lumber, bottles, boxes, moldy pants and dead cats." In the summer when they swim in the East River they must "push dead swollen dogs and vegetables" from their faces. And they have to learn to live with the rampant anti-Semitism rife in an area that at the turn of the century was home to the poor of many different ethnic groups. Gold writes about his protagonist's encounter with a group of Italian boys on Mulberry Street, the main stem of the Italian quarter, separated from the Jewish ghetto by the Bowery. Asked where he lived, he answered, "Chrystie Street," at which they shouted, "Hooray, a Jew, a Jew!" and beat him up. Bruised and breathless, and still listening to the shouts of "Christ Killer," he felt safe only when he "came to the Bowery, and managed to cross it into . . . [his] own Jewish land."

Like Ornitz, Gold writes at length about the Lower East Side gangs, which one joined "for self-protection," and about the prostitutes, who in good weather "sat on chairs along the sidewalks," gossiping, knitting, and chewing sunflower seeds. Winking and jeering, they "made lascivious gestures at passing males" and "called their wares like pushcart peddlers."

It would not be an exaggeration to say that Gold found little that was pleasant or attractive in ghetto life; nevertheless, there are several colorful and quite charming descriptions of the area. He writes, for example, about the pleasures and temptations of summer on the Lower East Side, including "the mysterious lemonade man" dressed in exotic Eastern garb and "the fortune-teller with a hand-organ and a parrot." He writes, too, about the wine cellars, so popular at the time, where "people talked, laughed, drank wine, [and] listened to music," and his sketch of Moscowitz's famous wine cellar on Rivington Street (the same Moscowitz was later to open a famous Roumanian restaurant on Second Avenue) is particularly good.

There is also a rather pleasant description of a visit to Bronx Park and his mother's delight when she discovers wild mushrooms, which remind her of her homeland. The theme of pastoral nostalgia is very common in the immigrant literature of this period, for many of those crowding into tenements had come from small towns in Eastern Europe and sorely missed the fresh air and foliage, which were almost totally absent from their new surroundings. The trip to and from Central Park on the El was decidedly unpleasant, however, with

excited screaming mothers, fathers sagging under enormous lunch baskets, children yelling, puking and running under everyone's legs . . . sweating bodies and exasperated nerves—grinding, lurching train, sudden stops when a hundred bodies battered into each other, bedlam of legs and arms, sneezing, spitting, cursing, sighing—a super-tenement on wheels.

The image of a tenement on wheels reappears, but in quite another sense, when Gold speculates about the population changes that occurred on the Lower East Side each decade as Jews managed to make enough money to move "to a better part of the city. At that time, the Jews with a little money were moving to the Bronx and to parts of Brooklyn. There was a great land boom in those places. . . ."

At one point in the story of the Gold family's crushing defeat in America, there is a chance for them to move to Brooklyn's Borough Park, at that time a suburb

of half-finished skeleton houses and piles of lumber and brick. Paved streets ran in rows between empty fields where only the weeds rattled. Real estate signs were stuck everywhere. In the midst of some rusty cans and muck would be a sign shouting "This Wonderful Apartment House Site for Sale!"

Gold describes his family's journey through the swampy fields of Borough Park to a block containing eight wood houses, "each an exact copy of its ugly neighbor." They are urged to buy, because "in five years it will be worth double the price. . . . All the refined Jewish businessmen are buying here." With its electric lights and modern water closet, it seems a fine house, but his mother refuses to buy it, explaining, "I will be lonesome here. I am used only to plain people; I will miss the neighbors on Chrystie Street."

A book that is sometimes compared to *Jews Without Money* because it is about a young boy, the son of immigrant parents, growing up on the Lower East Side is Henry Roth's *Call It Sleep*. It is, however, quite different from Gold's book in a number of respects. First, it is primarily about the inner, subjective world rather than about the outer, objective one, and therefore many of the descriptions of ghetto life are filtered through the imagination and colored by the fears and anxieties of its young protagonist, David Scherl. Furthermore, while Gold intimates that revolution will bring about the many changes necessary to make life on the Lower East Side tolerable, no amount of social change can solve the problems that beset David, who, terrified of his bitter father, his strange surroundings, and his dawning sexual awareness, feels safe only in the presence of his sensitive and nurturing mother. Finally, Roth's lyrical, symbolic novel is a far richer and more complex literary work than the polemical *Jews Without Money.*

That Roth considered the Lower East Side an important, even necessary element in his art can be seen in his third-person response to a query about his failure to write another novel, which appeared in a *New York Times* interview dated April 15, 1971:

Continuity was destroyed when his family moved from snug, orthodox 9th Street, from the homogenous East Side to rowdy, heterogeneous Harlem. . . . That which informed him, connective tissue of his people, inculcated by cheder, countenanced by the street, sanctioned by God, all that dissolved when his parents moved from the East Side. . . .

No longer "at home," Roth stopped writing.

His one novel is among the classics of Jewish-American literature, and its excellence becomes apparent as soon as one reads the prologue. Set on a spring day in 1907, "the year that was destined to bring the greatest number of immigrants to the shores of the United States," it depicts a group of newcomers aboard the *Peter Stuyvesant,* a small steamer, which was carrying them from Ellis Island to New York. Among them were "natives from almost every land in the world, the jeweled close-cropped Teuton, the full-bearded Russian, the scraggly-whiskered Jew," as well as "Slovak peasants with docile faces, smooth-cheeked Armenians, pimply Greeks, Danes with wrinkled eyelids." Roth describes their colorful costumes and their "astonished cries, ... gasps of wonder, [and] reiterations of gladness" when they set foot in the city and were once again united with family and friends.

There are some interesting passages about Brownsville in Brooklyn where the Scherls first went to live, but the best descriptions are of Ninth Street and Avenue D, where they moved in order to be near to the stables after Mr. Scherl had obtained employment as a milkman. The neighborhood was as frightening to David as it was convenient for his father:

For David it was a new and violent world as different from Brownsville as quiet from turmoil. Here on 9th Street it wasn't the sun that swamped one as one left the doorway, it was sound—an avalanche of sound. There were countless children, there were countless baby carriages, there were countless mothers. And to the screams, rebukes and bickerings of these, a seeming endless file of hucksters joined their bawling cries. On Avenue D horse-cars clattered and banged. Avenue D was thronged with beer wagons, garbage carts and coal trucks. There were many automobiles, some blunt and rangey, some with high straw poops, honking. Beyond Avenue D, at the end of a stunted, ruined block that began with shacks and smithies and seltzer bottling works and ended in a junk heap, was the East River on which many boat horns sounded. On 10th Street, the 8th Street Crosstown car ground its way toward the switch.

Roth writes, too, about other nearby streets, most of which frighten David, reflecting as they do the turbulence of his inner life. Perhaps the finest descriptions of all are of the waterfront area. Here David is accosted by a gang of boys who taunt him for being a "Sheeny," and here David begins the process of rebirth after receiving an electric shock when he pushes the handle of a zinc milk ladle into the slot between the streetcar tracks. A truly apt conclusion for a novel that has consistently used New York street scenes to portray a Jewish boy's innermost fears, loneliness, and confusion. For although Roth does not describe tenement life in the same kind of detail as Gold, in his depiction of David's fear of tenement cellars and dark stairways, in his description of the boy's getting lost in Brownsville and being tormented by a group of anti-Semitic boys near the docks, he has in his own way made the city an integral part of his novel. And at the end, when David's transfiguration is about to occur, New York life comes into prominent focus.

Fleeing from his enraged father, David runs past "the old wagon yard . . . the empty stables, splintered runways, chalked doors, the broken windows holding still their glass like fangs in the sash, exhaling manure—damp, rank." Passing the warehouse and the dump heap, David approaches the trolley tracks, and a montage of waterfront life bursts forth. There is a scene in Callahan's beer saloon, where "in the blue, smoky light . . . the pale fattish barkeep jammed the dripping beertap closed and leaned over the bar and snickered," no doubt at his customers—a hunchbacked sooty-faced coal heaver and assorted whores. There is also a sketch depicting a motorman's confrontation with an Armenian peddler whose cart, loaded with halvah, litchie nuts, and other delicacies, was parked directly in front of the trolley tracks. Voices from the Salvation Army were heard, singing, "Open the door to Jesus," and another voice shouted that now, as in the past, the capitalists would betray the oppressed masses.

All these activities are, however, interrupted when David, milk ladle in hand, touches the trolley rails and a flash of lightening bursts forth. Work and play are suspended, and on Avenue D the crowd swells, children run and screech, and a veritable polyglot of lament is heard, reflecting the many different ethnic and religious groups living the the area. One shouts, "Holy mother O' God! Look! Will yiz!"; another, "Oy! Oy Vai! Oy Vai! Oy Vai!"; and still another, "Bambino! Madre Mia!" The crowd witnesses, but is unable to perceive, the transfiguration of a young boy on a New York street, in a city that has been throughout the novel the symbolic setting that reflected his inner life, which is now transformed from the landscape of his terror to the scene of his triumph.

Another novel set on New York's waterfront but located considerably farther uptown—in the Upper East Forties—is Sholem Asch's *East River*. Although he writes about many families living in the neighborhood, including the poor Irish, his attention is focused primarily upon the Davidowskys. The father, Moshe Wolf, is a hard-working grocer who, because there is no neighborhood synagogue, often spends the Sabbath on the Lower East Side, and through his sons, Nat and Irving, Asch relates the history of the garment industry and the growth of labor unionism and Socialism in New York City. But as the title implies, the novel is more about the East River and its environs than about any particular family.

Once the site of farmhouses, there were brownstones in the area by the eighteen sixties, but after the building of the Second and Third Avenue Els and the development of river-front industry, the neighborhood began to deteriorate. By the early twentieth century, it had become a slum area inhabited by a number of ethnic groups, and it was not until the twenties that the neighborhood began to undergo renewal. At present it is one of New York's most fashionable and affluent sections.

Writing about the region at the turn of the century, Asch describes the riverfront as "one extended stable for Manhattan's horses." Here, where even the strong smell of horses could not overpower the fumes of raw whiskey, there were storehouses, warehouses, and granaries lining the shore. Longshoreman "unloaded sand, rolled iron drums filled with gasoline, or beer casks bound with iron hoops, carried bricks, or hauled sacks of sugar and salt." All in all, it was a vital, noisy area:

From early in the morning, before the full light of day had emerged, there came through the open tenement windows the clatter of truck wheels and the pounding of heavily shod horses' hoofs on the cobblestones of the street. Wagons jammed with milk cans, beer wagons drawn by powerful brewery horses, grain wagons, wagons heaped high with vegetables and fruits, crowded the East River streets and belabored the air with the deafening sounds of clanking iron and creaking wood.

Later in the morning hordes of people rushed to the trolley cars and El train, which "raced along like an iron monster splitting the ears with a deafening clatter of iron wheels on iron rails."

Clearly the river brought industry to the area, and with it noise, filth, and decay. But it was also a blessing to the residents of the neighborhood. Although having limited access to the river because the dead-end streets were "hemmed in by fences erected by the owners of the feed storehouses and stables," the children "find relief from the overpowering heat" by diving off rotting, abandoned docks, disregarding "the perils of . . . falling timbers." In addition, Asch explains that Forty-eighth Street had two yards that opened onto the river and that Democratic politicians had control of one of them, distributing tickets of admission to local residents to win and keep support for the local Tammany club.

As indicated earlier, Asch also writes about the garment industry, which employed many of the area's inhabitants. One of the Davidowsky brothers becomes a wealthy manufacturer, while his brother joins the ranks of the Socialists, who attack the manufacturers, particularly those who employ the "bundle system," which had infested the whole neighborhood with "the plague of homework—the bundles of cut material which the contractors sent to the tenement flats to be sewn together into finished garments." Like *Comrade Yetta* and *The Rise of David Levinsky, East River* contains much about the development of unions in the garment industry, but most memorable is its depiction of the tragic fire that occurred in 1911 in the factory of the Triangle Shirtwaist Company, which played an important role in strengthening the ILGWU (International Ladies Garment Workers Union) and in bringing about legislation to protect factory employees.

The factory occupied several floors in the Asch building on Washington Place, near Greene Street, the present site of New York University's Brown Building. Most of its employees were young women who worked for approximately nine and one-half hours a day, six days a week, and earned a weekly average of $15.50.

The fire—which started when a match fell on the floor and a piece of material caught fire—spread quickly, and many lives were lost because the owners had sealed off the rear exit in an attempt to check theft. Thirty-four bodies were found piled up in front of the rear door, and in all one hundred and forty-six workers died in the fire. Public indignation was great, and a hundred thousand East Siders followed the funeral procession, demanding that the cause of justice be served. Although the owners were indicted on charges of manslaughter, they were never convicted.

One of the characters in *East River* is employed at the Triangle Shirtwaist Company, and after describing the physical layout of the plant, Asch goes on to depict in painful detail what happened when the fire started and moments later "remnants of material and trimmings, silks, linings, padded cotton, the oil-soaked rags which the girls used to clean the machines" burst into flame. Screaming, gagging, and choking, many of the girls pushed toward the rear exit; those closest to the door began "beating at it with their fists, tearing at it with fingers, clawing at it with their nails." Others, more fortunate, fled in other directions, and Asch describes both the miraculous escape of one of the girls through a window and the street scene below. All in all, the eight or nine pages dealing with this catastrophe are a unique contribution to New York City fiction, and so is Asch's treatment of the East River area, which is hardly a typical setting for a novel about New York Jews in the first decades of the twentieth century.

Another novel about New York Jews during this period that is not set on the Lower East Side is Ludwig Lewisohn's *The Island Within*. Its setting is the Upper West Side, and it is about German Jews, so often derisively referred to in novels about the Lower East Side—and in *East River* as well—but rarely treated in any depth. Although Lewisohn's novel opens in 1840 in Vilna, Poland, it is for the most part the story of Reb Mendel ben Reb Jizchock's American-born descendent Arthur Levy, who searches for his identity as an American Jew.

The son of wealthy Americanized parents, Arthur's experiences are a far cry from those of young Michael Gold, for example. His father, Jacob, an Eastern European immigrant who married the American-born daughter of a German-Jewish family and quickly adopted her values and life style, had at first worked in a small department store on lower Sixth Avenue that

did an enormous trade with the poorer Irish of the lower West Side, who were shy of entering the more imposing and glittering establishments near at hand. Then poor Italians flooded those streets, and they too came for their underwear and children's clothes and overalls and cheap furniture . . . .

Soon Jacob has accumulated enough capital to start his own business, and success lies at hand. In the early 1890s, when "the World Building was the tallest in New York,"[5] Arthur's parents live in an apartment on West

Eightieth Street; later, at a time when architects were beginning to experiment with new styles on the Upper West Side, they purchase a house on Ninety-first Street, near West End Avenue:

Jacob would have preferred one of those newer-styled houses in yellow brick with great bay windows. But Gertrude [his wife] . . . preferred the unquestionable gentility of a brownstone front with a stoop on which one could sit in the spring evenings.

The Levys have little interest in religion, but when on the occasion of his son's birth, Jacob has a yearning to attend synagogue, he does not do so because he is "far away from the old-fashioned *shools* downtown into which a man could drop informally to pray." The Reform temples on the Upper West Side are "open, like Protestant churches, for formal worship on Sabbath eve and morning."

Actually, what Arthur's parents for the most part want is to be as little identified with their Jewish heritage as possible, to be Americans, with just a touch of German. They enjoy going to Luchow's—which opened in 1882 and is still in operation at 110 East Fourteenth Street and which still remains famous for its German specialities—and to a "delightful little German cellar restaurant on an Eighth Street corner called 'Zum Prelaten.' "

They socialize with other German Jews and with "aristocratic Sephardic families who had come to America . . . before the American Revolution," and they consider themselves superior to the Eastern European Jewish immigrants, whom Arthur thinks of as totally alien to himself, "repulsive, in fact: dirty, sunk in superstition, loud, Oriental without being picturesque, jabbering in a mongrel jargon, smelling of garlic."

Instead of sending their son to City College, where he would meet and mingle with the sons of Russian-Jewish immigrants, the Levys send Arthur to Columbia, which was established at its present Morningside Heights location in 1897, and there is an excellent description of the university in 1910, when the new buildings

still gleamed and glittered in their efficient newness and splendor. . . . One walked on this quadrangle with the erectness of a man. One sat in a capacious chair in that great domed library and had attendants bring one books and partook somehow of the dignity of learning. One had a considerable freedom in the choice of courses and studies; one could leave the campus between classes and loiter by the brilliant gold-flecked river under the yellowing poplars.

Arthur becomes a psychoanalyst, and the book provides an in-depth study of assimilated Jewish intellectuals in New York during the nineteen twenties as well as of the virulent anti-Semitism that swept America in the period after World War I. But his status as an assimilated Jew disturbs him, and he begins a long search to discover the meaning of Judaism and his own relation to it. He studies with an Orthodox rabbi who helps him to make a religious commitment, and at the conclusion of the novel Arthur has undertaken a mission to help European Jewry.

The conclusion is a welcome change from that of so many of the works discussed in this chapter which deal with Jews like David Levinsky who repudiate the past and their religion to become American. Arthur is an American Jew in search of a past that his assimilated parents have denied him, and clearly it is symbolic that at the end of the novel he journeys to Europe not only to help his fellow Jews but also to discover his heritage, an obvious reversal of the pattern whereby many, though certainly not all, Jewish immigrants coming from Europe to America abandoned their own rich and meaningful tradition.

5

SKYSCRAPER CITY

Perhaps the single most important development in the physical appearance of New York City during the early years of the twentieth century was its transformation into a "skyscraper city." The widespread use of steel-skeleton construction, first employed in the eleven-story Tower Building at 50 Broadway, which was completed in 1889, permitted the erection of high yet structurally sound buildings like the twenty-one story Flatiron Building, built in 1902, which for some years was New York's architectural showplace. It lost its special status, however, as new structures like the forty-seven-story Singer Building (1908) and the sixty-story Woolworth Building (1913)—known as the "cathedral of commerce" and for over twenty years the world's tallest building—were erected.

New York, which as early as 1905 was referred to as "a city of giants"[1] by a visiting Frenchman, could boast of more than skyscrapers. As a result of the City Beautiful movement, it was adorned with many handsome architectural monuments and statues. Fifth Avenue—the city's finest residential street—was lined with replicas of French châteaus and Italian villas inhabited by first- and second-generation millionaires, and the building boom on the West Side continued as New Yorkers flocked to live in the apartment houses, family hotels, and private dwellings that were being constructed there.

The city had several huge department stores and was by every measure thriving economically. By 1900 there were nearly forty thousand manufacturing companies in New York that annually produced more than 1,300,000,000 dollars worth of goods. Thirty-seven percent of all American exports and 67 percent of its imports passed through New York's bustling port. It was a period of great expansion on Wall Street, which by now controlled financial dealings all over the United States and in many foreign countries as well.

Thanks to Thomas A. Edison, New York had become a brilliantly lit city, especially in its theatre district—now known as the "Great White Way"—which had moved uptown and now had its center at Broadway and Forty-second Street. Electricity had also been put to use to improve the city's transportation system. The Els were electrified, and electrified cable cars and trolleys were more and more supplanting horsecars. Other improvements were soon to come. In 1904 the subway was opened, and three more bridges—the Williamsburg, the Manhattan, and the Queensboro—were constructed across the East River in an attempt to shorten the distance between Manhattan, the hub of the metropolis, and the other boroughs comprising Greater New York, which were growing in population and supplying a significant percentage of the city's work force. In addition, the production of large quantities of automobiles had begun. Interest in cars, stimulated by the automobile show held in Madison Square Garden in 1900, was great; and automobiles began to be seen in place of horse-drawn carriages on New York City streets.

There were many cultural developments in the city as well, among them the opening in 1902 of the section fronting on Fifth Avenue of the Metropolitan Museum of Art, the construction of the New York Public Library Building on Fifth Avenue, between Fortieth and Forty-second streets, on the former site of the Croton Reservoir (1898–1911), and the establishment of over sixty branch libraries financed by Andrew Carnegie, who some years earlier had donated funds to build Carnegie Hall.

The construction of skyscrapers, residences, and public buildings, the tearing down of old structures, the roaring of the El trains overhead, the din of subway excavations and automobile traffic was transforming New York City into a noisy metropolis that seemed to many an emblem of the growth, change, energy, and material progress that lay ahead in the new century.

The city was hardly a symbol of material progress to those who wrote about its poorer inhabitants, however. Among them was William S. Porter, who is better known by his pseudonym O. Henry. O. Henry, who arrived in New York in 1902, lived at several addresses in Manhattan, including 49 East Ninth Street and 55 Irving Place. Although he wrote about many aspects of New York life, he is best remembered for his descriptions of its working poor, the shops in which they found employment, the rooming houses in which they took lodgings, and the cheap restaurants in which they ate their meals.

In his preface to *The Four Million,* a collection of stories set in New York City, O. Henry alludes to the phrase "the Four Hundred," which supposedly had its origin in 1892 when one of Mrs. William Astor's contemporaries remarked that the Astor ballroom was able to accommodate four hundred, that being the total number of people then comprising fashionable New York society; and he explains that his own title reflects his interest in *all* New Yorkers.

Among the most memorable stories in this collection is "The Skylight Room," which is about a young woman who nearly dies of starvation in an East Side rooming house supposedly modeled on "Ma" Ettinger's house on East Ninth Street, where O. Henry himself lived for a time. The accommodations ranged from the exclusive "double parlors" to the pitiful "Skylight Room" on the fourth floor, which "occupied 7 x 8 feet of floor space at the middle of the hall" and contained "an iron cot, a washstand and a chair. A shelf was the dresser. Its four bare walls seemed to close in upon you like the sides of a coffin."

"The Furnished Room" is also about rooming houses and their occupants, who are as "restless, shifting, fugacious as time itself. . . . Homeless, they have a hundred homes. They flit from furnished room to furnished room, transients forever—transients in abode, transients in heart and mind." Set in "the red brick district of the Lower West Side," the story is about one such transient in search of lodgings who accompanies the landlady up the dank and dimly lit staircase, treading on carpet that appeared "to have degenerated in that rank, sunless air to lichen or spreading moss . . . and was viscid under the foot like organic matter." Despite misgivings about the tattered upholstery, the "chipped and bruised" furniture, and "the couch [which] distorted by bursting springs, seemed a horrible monster that had been slain during the stress of some grotesque convulsion," he takes the room.

It is likely that among his fellow roomers were one or more of New York's shopgirls. O. Henry writes with compassion about these girls, girls like Masie who in "A Lickpenny Lover" sells gloves in New York's "Biggest Store,"[2] which employs three thousand salesgirls, and Dulcie, whose budget is discussed in "An Unfinished Story." Dulcie pays two dollars a week for her tiny room, and struggling to make ends meet, splurges only on Sunday mornings, when she spends twenty-five cents for breakfast in Billy's restaurant. The rest of the week she lives frugally:

On week-days her breakfast cost ten cents; she made coffee and cooked an egg over the gaslight. . . . She had her lunches in the department store restaurant at a cost of sixty cents for the week; dinners were $1.05. The evening papers . . . came to six cents; and two Sunday papers—one for the personal column and the other to read—were ten cents. The total amounts to $4.76.[3]

O. Henry's stories are replete with references to the inexpensive, noisy places where girls like Masie and Dulcie ate and to the particular stresses of their jobs, not the least of which were the long, tiring hours, the constant scrutiny from the floorwalkers, and the propositions from male customers. Yet no stranger to other aspects of New York life, O. Henry also writes about its streets and squares, its theatres, restaurants, and cafés, including Scheffel Hall, a German restaurant and taproom on Third Avenue at Seventeenth Street, which he calls Rheinschloss, and the opulent and gay Mouquin's, a gathering place for artists and writers on Thirty-eighth Street and Sixth Avenue.

Lively Shubert Alley is another of his subjects, and so is Broadway, the "Gay White Way," which in "Man About Town" is depicted with its thousands of electric lights and at least as many pedestrians, among them "diners . . . shop-girls, confidence men, panhandlers, actors, highwaymen, millionaires and outlanders." In "The Love-Philtre of Ikey Schoenstein," he even writes about the Blue Light Drugstore, located "between the Bowery and First Avenue, where the distance between the streets is the shortest."[4] He is impressed because the establishment "does not consider that pharmacy is a thing of bric-a-brac, scent and ice cream sodas; scorning "the labour-saving devices of modern pharmacy," it makes its own pills, "macerates its opium and percolates its own laudanum and paregoric."

In "A Bird of Bagdad" O. Henry extols the strengths and acknowledges the weaknesses of Fourth Avenue—now called Park Avenue South above Fourteenth Street. "Born and bred in the Bowery," its northward stretch is "full of good resolutions," and crossing Fourteenth Street, it swaggers "for a brief moment proudly in the glare of the museums and cheap theatres." It cannot, however, compete with "its high-born sister boulevard to the west, or its roaring, polyglot, broad-waisted cousin in the east," for soon

come the silent and terrible mountains—buildings square as forts, high as the clouds, shutting out the sky where thousands of slaves bend over desks all day. On the ground floors are only little fruit shops and laundries and book shops. . . . And next—poor Fourth Avenue!—the street glides into medieval solitude. On each side are the shops devoted to "Antiques."
With a shriek and a crash Fourth Avenue dives headlong into the tunnel at Thirty-fourth and is never seen again.

Despite his descriptions of its lively streets, gay cafés, and quaint shops, more often than not O. Henry portrays the city as a depressing and lonely place, and in "Squaring the Circle," explains that its straight geometrical lines "coldly exhibit a sneering defiance of the curved line of nature." Yet in quite another mood he staunchly defends the city against its detractors in "Between Rounds," claiming that its hardness is only on the surface:

Silent, grim, colossal, the big city has ever stood against its revilers. They call it hard as iron; they say that no pulse of pity beats in its bosom; they compare its streets with lonely forests and deserts of lava. But beneath the hard crust of the lobster is found a delectable and luscious food.

There is, in most of O. Henry's stories, a sense of hope for those who struggle to survive in the harsh or seemingly harsh city and an admiration for a kind of decency and dignity that his characters maintain even under the most trying circumstances. In this sense, O. Henry is like Betty Smith, whose impoverished residents of Brooklyn's Williamsburg in the early years of the twentieth century may be without life's comforts—or even, at times, its basic necessities—but who are noble in their struggle to maintain their independence and their integrity.

Although she wrote other Brooklyn novels, Smith's most famous work is, of course, *A Tree Grows in Brooklyn.* With its symbolic Tree of Heaven that "grew in boarded-up lots and out of neglected rubbish heaps and . . . out of cement," it is truly an inspiring portrait of a lower-class Irish-German family living in Williamsburg from 1912 to 1919. With its vivid descriptions of the neighborhood's mixed racial and ethnic population, its tenements, schools, shops, and saloons, it is one of the best Brooklyn novels ever written.

The first chapter is a veritable street map of the area. Francie, the young protagonist, and her brother Neely take a trip to see the junkman. They go "up Manhattan Avenue, past Maujer, Ten Eyck, Stagg to Scholes Street. Beautiful names for ugly streets." Later Francie passes the Jewish district, which "started at Siegal Street, took in Moore and McKibben and went past Broadway," and on Graham Street she is fascinated by

the filled pushcarts—each a little store in itself—the bargaining, emotional Jews and the peculiar smells of the neighborhood: baked stuffed fish, sour rye bread fresh from the oven, and something that smelled like honey boiling.

Smith describes the ethnic composition of Francie's neighborhood in even more detail in *Maggie Now*:

It was a swarming neighborhood. Fifty percent of the population were Irish and German with a few English and Scottish families. There was a neighborhood saying that the Irish and the Germans "got along good together." Evidently this was so as there was a great deal of intermarriage between the Germans and the Irish.

The Jews and the Italians were called foreigners by the Irish and the Germans, presumably because they were not Nordic. There were some Dutch families left over from the time when Brooklyn had been called Breuckelen. They were classified with the Germans. Because there were some similarities in their language, Germans were called Dutchmen. Then there were Poles, Hungarians, Swedes, some Chinese who lived among bundles of laundry in rooms back of one-windowed stores, sloe-eyed Armenians and swarthy Greeks.

There were even some Indians. They were of the Canarsie tribe and they made their homes in run-down, abandoned, one-windowed stores.

Francie first lived in a Bogart Street tenement next door to a stable, but later the Nolans moved to the more refined Lorimer Street. Although still in Williamsburg, it was nearer to the Greenpoint section and was "peopled by letter carriers, firemen and those store owners who were affluent enought not to have to live in the back of the store." Still later, the family moves to a dilapidated railroad flat on nearby Grand Street. Lacking the bathroom and stoop the Nolans had enjoyed on Lorimer Street, its best feature is the roof, from which Francie can see "a whole new world," including "the lovely span of the Williamsburg Bridge,"[5] and in the distance the Brooklyn Bridge and Manhattan, "a fairy city made of silver cardboard."

Her horizons gradually broadening, Francie one day walks a few blocks, turns a corner, and finds herself in a section of Brooklyn inhabited by "fifth and sixth generation Americans." Contrasting this neighborhood with her own, where having been "born in America . . . was equivalent to Mayflower standing," she concludes that "only in a great sprawling place like Brooklyn could there be such a sharp division."

On another occasion she goes with her father to Bushwick Avenue, which

was the high-toned boulevard of old Brooklyn. It was a wide, tree-shaded avenue and the houses were rich and impressively built of large granite blocks with long stone stoops. Here lived the big-time politicians, the monied brewery families, the well-to-do immigrants who had been able to come over first class instead of steerage.

Although a visit to Bushwick was an unusual treat, there were many exciting events in Francie's own Williamsburg. Smith writes about the three-piece band that came around every week and played on the street and about the organ-grinders; according to her, "there was always music. There were song and dancing on the Brooklyn streets in those long-ago summers. . . ."

Some of the most memorable events in Williamsburg were sponsored by Tammany Hall, which "got the children young and educated them in the party ways." To woo them, there were boat rides and picnics, and on Election Night the children danced around big bonfires and ate roasted potatoes which they called "mickies."

On Thanksgiving Day they dressed up in costumes and went around to shops begging for treats. On a more regular basis they attended the theatre, for at that time "there were many good stock companies in the neighborhood: Blaney's, Corse Payton's and Philip's Lyceum. . . . [which] the children called. . . . 'The Lyce' and then changed that into 'the Louse.'"

Recreation for their fathers centered largely around the Williamsburg barrooms. One particularly memorable scene, which takes place in McGarrity's saloon in 1916, consists mainly of snatches of conversation about the issues of the time: prohibition, the woman's vote, automobiles and airplanes, movies, and the war. The voices rail at the upcoming prohibition, doubt that women will ever get the vote, contemplate a future when horses will be things of the past, consider airplanes a fad, discuss the closing of Brooklyn theatres and the advent of the movies, and argue about whether or not Woodrow Wilson will keep them out of the war.

Smith does more than merely describe aspects of Brooklyn life; she also conveys a special feeling about the borough and depicts the attitude of Brooklynites toward Manhattan. From the beginning of *A Tree Grows in Brooklyn,* Manhattan is perceived by Francie as a different—and quite glamorous—world. She decides that someday she will cross the bridge, make her way uptown, and visit "such legendary places as Reisenweber's and the Waldorf,"[6] and when her brother gets a job in Manhattan, Francie is envious because every day, while Neely "crossed the great Williamsburg Bridge and went into the strange city," she walked to her work on the north side of Brooklyn.

Later, however, when she finally gets a job in Manhattan, she finds the borough, with its crowds and high buildings, less enchanting than she had imagined it to be. The bridge, too, is a disappointment because crossing it does not "make her feel lika gossamer-winged fairy flying through the air." Eventually there is the realization that Brooklyn, not Manhattan, is the enchanted place. Francie tells Neely that Brooklyn is "a magic city and it isn't real." Later in the book when Francie and a beau walk across Brooklyn Bridge—which was, by the way, and probably still is, a popular lovers' lane—she says, "Brooklyn's better." She goes on to explain that although it doesn't have skyscrapers, "there's a *feeling* about it—Oh, I can't explain it. You've got to live in Brooklyn to know."

The feelings with which Brooklynites view Manhattan are also discussed in Smith's novel *Tomorrow Will Be Better.* Set several years later in the same neighborhood, the book describes its protagonist's yearning to work in Manhattan, which she considers "a glamorous place" and "a new world." Margy's attitude antagonizes her mother, Flo, who is one of those loyal Brooklynites whose fighting loyalty to her birthplace had been inherited from her parents. They and their neighbors had seriously considered setting up cannon and ramparts to fight a civil war for Brooklyn's liberty back in the old days when Brooklyn, a great American city in its own right, was absorbed by the census-hungry New York City and demoted to "borough."

Flo's loyalty to Brooklyn is perhaps best expressed when she berates her daughter for having wasted time seeking employment in Manhattan:

"I told you you'd stand a better chance in Brooklyn. I told you it was silly to go so far away from home to work. I told you that there's everything in Brooklyn that you could find or see in New York."[7]

Henry Miller, born in the Yorkville section of Manhattan in 1891 and raised in Brooklyn—first in Williamsburg and then in Bushwick—often writes about Brooklyn, but his attitude is far different from that of Betty Smith or her characters. Although the tone is sometimes nostalgic or even maudlin, much of his writing suggests that he perceived Brooklyn as antithetical to the aesthetic and the ecstatic, which he sought in art and in sex, in Europe and then in Big Sur, California. Brooklyn philistinism was a frequent subject of his; in *Tropic of Capricorn* he describes Myrtle Avenue as "a street [where] no saint ever walked . . . nor any poet," and he refers to himself as "just a Brooklyn boy . . . which is to say one of the last and least of men."

In "The 14th Ward" Miller writes about the Williamsburg of his youth, about the "steel-gray battleships in the Navy Yard," the neighborhood saloons, a burlesque house called the Bum, and a tin factory located opposite his home on Driggs Avenue, where he lived until he was ten:

Where others remember of their youth a beautiful garden, a fond mother, a sojourn at the seashore, I remember, with a vividness as if it were etched in acid, the grim soot-covered walls and chimneys of the tin factory opposite us and the bright, circular pieces of tin that were strewn in the street, some bright and gleaming, others rusted, dull, copperish, leaving a stain on the fingers; I remember the ironworks where the red furnace glowed and men walked toward the glowing pit with huge shovels in their hands, while outside were the shallow wooden forms like coffins with rods through them on which you scraped your shins or broke your neck.

In the same piece Miller describes his family's move to Decatur Street in the German-American Bushwick section, which he describes as "a cemetery, a *Lutheran* cemetery, where the tombstones were always in order and the wreaths never faded." The same note reappears in "Reunion in Brooklyn." Here Miller writes about his return from Greece to visit his dying father, and his realization that the whole borough is moribund:

In Brooklyn, so it seemed to me, they were dying of malnutrition of the soul. They lived on as vegetable tissue, flabby, sleep-drugged, disease-ridden carcasses with just enough intelligence to enable them to buy oil burners, radios, automobiles, newspapers, tickets for the cinema.

When Miller rhapsodizes elsewhere over the monumental achievement of John A. Roebling, it is not because the bridge links what he thinks of as the moribund borough of Brooklyn to the city's thriving commercial and cultural center, Manhattan, but because it is for him a bridge to the past and a symbol of transcendence. If Brooklyn represents death through intellectual inertia and philistinism, feverish and chaotic Manhattan is emblematic of the alientation and negation of modern urban life, another kind of death.

In "The Tailor Shop," an account of the years before and after World War I that he spent working in his father's midtown Manhattan shop, Miller appears to despise the present, when "riveters are sewing up the ribs of the coming skyscrapers," and to despair of the future, which promises to be "a world made entirely of merchandise which rises box on box like a paper factory, f.o.b. Canarsie." Alienation his most pressing theme, he finds himself "swimming in the crowd, a digit with the rest" and rages against the "steel and concrete hedging me in. . . . The new world eating into me, expropriating me."

Whether he writes in *Black Spring* about the Bowery, with "its pimps, cooks, cokies, panhandlers, beggars, touts, gunmen . . . [and] drunken micks," or Fourteenth Street, which he calls a "line of pus" separating the city's Jewish and Gentile populations, or describes in *Tropic of Capricorn* Brooklyn's spiritually improverished residents or contemporary Broadway from Times Square to Fiftieth Street, with its "hamburger sandwiches . . . slot machines . . . free toilets . . . sanitary napkins, mint jujubes, billiard balls, sugared sweet and powdered urine," Miller's New York is—with a single exception—a landscape of despair. The exception is the Jewish quarter on the Lower East Side, which Miller—himself a non-Jew—describes in "The Ghetto (N.Y.)" as the only vital part of the city:

All the glamour of New York is squeezed into this pullulating area which is marked off by formaldehyde and sweat and tears. . . . The rest of New York is an abstraction; it is cold, geometrical, rigid as *rigor mortis* and, I might as well add, *insane*—if one can only stand apart and look at it un-dauntedly. Only in the beehive can one find the human touch, find that city of sights, sounds, smells which one hunts for in vain beyond the margins of the ghetto. To live outside the pale is to wither and die. Beyond the pale there are only dressed-up cadavers. They are wound up each day, like alarm clocks. They perform like seals; they die like box-office receipts. But in the seething honeycomb there is a growth as of plants, an animal warmth almost suffocating, a vitality which accrues from rubbing and glueing together, a hope which is physical as well as spiritual, a contamination which is dangerous but salutary.

Brooklyn Heights, just across the river from the Lower East Side so beloved by Henry Miller, is the setting for Ernest Poole's *The Harbor*. A fictional history of the city's waterfront commerce over several decades beginning in the eighteen eighties, Poole's novel, which describes the three phases of New York's waterfront commerce—the original mode of small, competitive businesses, the transfer of control to large corporations, and the eventual struggle of unions to gain power—opens with some fascinating descriptions of the Heights, where Bill, the son of a prosperous merchant, grows up in a "narrow brownstone house" on a "sedate old street."

From Poole's description of the back windows that overlook the harbor it would appear that the brownstone is located on Columbia Heights, one of the most fashionable streets in "one of the quietest, the cleanest, and the finest [neighborhoods] . . . of any in the country." Columbia Heights was then lined with brownstone mansions, many of which belonged to merchants like Bill's father, whose ships were docked at nearby piers. These piers ran back to warehouses, the roofs of which, when planted, made fine backyard gardens. Poole writes about the street's

old-fashioned houses . . . a few of red brick, but more of brown stone with spotless white-sashed windows which were tall and narrow and rounded at the top. There were no trees, but there were many smooth, orderly vines. Almost all the houses had wide, inviting doorways . . . but the people they invited in were only those who lived quietly here, shutting out New York and all the toots and rumblings of the ships and warehouses and docks below, of which they themselves were the owners.[8]

Not far from Bill's house, on nearby Orange Street, was—and is— the historic Plymouth Church of the Pilgrims founded by Henry Beecher Ward in 1847. Here the young protagonist, unmoved by the history of the famous church, which was the center of so much abolitionist activity and whose worshippers at one time or another included Abraham Lincoln, Horace Greeley, Mark Twain, and Booker T. Washington, must endure his "Sabbath torture."

Clearly it is not the church but the harbor that captures the youth's imagination. Its sights and sounds are always with him. At noon he watches the laborers, "some nearly naked, some only in shirts, men with the hairiest faces," sitting against the warehouse wall eating lunch and taking "long drinks of a curious stuff all white on top." At night in his bed he listens to "hoots and shrieks from ferries and tugs, hoarse coughs from engines along the docks, the whine of wheels, the clang of bells, deep blasts and bellows from steamers."

Sometimes, having escaped the watchful eye of his mother or nurse, he explores the waterfront with the dirty and ill-clad children "who live in poorer and smaller houses down below." They play in the dock sheds and warehouses, climb on freighters, and search for treasures in the "dark holds of the square-rigged ships called 'clippers,'" where they find "curious mottled wood, huge baskets of sugar, odorous spices, indigo, camphor, tea, coffee, jute and endless other things" that came from far-away exotic places like "Manila, Calcutta, Bombay, Ceylon."

While the youths find romance and excitement on the Brooklyn water-front, Bill's father and other merchants like him find themselves beset by many problems, for

the harbor had changed and . . . mammoth corporations, great foreign shipping companies [were] combining in agreement with the American railroads to freeze out all the little men and to take to themselves the whole port of New York.

Eventually Bill's father is forced to sell out to a huge company whose holdings include over two miles of docks and warehouses, but Bill's inter-est in the harbor does not end with his family's setback or his own boyhood. He becomes a writer whose subject is the city's port and a chronicler of the changes that have occurred in the shipping industry:

The sails were gone. . . .
Gone, too, were the American sailors. All races of men on the earth but ours seemed gathered around this hog of the sea. From barges filled with her cargo, the stuff was being heaved up on the dock by a lot of Irish bargemen. Italian dockers rolled it across to this German ship, and on deck a Jap under-officer was bossing a Coolie crew. . . .
The Old East with its riches was no longer here. For what were these Coolies doing? Handling silks and spices? Oh, no. They were hoisting and letting down into the hold an automobile from Dayton, Ohio, bound for New South Wales. Gone were the figs and almonds, the indigo, ivory, tortoise shells.

His focus no longer exclusively on the Brooklyn harbor, Poole also writes about the North River piers and about West Street, which in Revo-lutionary days had been underwater. Although in 1811 the bank was ex-tended and raised to permit the building of docks, these docks were not used much until 1870, and it was not until 1890 that West Street displaced South Street as the city's main gateway for water traffic. Poole's portrait

of the bustling Manhattan docks in the early years of the twentieth century is memorable, but his best descriptions remain those of the Brooklyn
waterfront.

In the course of the novel his protagonist, Bill, progresses through
several stages. As a boy, he is enthralled by the excitement and romance of
the Brooklyn harbor. As a young author, he is both a historian and critic
of New York's waterfront industry. For a time a participant in a program
of renovation that will make New York the greatest port in the world, he
later becomes involved in unionizing dock workers and stokers, whose
miserable working conditions are depicted in the book. What remains unchanged, however, is the abiding interest of both the author and his protagonist in the docks, the longshoremen, the boats, the bridges, and the
warehouses of New York City. In *The Harbor* is found a full and rich
treatment of a subject rarely if ever dealt with in New York fiction.

Although in physical distance not too many miles away from some of
the docks described by Poole, the concert halls and opera houses depicted
in James Huneker's *Painted Veils* and Willa Cather's *The Song of the Lark*
seem to belong wholly to another world. Poole writes about New York's
brisk waterfront commerce; Huneker and Cather depict the city as a
thriving cultural and artistic center.

Huneker's novel, published in 1920, was considered quite daring for
its time. It traces the musical career of Easter Brandes over several decades.
The book opens with Easter's arrival in New York City. She has taken
quarters on Twenty-fifth Street, close to Madison Square, in a hotel called
Maison Felicé, which "was in reality two old-fashioned houses with high
steps and brown stone façades . . . [and was] one of those semi-hotels with
table d'hôtes so popular in New York two or three decades ago." Its clientele is for the most part bohemian, but few if any of the aspiring artists,
writers, and musicians who live there will achieve the success of Easter
Brandes, who will one day sing at the Metropolitan Opera House.

There are many interesting descriptions of the city during the late
eighties and nineties, particularly of well-known restaurants like Martin's,
on Ninth Street and University Place, and, of course, of the city's opera
houses, concert halls, and music conservatories, but particularly memorable are a number of lengthy and at times lyrical passages describing New
York some decades later, after it has been transformed into a skyscraper
city.

At one point in the novel Easter and some of her friends are having coffee at the Vienna Café, next to Grace Church. One member of the party is
particularly taken by the scene before him, which makes him reflect "that
in no other spot of this planet is the tempo of living faster." Contempla-
ting the city's hard surfaces, abrupt rhythms, incessant noise, and huge
proportions, he yet concludes that it has a beauty of its own:

Its specific beauty savours of the monstrous. The scale is epical. Too many buildings are glorified chimneys. But what a picture of titanic energy, of cyclopean ambition. Look over Manhattan from Washington Heights. The wilderness of flat roofs in London; the winning profile of Paris; the fascination of Rome as viewed from Trinata dei Monti; of Buda from across the Danube at Pest—these are not more startingly dramatic than New York, especially when the chambers of the west are filled with the tremendous opal of a dying day, or when the lyric moonrise paves a path of silver across the hospitable sea. . . .

Another character, looking out the window of a Lexington Avenue apartment at dusk, thinks that "the magic of New York" can best be appreciated at night, when it glows with a "mysterious melancholy beauty":

He saw a cluster of blazing lights across at the West Side Circle, a ladder of fire the pivot. Further down theatre-land dazzled with its tongues of flame. Literally a pit, white hot. Across in the cool shadows of the east are level lines of twinkling points. The bridges. There is always the sense of water not afar. The hotels are tier upon tier starry with illumination. The avenues, long shafts of bluish-white electric globed fire. . . . In the moonlight mansions on Fifth Avenue seem snow-driven. . . . The park as if liquified, flowed in plastic rhythms, a lake of velvety foliage, a mezzotint dividing the east from the west. Sudden furnace bonfires leap up from the Brooklyn side; they are purely commercial. . . . Battery Place and the Bay are operatic, the stage for a thrilling fairy spectacle. The dim, scattered plain of granite house-tops are like a petrified cemetery of immemorial Titans. At night, he mused, the city loses its New World aspect. It reveals the patina of Time. It is a city exotic, semibarbaric, the fantasy of an oriental sorcerer who had been mad enough to evoke from unplumbed and forgotten seas the long lost Atlantis. . . .

In still another impressionistic nocturnal scene, the "undulating blur of blue and grey and frosty white, . . . [the] ebon silhouettes of hushed brassy places, and the shimmering wet night" are described as evoking "the exasperating tableau of a petrified Venice."

The style of *The Song of the Lark* is quite different from that of *Painted Veils,* and Cather's novel contains none of the long, lyrical descriptions of the city that are found in Huneker's work. Nonetheless, it too depicts New York's musical world, and its protagonist, Thea Kronberg, is, like Easter Brandes, invited to sing at the Metropolitan Opera House. Several scenes are set there, and on one occasion it is depicted through the eyes of an out-of-towner who is visiting the opera house for the first time and is impressed by

the height of the audience room, the rich color, and the sweep of the balconies. . . . He watched the house fill with a growing feeling of expectation. When the steel curtain rose and the men of the orchestra took their places he felt distinctly nervous. The burst of applause which greeted the conductor keyed him still higher. . . . When the lights went down and the violins began the overture, the place looked larger than ever; a great pit, shadowy and solemn. The whole atmosphere, he reflected, was somehow more serious than he had anticipated.

Cather also writes about New York's less venerable but nonetheless famous institution, Weber and Fields'. Located on Broadway and Twenty-ninth Street, this was a music hall where Joe Weber and Lew Fields, a team of slapstick comedians, performed. Their vaudeville shows, which featured such famous entertainers as Lillian Russell, were a major New York attraction, and opening-night tickets were auctioned off for sometimes un-believably high prices.

While in New York, Thea lives on Riverside Drive, in an apartment hotel "as impersonal as the Waldorf, and quite as large. It was above 116th Street, where the Drive narrows, and in front of it the shelving bank dropped to the North River." But when we think of Cather's New York fiction, we think not of the Upper West Side, but of Madison Square, where an important section of *My Mortal Enemy* is set, or perhaps of Washington Square, where the protagonist of "Coming, Aphrodite!" has his studio. In these works, as in *The Song of the Lark,* Cather depicts a city rich with art and culture.

My Mortal Enemy is about a young girl who comes East for a visit. Nellie, who will be staying at the Fifth Avenue Hotel, gets her first glimpse of the city from the Jersey City ferry:

The snow blurred everything a little, and the buildings on the Battery all ran together—looked like an enormous fortress with a thousand windows. From the mass, the dull gold dome of the *World* building emerged like a ruddy autumn moon at twilight.

Soon after her arrival, Nellie becomes acquainted with Madison Square. Her aunt, who lives on Madison Square, tells her, "To me this is the real heart of the city; that's why I love living here," and Nellie's own impressions are quite favorable:

Madison Square was then at the parting of the ways; had a double personality, half commercial, half social, with shops to the south and residences to the north. It seemed to me so neat, after the raggedness of our Western cities; so protected by good manners and courtesy—like an open-air drawing room. I could well imagine a winter dancing party being given there, or a reception for some distinguished European visitor.

The snow fell lightly all the afternoon, and friendly old men with brooms kept sweeping the paths. . . . The trees and shrubbery seemed well-groomed and sociable, like pleasant people. . . . Madison Square

Garden, new and spacious then, looked so light and fanciful, and St. Gaudens' Diana . . . stepped out freely and fearlessly into the grey air. I lingered long by the intermittent fountain. Its rhythmic splash was like the voice of the place. It rose and fell like something taking deep, happy breaths, and the sound was musical."[9]

Noticing an old man selling bunches of English violets, Nellie says, "Here, I felt, winter brought no desolation; it was tamed, like a polar bear led on the leash by a beautiful lady."

Nellie remains in the Square until "the street lamps flashed out all along the Avenue, and soft lights began to twinkle in the tall buildings while it was yet day," and then goes to her aunt's "old brownstone house on the north side of the square." During her stay in New York she visits Grace Church, takes a hansom cab through Central Park, goes to the theatre, and dines at Martin's, but the most memorable experience of all is the New Year's party given by her aunt and uncle and attended by singers and actors, many of who came "with traces of make-up still on their faces." Among them is Helena Modjeska, considered one of the greatest tragic actresses of her time. Much of the conversation is about the current theatre scene, especially Sarah Bernhardt's controversial Hamlet, and there is also some discussion of Jean de Reszke's return to the Metropolitan after a prolonged absence.[10] Nellie finds herself as much dazzled by New York's glittering theatrical and musical personalities as she is by the city's beauteous sights, not least among them Madison Square.

"Coming, Aphrodite!" is set on another of New York's famous squares and treats a different aspect of artistic life in the city. Its protagonist, Don Hedger, is a painter who lives "on the top floor of an old house on the south side of Washington Square." He does his shopping on West Houston Street and walks his dog along University Place or West Street, but, clearly, Washington Square dominates Cather's story. From there Hedger watches

the stages pull out;—that was almost the very last summer of the old horse stages on Fifth Avenue. The fountain had but lately begun operations for the season and was throwing up a mist of rainbow water. . . . Plump robins were hopping about on the soil; the grass was newly cut and blindingly green. Looking up the Avenue through the Arch, one could see the young poplars with their bright, sticky leaves, and the Brevoort glistening in its spring coat of paint, and shining horses and carriages,—occasionally an automobile, mis-shapen and sullen, like an ugly threat in a stream of things that were bright and beautiful and alive.[11]

It is here in Washington Square that Hedger first sees Eden Bower, and the place of their meeting is important since his attitude toward women is always described in relation to particular places. We learn, for example, that he liked "the silk-shirt factory girls who came to eat their lunch in Washington Square," but "felt an unreasoning antipathy toward the well-dressed women he saw coming out of big shops, or driving in the Park," believing "them to be artificial and, in an aesthetic sense, perverted."

Later Hedger exchanges a few words with Eden near the bronze statue of Garibaldi on the east side of the Square, which leads to lunch at the Brevoort.[12] A romance develops but suffers a setback when Hedger, hostile to conventional ideas of success, senses that Eden would like him to become a rich and famous artist. In anger he leaves her, hurrying "through Sullivan Street off toward the river," where he could "be among rough, honest people . . . [and] where the big drays bumped over stone paving blocks and the men wore corduroy trowsers [sic] and kept their shirts open at the neck."

Leaving the city for a few days, he returns only to discover that Eden has left. Years later when she returns from Europe a famous opera star, she discovers that Hedger, who in his young manhood despised conventional notions of success, has indeed become a rich and famous artist.

Like Cather, Ellen Glasgow is not usually thought of as a New York writer. While Cather is generally associated with the Midwest and is best known for novels like *My Antonia* and *O Pioneers!* Glasgow's best-known works are set in Virginia. But both lived for a time in New York City, and Glasgow wrote *Life and Gabriella* while living at 1 West Eighty-fifth Street.

To be sure, the novel opens in Virginia, but soon after her marriage to George Fowler, Gabriella moves to New York. Her first impressions are none too favorable and are somewhat reminiscent of Edith Wharton's feelings about the "chocolate-coloured" city as she notices the "depressing examples in brownstone of an architecture, which . . . was trying rather vaguely to express nothing." Dismayed when her carriage stops on Fifty-seventh Street "before one of the solemn houses which stood, in the dignity of utter ugliness in the middle of the long block," Gabriella thinks that she will never be able to recognize her house among so many identical ones.

More memorable though than the descriptions of the midtown area are those of the Upper West Side, where Gabriella visits her sister-in-law and later, after George has left her, finds an apartment. George's sister Patty lives in a studio on the top floor of "a small dingy apartment house," but eager to move downtown because travel expenses are high "when one lives so far uptown," she announces that she has found a new studio downtown and will be living over a stable. "How could you possibly live there?" asks her distraught mother, and then goes on to express her view that the Lower East Side "is just as bad as up here."

Years later when Gabriella tells her daughter that they will be moving into "the old Carolina over on the West Side near Columbus Avenue," the child, who has been brought up on Fifty-seventh Street in her grand-parents' house, cries, "It's a horrid street. . . . I got my white shoes dirty, and there were banana peels all about. A man has a fruit-stand in the bottom of our house. Don't let's go there to live, mother."

They move there, nevertheless, and in the summer, from the window of their stifling apartment, Gabriella can see "the small shopkeepers seated in chairs on the sidewalk," the Jewish tobacco merchant's shop "pressed like a sardine between a bakery and a dairy," and "unwashed children . . . [swarming] like insects over pavements."

Gabriella supports herself and her children by working in a fashionable women's clothing shop on Fifth Avenue and after many years is able to purchase a row house in London Terrace, located on Twenty-third Street between Ninth and Tenth Avenues.[13] Although she does not like the West Side neighborhood, which she describes as "too far away," she is convinced by Polly, a fellow Virginian who for years has lived with Gabriella and helped to raise her children, to buy the house because it has "a little yard in front with an elm tree and a rose-bush and plenty of space for flowers." Polly argues that "there ain't many places in New York where you can have a flower-bed in the front yard," and that "it's a real comfortable house, more like Richmond than New York." In fact, the whole neighborhood, with its three-story row houses set back twenty or thirty feet from the street and fronted by large lawns, seems quiet and rural.

Many other city scenes are described: elegant Fifth Avenue where Gabriella forges a successful career for herself in the world of women's fashions, the Broadway crowds hurrying to and from work, the traffic on Forty-second Street. Like so many other New York novels, the book is concerned with a newcomer to the city, Gabriella's first impressions of it, and the destiny that she meets there. What is unique about *Life and Gabriella* are the occasional moments when Glasgow discovers a New York scene reminiscent of Richmond. Polly's comments about London Terrace have already been mentioned, but there is another instance when Gabriella, passing the corner of Sixth Avenue, notices a young Italian selling peanuts, which he is roasting on a kerosene stove. Nearby, children are

dancing to the music of a hand-organ, which ground out a melancholy waltz; and from a tiny flowerstall behind the stand of a bootblack there drifted the intense sweetness of hyacinths. An old negro, carrying a basket of clothes, passed her in the middle of the block, and she thought: "that might have been in Richmond—that and the hand-organ and the perfume of hyacinths."

The working girl is a recurrent figure in New York fiction set during the early years of the twentieth century, and even Sinclair Lewis put aside his preoccupation with Main Street long enough to write *The Job: An American Novel.* The book—probably the most detailed fictionalized account of office work ever written—opens in Panama, Pennsylvania, in 1905, and is about Una Golden, who with her widowed mother comes to New York to pursue a secretarial career. Una's first impressions of the sky-line—related some seventeen pages later—are quite unremarkable; of somewhat greater interest, however, is her initial reaction to the subway, "which was still new and miraculous in 1905." Una is terrified by the surging crowd, the deafening roar, the darkness, and most of all by "the sense of being powerlessly hurled forward in a mass of ungovernable steel."

Her fear of the subway, which to Una becomes emblematic of the city's power, persists long after she has become acclimated to New York. Although she appreciates the "heroic side" of the spectacle and is awed by the engineering genius that created it, Una thinks of subway travel as "ruffling and fatiguing to a man" and a "horror" to a woman.

Una and her mother find temporary lodgings on Amsterdam Avenue, which is, on the whole, a disappointment, with "its walls of yellow flat-buildings cluttered with fire-escapes, the first stories all devoted to the same sort of shops over and over again," but she is impressed by West End Avenue, where she begins to find "the city of golden rewards." Here she has glimpses of elegant hallways with palm trees and "marble and mahogany and tiling," of uniformed attendants, and of couples in formal attire setting out for an evening's entertainment.

Even lovelier than West End Avenue is Riverside Drive, where the city "bares her exquisite breast and wantons in beauty. Here she is sophisticated, yet eager, comparable to Paris and Vienna. . . ." The Goldens, however, are in no position to afford an apartment on either fashionable West End Avenue or elegant Riverside Drive and eventually take a flat on 148th Street in a new but barren tenement that was "one of . . . a mile of yellow brick tenements; it was named after an African orchid of great loveliness, and it was filled with clerks, motormen, probationer policemen, and enormously prolific women in dressing saques."

Una attends secretarial school and then holds a variety of office positions, one of them in an "ugly building of brownstone and iron Corinthian columns resembling an old fashioned post office, and typical of all that block on Church Street." Another is in the Septimus building on Nassau Street that is occupied for the most part "with offices of fly-by-night companies," and still another is in the Zodiac Building on Thirty-fourth Street. Lewis describes the crowds inside the Zodiac's lobby "examining the black-and-white directory board with its list of two hundred offices, or waiting to surge into one of the twelve elevators—those packed vertical railroads," and he writes about the "whole village life" that thrived on the lobby level dominated by the elevator men, the barbers, and the cigar-stand operator.

Lewis also records Una's tentative and sometimes fearful exploration of New York. Because she has adopted her mother's view that most sections of the city "weren't quite nice," Una is reluctant to visit "the proliferating East Side" and Fifth Avenue and for a long while "knew the picturesqueness neither of wealth nor of pariah poverty." Gradually, however, her experience broadens. A beau takes her to the Lower East Side and to Gramercy Park; he shows her "the Princeton Club, the Columbia Club, the National Arts, and the Players'," as well as Stuyvesant Square, "a barren square out of old London, with a Quaker school on one side, and the voluble Ghetto on the other."[14]

On her own, during lunch hours, Una visits City Hall, Newspaper Row,[15] and the Curb Market on Broad Street,[16] where she "marvelled at the men with telephones in little coops behind open windows." When she can get a fifty-cent ticket she attends the theatre and occasionally eats a meal at Childs, "one of the string of Vance-eating places, a food-mill," which in an effort to achieve distinction used "imitation rafters, a plate-rack aligned with landscape plates," and tables for four instead of the long tables generally found in restaurants of this type.

Lewis writes, too, about Una's search for rooms after her mother has died, which was "not so splendid a quest as she had hoped." Her encounters with landladies are, in fact, reminiscent of those described by O. Henry, but Una finally finds a room in a railroad apartment on Lexington Avenue. Later, during a brief and unhappy marriage, she lives in "a room in a family hotel on a side street near Sixth Avenue" and comes to know the sense of rootlessness and desolation felt by

the blank procession of phantoms who haunt cheap family hotels, the apparitions of the corridors, to whom there is no home, nor purpose, nor permanence. Mere lodgers for the night, though for score on score of tasteless years they use the same alien hotel room as a place in which to take naps and store their trunks and comb their hair and sit waiting—for nothing.

It is not until she divorces her husband and finds challenging work in the real-estate field that Una achieves a sense of fulfillment and independence. No longer compelled to choose between being an idle wife or a harried office worker beleaguered by tedious and repetitious tasks, the petty jealousies of coworkers, and the condescension of employers, Una, like Glasgow's Gabriella, manages to carve out a meaningful life for herself in the big city. Clearly the struggles and the triumphs of these "new women" are not those of Edith Wharton's protagonists Lily Bart in *The House of Mirth* and Undine Spragg in *The Custom of the Country,* both of whom have been brought up to believe that a woman's status and wealth can—and should—be conferred by marriage rather than earned by individual effort.

While both of Wharton's novels deal with the quest of young women for affluent and socially prominent husbands, their more important subject is the assault upon New York's old established families by the new rich and the ways in which vulgarity and coarseness made inroads into the bastions of tradition and gentility in the early years of the twentieth century. Although in *The Age of Innocence* New York's old families were keeping the new millionaires out of their opera house and out of their own circle, some decades later these tycoons were finding acceptance among New York's untitled aristocracy.

Even the fabulously wealthy but uncouth Sim Rosedale, whose portrait in *The House of Mirth* is tinged with overtones of anti-Semitism,

was making his way through the dense mass of social antagonisms. Already his wealth and the masterly use he had made of it were giving him an enviable prominence in the world of affairs, and placing Wall Street under obligations which only Fifth Avenue could repay. In response to these claims, his name began to figure on municipal committees and charitable boards; he appeared at banquets to distinguished strangers; and his candidacy at one of the fashionable clubs was being discussed with diminishing opposition. He had figured once or twice at the Trenor dinners and had learned to speak with just the right note of disdain of the big Van Osburgh crushes. . . .

Rosedale is considering the purchase of a house on Fifth Avenue, whose former owner had "filled a picture-gallery with old masters [and] entertained all New York in it," and many other newly rich families like the Brys are building mansions there. Indeed, in *The House of Mirth* and in *The Custom of the Country* Wharton updates the portrait of Fifth Avenue that appeared in *The Age of Innocence,* set some thirty years earlier.

More and more residents had begun to move uptown, as such shops as Altman's (1906), Oppenheim and Collins (1907) and Best and Company (1910) began to be located on Fifth Avenue in the Thirties. In the early years of the new century, many mansions were built uptown, some as far north as Eighty-sixth Street, and most of the city's best-known millionaires such as the Vanderbilts, the Whitneys, the Guggenheims, and the Fricks lived above Fiftieth Street.[17] Unfortunately very few of the houses that once lined Fifth Avenue before World War I stand today, for what was once known as "Millionaire's Row," is now almost completely commercialized.

It is nothing less than Fifth Avenue to which Undine Spragg, the protagonist of *The Custom of the Country,* aspires. Early in the book she looks out of her hotel window toward Central Park. "Beyond the Park lay Fifth Avenue—and Fifth Avenue was where she wanted to be!" As it turns out, Undine marries into an old, aristocratic Washington Square family, giving herself "to the exclusive and the dowdy when the future belonged to the showy and the promiscuous."

It is Undine's husband, Ralph, who best articulates the differences between Washington Square and Fifth Avenue. He describes Washington Square as a "Reservation," claiming "that before long its inhabitants would be exhibited at ethnological shows," and speaks of the "restrictions and exclusions of the old code." He rails against the "social disintegration expressed by widely different architectural physiognomies at the other end of Fifth Avenue," and referring to the newly rich as "Invaders," explains that

the daughters of his own race sold themselves to the Invaders; the daughters of the Invaders bought their husbands as they bought an opera-box. It ought all to have been transacted on the Stock Exchange.

Ralph's reference to the stock exchange is not without contempt, for while the new families made their fortunes on Wall Street, the old were loath to participate in transactions which they considered to be of questionable morality. Thus, the old landed gentry not only had honor, dignity, and impeccable morals but also had depleted fortunes.

After her marriage to Ralph, Undine does not live "within the sacred precincts of fashion" but on West End Avenue, where she must suffer

the incessant pin-pricks inflicted by the incongruity between her social and geographical station—the need of having to give a west side address to her tradesmen, and the deeper irritation of hearing her friends say: "Do let me give you a lift home, dear—Oh, I'd forgotten! I'm afraid I haven't the time to go so far—."

It is not until she divorces Ralph and marries the coarse and unprincipled Elmer Moffatt, who has made his millions on Wall Street, that she is able to realize her dream of living on Fifth Avenue. "Said to be one of the six wealthiest men east of the Rockies," Moffatt gives his bride "a necklace and tiara of pigeon-blood rubies belonging to Queen Marie Antoinette, a million dollar cheque, and a house. . . . [on] Fifth Avenue, which is an exact copy of the Pitti Palace, Florence."

Like Wharton, Henry James was a chronicler of the changes in New York City as commerce and wealth gained supremacy over the values and traditions held by the old established families. In "The Jolly Corner" he depicts Spencer Brydon's return to New York to check on his properties after a stay of more than thirty years in England. Like James himself, who had lived abroad for many years before he visited New York in 1904, he was greatly shocked by what he saw:

It would have taken a century, he repeatedly said to himself . . . to pile up the differences, the newnesses, the queernesses, above all the bignesses, for the better or the worse, that at the present assaulted his vision wherever he looked.

To James, as to H.G. Wells, who visited New York in 1906, the city was a fascinating yet frightening monument to materialistic progress. Brydon, like James, "missed what he would have been sure of finding, . . . found what he would never have imagined," and was particularly dismayed by "the 'swagger' things, the modern, the monstrous, the famous things." Lost "among the dreadful multiplied numberings [of houses] which seemed to him to reduce the whole place to some vast ledger-page," depressed by "the vast wilderness of the wholesale" that lay before him, he finds comfort in his friend Alice Staverton, whose house on Irving Place calls to mind New York's old-fashioned dignified past. Alice herself "stood off, in the modern crush when she could," remembered as a better time "their quite far-away and antediluvian social period and order," and still clung "to memories and histories."

Brydon's own "memories and histories" give way to the realities of the present as he witnesses the conversion of one of his properties into several apartments. Although he appears to be fascinated by the details of the construction and imagines that had he remained in New York he might himself have been "the inventor of the sky-scraper," his feelings on the subject are ambivalent. He would never, for example, permit his cherished house on the "jolly corner" to be converted into flats because there are "values other than the beastly rent-values."

Although the "jolly corner" is not identified, we learn that this fine brownstone house with its silver-plated doorknobs, mahogany doors, high windows, and gleaming wooden floors, which for Brydon symbolizes his own past as well as the genteel past of the city, is located on a street "now . . . generally dishonored and disfigured in its westward reaches." The street meets with "the comparatively conservative Avenue . . . [that] still had pretensions . . . to decency [although] the old people had mostly gone, the old names were unknown."

Like Wharton, James is lamenting the passing in New York of the old patrician families, the triumph of "wealth and force and success." While he cherishes all emblems of the city's past, he is appalled by what New York has become. At one point in the story Brydon wonders, "How could any one—of any wit—insist on any one else's 'wanting' to live in New

York?" and his final negative judgment of the city occurs when he has a confrontation with a ghost who represents the vastly wealthy but ravaged and unhappy person he might have become had he remained in New York, where "there are no reasons . . . but dollars."

The theme of the return to New York by one long absent also appears in "Crapy Cornelia." Cornelia Rasch returns from Europe in time to stop White-Mason from proposing to the wealthy Mrs. Worthingham, who is "the very essence of the newness and freshness and beautiful, brave, social irresponsibility." The latter is without "instinct for any old quality or quantity or identity" and has no appreciation for "the New York of his [White-Mason's] already almost legendary past."

The self-serving White-Mason has planned to marry Mrs. Worthingham, nonetheless, and to go abroad, for he cannot bear living in a city bereft of its traditions and its history. He knows that he could stay on "in *his* New York, that is in the sentimental, the spiritual, the more or less romantic visitation of it," but doubts whether he can remain in Mrs. Worthingham's New York, where "the angular facts of current finance were as harsh and metallic and bewildering as some stacked 'exhibit' of ugly patented inventions."

The return of Cornelia, who shares with him a sense of the past and a dedication to its traditions, causes him to recognize the absurdity of his intentions. Together he and Cornelia relive the times they spent "south of Thirteenth Street and north of Washington Square [during] those spacious, sociable, Arcadian days that . . . were so different from any of these arrangements of pretended hourly time that dash themselves forever to pieces as from the fiftieth floors of sky-scrapers." They admire lovely old objects from the 1860s and speak with contempt of Mrs. Worthingham's "awful things" that are "the newest of the new." A moral coward but nonetheless an insightful critic of the "new" era, White-Mason offers neither love nor marriage to Cornelia, whom he uses as a link to the Arcadian past and as a buffer against the vulgar present, in much the same way that Spencer Brydon uses Alice Staverton.

Clearly James's portrait of the city in "The Jolly Corner," "Crapy Cornelia," and other stories set in New York at the beginning of this century is far from flattering. The materialism, vulgarity, and coarseness, the decline of the old and the traditional, the reverence for the new and the big that he so vehemently objected to were, of course, to increase vastly during the postwar years, and one can only speculate about what his reaction would have been had he returned to visit New York again after World War I. As it happened he died in England in 1916, and thus was spared what to him would probably have been an infernal vision of New York City during the Jazz Age, the subject of the next chapter.

6

THE ROARING TWENTIES

While several of the works discussed in the previous chapter allude to World War I, the impact of that cataclysmic event on New York life and literature was relatively minor until 1917, when the United States abandoned its neutral position and declared war on Germany. Following the outbreak of the war in Europe in 1914, the stock market had closed for four months, and savings banks had paid depositors only upon sixty days notice. With the great demand for munitions, however, the economy had altered rapidly, and there followed an inflationary period in America that lasted until the Great Depression.

Following the war, there was a great sense of power and prosperity throughout the United States; high living, big spending, good times—a determined effort to forget the war—characterized the Jazz Age, and during this period, New York was the pleasure capital of America.

Prohibition ushered in the age of the speakeasy, and there were said to be as many as thirty thousand speakeasies in New York, the greatest number located on the West Side, between Fortieth and Sixtieth Streets. It was in the postwar period, also, that New Yorkers discovered Harlem's nightclubs, and Harlem quickly gained a reputation for being the city's most exotic entertainment center.

Large, lavish hotels and restaurants were filled with freely spending patrons at all hours of the day and night. More pleasures and thrills were made easily accessible to New Yorkers with the completion in 1920 of the subway extension to Coney Island. The introduction of sound to films in the late twenties led to the construction of gigantic and garish movie palaces like the Roxy (1926). In 1925 the new Madison Square Garden was erected on Eighth Avenue, between Forty-ninth and Fiftieth streets.

In a decade that put a premium on bigness, several huge department stores were built along Fifth Avenue, and many of its former residents were now living on Park Avenue, where luxury apartment houses had been constructed during the postwar building boom. The bigness, prosperity, and excitement of the city commented on by European visitors in the prewar years had by now increased appreciably, and the English author W. L. George compared postwar New York to Brobdingnag, the country of the giants in *Gulliver's Travels:*

The American does not realize what a shock New York can be to a European who has never before seen a building higher than ten floors; the effect is bewildering. The monster hotel where the stranger makes his first acquaintance with America is itself a shock. I began in a hotel which seems to have two thousand bedrooms and to carry a rent roll of $20,000 a day. In other words, this is Brobdingnag, the land of the giants. Gigantic chaos, that is the first feeling I had in New York. . . . Fifth Avenue, people so many, traffic so thick that one has to take one's turns at a crossing, that police control has become mechanical, beyond the power of man. Then one goes into a store; one wanders through endless departments, on endless floors, one goes through tunnels and never comes out by the same block as one went in. There is so much in the streets; everything hurries —motor cars, street cars, railway cars. In the restaurants endless vistas of napery and crystal extend away. One goes up Broadway at night to see the crowded colored signs of the movie shows and the theatres twinkle and eddy, inviting, clamourous, Babylonian![1]

While many artists and writers attacked the gross materialism, taste-lessness, and false optimism that characterized American life in general and New York life in particular during the twenties, large numbers came to live in what was indisputably the intellectual and cultural capital of the nation. Most found rooms or studios in Greenwich Village, a bohemian colony reminiscent of Paris's Montmartre. It was in New York, for example, that Alfred Stieglitz's 291 Gallery first exhibited Cubist art, and no doubt the most momentous cultural event of the decade was the open-ing of the Museum of Modern Art in 1929.

Unique among the writers of the period was F. Scott Fitzgerald, who partook more in the city's glamour and excitement than its intellectual or cultural life and whose legacy to us is a vivid—if sometimes one-sided— fictional re-creation of New York during the Jazz Age. Called by Alfred Kazin "the only poet of New York's luxurious upper-class landmarks,"[2] Fitzgerald depicted the city as a gay, romantic dreamland where rich and beautiful young people indulged in high living and reckless freedom.

In stories like "May Day" and "The Rich Boy" Fitzgerald writes about "the movement and glitter of post-bellum New York," about the Biltmore, the Commodore, Delmonico's, and the Yale Club.[3] He describes Childs on Fifty-ninth Street, where a group of young revelers breakfast after a night of partying. So mundane at eight o'clock in the morning when its clientele consists "of poor people with sleep in the corners of their eyes, trying to look straight before them at their food so as not to see other poor people," it is at four in the morning both glamorous and exciting:

Within its pale but sanitary walls one finds a noisy medley of chorus girls, college boys, debutantes, rakes, *filles de joie*—a not unrepresentative mixture of the gayest of Broadway, and even of Fifth Avenue. . . . Over the marble-topped tables were bent the excited faces of flappers whose fathers owned individual villages. They were eating buckwheat cakes and scrambled eggs with relish and gusto, an accomplishment that would have been utterly impossible for them to repeat in the same place four hours later.

And Fitzgerald describes Fifth Avenue and Forty-fourth Street, where

the wealthy, happy sun glittered in transient gold through the thick windows of the smart shops, lighting upon mesh bags and purses and strings of pearls in gray velvet cases; upon gaudy feather fans of many colors; upon the laces and silks of expensive dresses; upon the bad paintings and the fine period furniture in the elaborate show rooms of interior decorators.

"The Freshest Boy" contains one of his most explicit descriptions of New York as a fulfilled dream. For its protagonist, Basil Lee, the city is "the long awaited heaven of romance." He watches the diners at the Manhattan Hotel, "investing them with a romance," and at the theatre the program "had a curious sacredness." In many respects Basil is reminiscent of Amory Lane, the protagonist of *This Side of Paradise* who as a prep-school student felt that New York "rivalled the dream cities in the Arabian Nights."

Later, when Amory is a student at Princeton, he continues to visit New York at every opportunity. Until the onset of Prohibition when "the great rendezvous . . . received their death wounds," his favorite places were the Knickerbocker Bar, the Biltmore Bar, and the Coconut Grove.[4] He also frequented the theatre, and dined at the Ritz,[5] the Princeton Club, and Delmonico's.

As the promising youth becomes a wasted young man, bored, restless, and jaded, his image of New York becomes increasingly tarnished. At one point, disgusted with his drinking and his partying, he is sickened by Broadway with its "babel of noise and . . . painted faces." He begs his companion, "Let's get off of this—this place! . . . This street, it's ghastly!" Later he becomes acquainted with other unpleasant aspects of city life, including the subway, where for the first time he encounters working-class New Yorkers:

He pictured the rooms where these people lived—where the pattern of the blistered wall-papers were heavy reiterated sunflowers on green and yellow backgrounds, where there were tin bathtubs and gloomy hallways and verdureless, unnamable spaces in back of the buildings; where even love dressed as seduction—a sordid murder around the corner, illicit motherhood in the flat above. And always there was the economical stuffiness of indoor winter, and the long summers, nightmares of perspiration between sticky enveloping walls . . . dirty restaurants where careless, tired people helped themselves to sugar with their own used coffee-spoons, leaving hard brown deposits in the bowl. . . .

Never before in his life had Amory considered poor people. . . . O. Henry had found in these people romance, pathos, love, hate—Amory saw only coarseness, physical filth, and stupidity.

That such disdain extends to New York's middle as well as to its laboring class is made apparent in *The Beautiful and Damned,* in which Fitzgerald describes the Marathon, a cheap Broadway cabaret that "imitates with a sort of shoddy and mechanical wistfulness the glittering antics of the great cafés of the theatre district." Its patrons are

the credulous, sentimental, underpaid, overworked people with hyphenated occupations: book-keepers, ticket-sellers, office-managers, salesman, and, most of all clerks—clerks of the express, of the mail, of the grocery, of the brokerage, of the bank. With them are their giggling, over-gestured, pathetically pretentious women, who grow fat with them, bear them too many babies, and float helpless and uncontent in a colorless sea of drudgery and broken hopes.

What Fitzgerald's protagonists want is the best romantic vision of New York that money can buy. They want the Plaza and the Biltmore, not the Marathon. Like Amory Blaine, Anthony Patch, the protagonist of *The Beautiful and Damned,* wants to enjoy the pleasures of a dazzling, opulent city. Although early in the novel he recognizes the artificiality of much of of the city's splendor, he revels in its pleasures, spending recklessly and living high until he has wasted not only his grandfather's millions but also himself.

In the novel, which opens in 1912 and concludes after the end of World War I, there is a description of Anthony's apartment on Fifty-second Street in a house that had been built in the 1890s and been subdivided into flats "in response to the steadily growing need of small apartments," as well as his impressions of Fifth and Sixth avenues, which seem to him to be "the uprights of a gigantic ladder stretching from Washington Square to Central Park."

Living on a generous allowance from his grandfather, Anthony and Gloria Gilbert, whom he eventually marries, have a taste for the glamorous and the spectacular. To him, New York is itself a spectacle, albeit "a transparent, artificial sort of a spectacle. . . . [with] its press-agented stars and its flimsy, unenduring stage settings, and . . . the greatest army of supers ever assembled." While the Plaza Hotel dominates the scene, there are many descriptions of the city's other fine restaurants and hotels, and of opening night at the theatre and its dazzling display of wealth and fashion:

There were opera cloaks stitched of myriad, many-colored silks and furs; there were jewels dripping from arms and throats and ear-tips of white and rose; there were innumerable broad shimmers down the middle of innumerable silk hats; there were shoes of gold and bronze and red and shining black. . . .

Fitzgerald describes Times Square at night, a veritable carnival with its crowds and noise and "revolutions of light, the growings and recedings of light—light dividing like pearls—forming and reforming in glittering bars and circles and monstrous grotesque figures." And later in the book, the whole city turns into a carnival when New Yorkers learn that Germany has surrendered. Fitzgerald depicts "the carnival, the feasting, the triumph" that took place in the streets, apartments, restaurants, and hotels of the city. One particularly memorable scene is set in the ballroom of the Astor Hotel, which is filled with "horn-blowing, kissing, coughing, laughing, drinking parties under the great full-bosomed flags which leaned in glowing color over the pageantry and the sound."

Although Anthony and Gloria join in the festivities, there is for them an undercurrent of unhappiness. Their marriage is foundering; their fortune wasted, their lives empty. Their indulgences have cost them a tremendous inheritance, and they are eventually forced to move from their small but elegant Fifty-seventh Street apartment, where postwar inflation has driven the rent up to two hundred and twenty-five dollars a month, to a flat renting for eighty-five dollars a month, located not far from where Fitzgerald himself had lived on Morningside Heights after his discharge from the army. From the window of this flat "on Claremont Avenue, which is two blocks from the Hudson in the dim hundreds," Anthony can see "a patch of vivid green trees . . . [on] Riverside Drive. Across the water were the Palisades, crowned by the ugly framework of the amusement park. . . ."

But wealth, not poverty, is the subject of The Beautiful and Damned, and for that matter, of most of Fitzgerald's fiction. The Patches do not live on Claremont Avenue for very long. Their litigation having been successful, they eventually inherit thirty million dollars, but by then both Anthony and his marriage are ruined. His millions cannot, in the final analysis, buy happiness.

The theme of The Great Gatsby is similar in that the fabulously wealthy Gatsby can surround himself with every conceivable luxury but cannot "buy" Daisy Buchanan, the woman he loves and without whom he will always be unhappy.

The Great Gatsby is not a New York City novel in the same sense as *The Beautiful and Damned.* Most of it is set outside the city limits on Long Island, the location of the fabulously wealthy Jay Gatsby's estate, but there are a number of scenes that take place in Manhattan as well as several descriptions of Queens, a borough much neglected in New York fiction.

While living in Great Neck, Long Island, in 1922, Fitzgerald made frequent trips into the city and became familiar with an area then known as the Corona Dumps, near Northern Boulevard, which in *The Great Gatsby* he calls the valley of ashes. In this desolate and lonely place visible to motorists and Long Island Railroad passengers alike, there is

a fantastic farm where ashes grow like wheat into ridges and hills and grotesque gardens; where ashes take the forms of houses and chimneys and rising smoke and, finally, with a transcendent effort, of ash-gray men who move dimly and already crumbling through the powdery air. Occasionally a line of gray cars crawls along an invisible track, gives out a ghastly creak and comes to rest, and immediately the ash-gray men swarm up with leaden spades and stir up an impenetrable cloud, which screens their obscure operations from your sight. . . .

There are several other scenes associated with the trip from Long Island to New York, including a description of Manhattan as seen from the Queensboro Bridge, its buildings

rising up across the river in white heaps and sugar lumps all built with a wish out of non-olfactory money. The city seen from the Queensboro Bridge is always the city seen for the first time, in its first wild promise of all the mystery and the beauty in the world.

Despite Manhattan's romantic promise, the scenes set there are for the most part unpleasant, if not actually brutal. The promise of beauty and romance is there as Daisy's husband, Tom, and his mistress, Myrtle, take Nick, the narrator of the novel, to visit their "love nest" on 158th Street. On the way, they drive along Fifth Avenue, "so warm and soft, almost pastoral, on the summer Sunday afternoon" that Nick "wouldn't have been surprised to see a great flock of white sheep turn the corner." However, soon after they arrive at their destination, described by Fitzgerald as "one slice in a long white cake of apartment houses," Tom breaks Myrtle's nose, and romantic illusion gives way to violent reality.

Later, when Nick meets Gatsby in a Forty-second Street "cellar," he finds him with Meyer Wolfsheim. A gangster reputed to have fixed the World Series in 1919, Wolfsheim speaks of a restaurant across the street, the old Metropole, which for him is "filled with faces dead and gone," and describes the night when Rosy Rosenthal was shot there.

Two scenes are set in the Plaza, neither of them pleasant. In the Palm Court, Nick learns about the romance between Gatsby and Daisy and is asked to arrange a rendezvous for them at his house. The critical scene during which Gatsby tells Tom of his love for Daisy also takes place in the Plaza.

When it is not the scene of violence or treachery, Manhattan is for Nick, a Midwesterner, a lonely place. Nick describes hurrying "down the white chasms of lower New York" on his way to work, lunching in dark, crowded downtown restaurants, having a gloomy dinner at the Yale Club. He senses and eventually comes to enjoy the excitement of the city, but still sometimes feels "a haunting loneliness" at twilight when he watches young clerks loitering "in front of windows waiting until it was time for a solitary restaurant dinner" or when later in the evening he walks along uptown streets "lined five deep with throbbing taxicabs," carrying to the theatre gay young couples who press together, laughing and joking.

On the whole it can be said that Fitzgerald's romantic image of New York appears more tarnished than ever in *The Great Gatsby*. The city still promises romance and beauty, but the promise is not fulfilled.[6] Alienation, violence, and corruption are more often than not associated with the city, and New York—along with the entire East Coast—is indicted at the end of the novel when Nick—the narrator and moral commentator—returns to the Midwest in search of his lost innocence.

Carl Van Vechten could perhaps be classified as a lesser F. Scott Fitzgerald in that he, too, is concerned with the wealthy in their pursuit of hedonistic pleasures in postwar New York and with the desperation and emptiness existent beneath the glitter. A chronicler of the changing forms of entertainment ushered in by prohibition, which eventually led to the closing of such established places as Sherry's (May 1919) and Delmonico's (May 1923), Van Vechten writes about the speakeasies that sprang up in midtown brownstones and about sophisticated New Yorkers' discovery of Harlem night spots.

Parties, which seems at times to be a guide to New York's "dives and resorts," deals with the visit of the elderly Grafin Adele von Pulmernal und Stilzerhl to the city. She is not interested in going to "the Museum of Natural History, the Metropolitan Museum of Art, the Bronx Zoo, the Aquarium, and the concerts of the Philharmonic Society." She prefers to visit speakeasies and nightclubs, and in the company of Van Vechten's other pleasure-seeking characters manages to visit quite a number of them, including the Wishbone, which occupies "the third floor of a brownstone house in the East Fifties" and attracts a mixed crowd, including those "whose names appeared on the passenger lists of the *Majestic* or the *Ile de France* and who headed the reports of balls at Palm Beach" as well as "painters, writers, chauffeurs, actors, sailors, soldiers and firemen."

While there are descriptions of numerous speakeasies and cabarets, some of them in Harlem, which by the twenties had become a famous entertainment center, not all the partying takes place there, and many revelers get drunk in their own or other people's apartments, for after the arrival of prohibition more cocktail parties "were held in one day in Manhattan than in a month elsewhere."

There are few pages in the novel that do not deal with parties, the most notable exception being a lengthy description of the perpetual changes occurring in the city during the boom years of the twenties. Comparing Manhattan to a flowing liquid, Van Vechten explains that it is not uncommon for New Yorkers to find that their banker's or lawyer's office "has disappeared in favour of a deep hole in the ground" or to discover that "a new and glittering tower, some fifty or more stories in height" has been built before they even noticed "the preparatory excavations." Equally commonplace are apartment dwellers who suddenly find their "splendid and uninterrupted view . . . blocked out by a taller neighbor," and "elevated and street-car lines . . . have been known to disappear in a week."

While change was always part of the New York scene, the pace has never before been so swift:

In Victorian days such landmarks as Delmonico's and Martin's moved northward every decade, the Harrigan Theatre became the Mansfield, and later the Garrick. Now, the changes are accomplished more swiftly. Almost before the last stone had been removed from the old Waldorf-Astoria, a new Waldorf-Astoria was rising on Park Avenue. Stanford White's Madison Square Garden with its celebrated replica of the Giralda Tower, *in Madison Square,* has been supplanted by a Madison Square Garden on Eighth Avenue. Maxfield Parish's mural decoration representing Old King Cole which so recently graced the Knickerbocker Hotel Bar has been transferred to the Racket Club, but what has become of Saint-Gauden's Diana nobody seems to know. . . .

McGowan's Pass Tavern, Jack's, Shanley's, Rector's, all have disappeared, while the new Casino in Central Park would not be on speaking terms with the old. . . . Negro Harlem has supplanted Chinatown and the Bowery in the affections of those who seek diversion at night. The Woolworth Building, once the eighth wonder of the world, is no longer solitary or even paramount.[7]

In *Peter Whiffle: His Life and Works,* Van Vechten also writes about the changing city, particularly about its older theatres, many of which have been demolished or left in a state of disrepair:

I stopped before the Thalia Theatre, as I have stopped so many times, to admire the noble facade with its flight of steps and its tall columns, for this is one of my dream theatres. . . . This is a theatre, in which, and before which, it has often amused me to fancy myself a man of wealth, when my first diversion would be a complete renovation—without any reconstruction or vandalism—of this playhouse, and the production of some play by Shakespeare, for to me, no other theatre in New York, unless it be the Academy of Music, lends itself so readily to a product of Shakespeare as the Thalia. As I write these lines, I recall that the old New York theatres are fast disappearing: Wallack's is gone; Daly's is no more; even Weber and Fields's has been demolished. Cannot something be done to save the Thalia, which is much older than any of these?

Elsewhere in *Peter Whiffle* Van Vechten writes about

one of those charming old brick houses with marble steps and ancient hand-wrought iron railings which still remain on East Broadway to remind us of the day when stately landaus drove up to deposit crinolined ladies before their portals.

Another of the charming old houses described by Van Vechten is where Peter Whiffle—would-be author and sometime philosopher—lives. It is located on Beekman Place in "that splendid row, just two blocks long, of mellow brownstone dwellings, with flights of steps, which back upon the East River and Fiftieth Street."

Perhaps more than anything else, Van Vechten's novel, most of which is set in postwar New York, is memorable for its depiction of the city's cultural life. The characters—most of them intellectuals or aesthetes—go to the Metropolitan Opera and to Carnegie Hall, to the Italian and Yiddish theatre. They discuss modern art, particularly the tremendous impact of cubism on New York artists, and galleries like Alfred Stieglitz's 291 [Fifth Avenue] that exhibited and promoted it.

Intellectuals and aesthetes, writers and artists are also the subject of Floyd Dell's *Love in Greenwich Village*. The book contains a colorful history of the area that in the twenties was a thriving artistic and intellectual community. Likening himself to an archaeologist, Dell presents "the spectacle of successive layers of ruin," describing the "happy Indian village, the busy Dutch settlement, the quiet English hamlet, the fashionable American suburb, and the proud Washington Square period" and explaining how the Village was transformed into a bohemian neighborhood as fashionable New York society moved uptown, leaving the area—except for the north side of Washington Square—to artists and writers who enjoyed cheap rent "because the rush of traffic could not make its way through little twisted streets that crossed and recrossed each other and never seemed to get anywhere else."

Dell credits the Liberal Club, which opened in 1913, with having transformed the area into a "neighborhood" by bringing artists and writers out of their small cliques and into the larger community. Frequented by Theodore Dreiser, Upton Sinclair, and Sherwood Anderson, among others, the Liberal Club was located at 137 Macdougal Street, above Polly's restaurant, another meeting place for Village residents.[8] Here, as in the other bohemian gathering places, camaraderie and freedom, art and ideas flourished, although only, as Dell explains, for a short time:

Greenwich Village could not remain forever islanded amid the roaring tides of commerce. Already the barriers were being broken down; Seventh Avenue was being extended southward, the new subway was being laid; in a little while the magic isolation of the Village would be ended. The tangle of crooked streets would be pierced by a great straight road, the beautiful crumbling houses of great rooms and high ceilings and deep-embrasured windows would be ruthlessly torn down to make room for modern apartment-buildings; the place would become like all the rest of New York City—its gay, proud life would be extinguished.

Yet the end came more swiftly than Dell expected, the Village being invaded by outsiders who arrived "with their pockets full of money and their hearts full of a pathetic eagerness to participate in the celebrated joys of Bohemian life." Tearooms and restaurants "responded by laying on villagy quaintness in thick daubs to tickle the fancy of the visiting bourgeoisie," compelling residents to search out as yet undiscovered places where the emphasis was on good, cheap food rather than on atmosphere:

But it was not merely a matter of food; a certain Village snobbishness was also involved. . . . Too many of them [the up-towners] had no manners; they flocked in to stare and giggle and make loud remarks; and they tried, half enviously and half contemptuously, to buy their way into Village companionship. . . . And what could we do about it? There they were; we could not put them out of our Village! We could only, if it came to that desperate pass, go away ourselves.

This, unhappily, was what finally occurred. At the end of the book Dell laments, "The Village—our Village—was dead and gone" and describes the new Village as a place of "uglification and pretense."

Like Floyd Dell, John Dos Passos was a Greenwich Village resident during the nineteen twenties, and *Manhattan Transfer* contains a number of autobiographical details. Jimmy Herf, the character that most resembles the author, lives for a time on Washington Square, as did Dos Passos in 1922, and there are references to various Village locations, such as the Syrian restaurant on Washington Street that Dos Passos himself frequented. *Manhattan Transfer* is, however, as the title suggests, not exclusively about one particular New York neighborhood, nor is it about a particular person. Its subject is nothing less than the whole of Manhattan itself, and the novel's very form, like the lives of its characters, is shaped by the modern metropolis.

Like the city, the novel is big and diverse; like modern urban life, it is fast-paced, sometimes frenetically so, fragmented, and disjointed. Not limited to a single decade, but primarily about the city during the twenties, *Manhattan Transfer* is the story of New York's multitudes: of newspapermen, actresses, businessmen, drifters, waiters, lawyers—representative New Yorkers—whose destinies cross in the big city. While some characters like Jimmy Herf, a newspaper reporter burned out by life in "the City of Destruction," and Ellen Oglethorpe, a successful but unhappy actress seduced by the city's wealth and glamour, are more developed than others, Dos Passos's emphasis is on New York itself, and his is a dazzling, panoramic view of the city, of the strains and stresses of life in the modern metropolis, and of the alienation and despair experienced by so many of its inhabitants.

"Crammed . . . [with] millionwindowed buildings," Dos Passos's New York is a vital and growing city, but its inhabitants, more often than not, are depleted and drained by life amidst the concrete and steel. In "Revolving Doors" he compares the gray-faced, exhausted workers gradually draining out of the downtown skyscrapers at five o'clock in the evening to sap draining out of trees at the first frost; in "Nine Day's Wonder" he describes the homeward journey of "shopworn" and "officeworn" New Yorkers when *"it's ebbtide in the downtown district, flood in Flatbush, Woodlawn, Dyckman Street, Sheepshead Bay, New Lots Avenue, Canarsie."*

Bent on pleasure, they seek escape from the grim monotony of their daily lives:

A nickel before midnight buys tomorrow . . . holdup headlines, a cup of coffee in the automat, a ride to Woodlawn, Fort Lee, Flatbush. . . . A nickel in the slot buys chewing gum. Somebody Loves Me, Baby Divine, You're in Kentucky Juss Shu' As You're Born . . . bruised notes of foxtrots go limping out of doors, blues waltzes (We'd Danced the Whole Night Through) trail gyrating tinsel memories. . . . On Sixth Avenue on Fourteenth there are still flyspecked stereopticons where for a nickel you can peep at yellowed yesterdays. Besides the peppering shooting gallery you stoop into the flicker A HOT TIME, THE BACHELOR'S SURPRISE, THE STOLEN GARTER . . . wastebasket of tornup daydreams. . . . A nickel before midnight buys our yesterdays.

Amidst the "seethe and throb," however, there is a perpetual sense of loneliness and despair, as expressed in the image of an old man plodding slowly and heavily along Broadway, a *"broken doll in the ranks of varnished articulated dolls."* Like other of Dos Passos's characters, he is more than a victim of age and infirmity; he seems to be a victim of urban life itself.

While many of Dos Passos's characters are defeated by city life, others appear to be victims of capitalism, which is attacked by a soapbox orator in "One More River to Jordan." Stationed in front of the Cosmopolitan Café on Second Avenue and Houston Street, he rails against the capitalists who

take our work and our ideers and our women. . . . They build their Plaza Hotels and their millionaire's clubs and million dollar theayters and their battleships and what do they leave us? . . . They leave us shopsickness an the rickets and a lot of dirty streets full of garbage. . . .

Dos Passos's descriptions of the city—and its beleaguered and sometimes despairing inhabitants—are not limited to the italicized passages quoted above and to the many others like them that introduce the chapters of *Manhattan Transfer*. The city is also depicted within the chapters themselves. Dos Passos writes about the poor Irish who live on West Fourth Street, near Sixth Avenue, where there is "the smell of stables" and the pavement is "littered with scraps of garbage and crawling children," and about the bars on Pearl Street, with their "yellow light off mirrors and brass rails and gilt frames around pictures of pink naked women." There are descriptions, too, of the "desolate empty pavements of 105th Street," where "a fetor of mattresses and sleep seeped out from the blocks of narrow-windowed houses. . . . [and] garbage cans stank sourly," of a group of small, dirty boys smelling like moldy bread who are fighting on the "soggy asphalt" of Tompkins Square Park, of Trinity Churchyard at noon, where officeworkers "are eating sandwiches among the tombs," a fit emblem of the fate they suffer entombed in the city's skyscrapers.

Defeat, despair, depletion, and poverty—these are not Dos Passos's only themes. Vast, complex, and multifaceted, New York is also depicted as a beautiful and affluent city. Dos Passos writes about the Astor Hotel, the Algonquin, the Ansonia, the Lafayette, and Huyler's.[9] And there is a description of Fifth Avenue on a Sunday afternoon as seen through the eyes of a passenger on the Washington Square bus:

On the shady side there was an occasional man in a top hat and frock coat. Sunshades, summer dresses, straw hats were bright in the sun that glinted in squares on the upper windows of houses, lay in bright slivers on the hard paint of limousines and taxicabs. . . . In an occasional storewindow, paintings, maroon draperies, varnished antique chairs behind plate glass. The St. Regis, Sherry's. . . . As they passed St. Patrick's she caught a whiff of incense through the tall doors open into gloom.[10]

In sum, Dos Passos does not write about a single neighborhood or a single class of New Yorkers. His is a richly complex portrait of a city that encompasses many neighborhoods, many kinds of people, and many contradictions. It is a powerful panoramic novel that captures the spirit of the city in the frenetic years following World War I.

Thomas Wolfe, another author who lived in Greenwich Village during the nineteen twenties, also wrote vast, sprawling novels that reflect in their very form the great size and energy of the city. A cumulative portrait of the artist as a young man in New York and a chronicle of the Southerner's love-hate relationship with the city, *Of Time and the River, The Web and the Rock,* and the posthumously published *You Can't Go Home Again* portray New York in a far more subjective manner than *Manhattan Transfer.* Whether his protagonist is called Eugene Gant *(Of Time and the River)* or George Webber *(The Web and the Rock* and *You Can't Go Home Again),* it is clear that his perceptions are those of Wolfe himself, who when he first came to New York believed that in no place in this world could the life of a newcomer be "more barren, more drab, more hungry and comfortless."

Here, Wolfe thought, dwelled

a race of mechanical creatures, who were as essential and inhuman a part of the city's substance as stone and steel and brick, who had been made of one essential substance and charged with one general and basic energy along with the buildings, tunnels, streets, and a million glittering projecticles of machinery, and who flowed by incessantly, were poured into tunnels or driven through the streets.

Likening New Yorkers to vermin and to rats swarming "up out of earth ... to push, claw, sweat, curse, cringe, menace, or contrive, in a furious round of dirty, futile, little efforts that got them nowhere, brought them nothing," Wolfe found etched on their faces "a common story of mean and ungenerous living."

Although he so often depicts the "iron-breasted" city as a wasteland, Wolfe's novels are curiously enough also a celebration of New York. He describes a friend for whom Manhattan's subways, restaurants, theatres, and shops are "simply magic," and to Esther Jack, George Webber's mistress, it is "a living, breathing, struggling, hoping, fearing, hating, loving, and desiring universe of life." At times even George is able to sense the magic and energy of the city so beloved by his friends and to feel "the mighty pulsations of a unity of hope and joy, a music of triumph and excitement that suddenly wove all life into the fabric of its exultant harmonies."

Wolfe's novels contain some memorable descriptions of particular New York locales. In *Of Time and the River* he writes about New York University, where he taught evening classes in the Brown Building, and about the Hotel Leopold—in actuality, the Hotel Albert—where he lived on University Place. In *The Web and the Rock* he describes the apartment near Columbia that George shared with several roommates, his little room on Fourteenth Street, and his flat on Waverly Place in "an old four-story house . . . that had fallen on evil days," which is reminiscent of the dilapidated building on East Eighth Street where Wolfe lived for a time with Aline Bernstein (Esther Jack). *You Can't Go Home Again* opens with a description of George's apartment on Twelfth Street, this one reminiscent of Wolfe's rooms on West Eleventh Street.

Many other New York locales are also depicted. One of the most compelling descriptions occurs in *Of Time and the River* where Wolfe writes about the Gashouse District,[11] which

with its wasteland rusts and rubbish, its slum-like streets of rickety tenement and shabby brick, its vast raw thrust of tank, glazed glass and factory building, and at length its clean, cold, flashing strength and joy of waters —[was] a district scarred by that horror of unutterable desolation and ugliness and at the same time lifted by a powerful rude exultancy of light and sky and sweep and water, such as is found only in America. . . .

Wolfe goes on to explain that the district, "one of the worst in the city," was infested by "young Irish toughs and gangsters" and was a place where "in pier and alley, on street and roof, children had learned the arts of murder, the smell of blood, the odor of brains upon the pavement."

Equally memorable is Wolfe's glowing portrait of the Lower East Side, which despite its poverty and squalor appears to George to be "the essential New York; by all odds the richest, the most exciting, the most colorful New York that he had known." There are memorable descriptions of Second Avenue, which during the twenties was a noted Yiddish theatre district, "a better Broadway—a Broadway with the warmth of life, the thronging sense of the community, a Broadway of a richer and more secure humanity,"[12] and Wolfe defines its particular kind of vitality as

a vitality that is not happy but that is burning with an insatiable hope, a feeling of immediate expectancy, the overwhelming sense that the thrilling, the exciting, the wonderful thing is just there within touch, and may be grasped at any moment.

Believing hope and vitality to be American characteristics, Wolfe concludes that Second Avenue and for that matter the Lower East Side, "even to its rusted cornices, its tenemented surfaces, its old red brick, . . . was American," more American, in fact, than Park Avenue.

Wolfe writes, too, about lower Broadway, its crowded, narrow streets "full of the old, rusty, and gloomy-looking buildings of another time, but also filled with the sensuous and basic substances of life and commerce," and about the Upper West Side, where Esther Jack and her husband live in a five-story brownstone which evokes "memories of primitive America, of '1887,' of '1893,' of '1904,'—that lost time which is more remote, more strange, and, to some men, more beautiful than the Middle Ages."

But the Jacks are soon to be forced out of their house by the "apartment house people ... [who] want to tear down this whole block and put up one of those awful places." Their method, as Esther explains to George, is to "put up big buildings all around you ... shut out all light and air ... [and] simply smother you."

The triumph of the "apartment house people" is apparent in *You Can't Go Home Again,* for the Jacks are now living in a luxurious Park Avenue flat. In the twenties, when it had been demonstrated that apartment houses could be constructed free of vibrations from the railroad below, Park Avenue—one of the city's widest thoroughfares—became a fashionable residential street that attracted many wealthy families in flight from the increasing commercialization of Fifth Avenue. Wolfe describes Park Avenue's "sheer cliffs of solid masonry," its towering buildings with "upper tiers and summits," its "pyramids of steel and stone."

A word about the reference to stone—or rock— and metal in the above quotation is in order here, for these are the images most frequently associated with New York City in Wolfe's novels. Repeatedly, he describes New York as "iron-breasted" or "stony-breasted," and at times the city itself appears to him to be hewn out of rock. Yet, in other moods, he sees a city that "foamed and glittered with ... life and color" and delights in the sights, sounds, and smells of New York, which he perceives as an enchanted place.

What remains consistent in Wolfe's depiction of the city, whether he is describing Park Avenue or Second Avenue, the Upper West Side or Greenwich Village, is a sense of its tremendous power and energy, and this feeling is also conveyed by Janet Flanner in her little-known novel *The Cubical City.*

The importance of New York in Flanner's novel is underscored by both the title and its opening paragraphs in which Delia Poole, a young free-thinking set designer from the Midwest, gazes out a window at

the electric flame and feathers of the colossal cock on the Heckscher building—neck arched in space, comb blazing, claws tightened to his nest of high lights gawdy [sic] above Fifth Avenue.[13]

The Heckscher Building topped with its splendid rooster is an apt opening image for a novel that portrays New York as a vigorously masculine city. Unlike Paris, which has "an old girl's countenance," and London, which displays "the grey phiz of a sour judge," New York's visage is that of "a young male . . . inventive, violent, spoiled, the face of a nervous, handsome and clever only son."

The Cubical City is particularly memorable for its vivid imagery. Flanner writes of Sixth Avenue traffic, of "verdant trams [that] shone like grass among the black flock of evening cabs with their bleating horns and the shepherding call of the police whistle," and of New Yorkers who live "in high homes . . . halfway beneath the unseen rock of the island below and the mist hanging in shelter and clouds far over the roofs," and of "the rich lava-colored brownstone of what had once been polite domestic seats . . . now turned into ruthless shops."

Elsewhere Flanner describes the "resurrection" of the city at dawn when night-shrouded streets that had resembled "paths pointed and cypress-shaped like walks in cemeteries with early workmen stumbling through them like hired mourners" are transformed by the soft light and "saved by the brightness" of a new day.

Several of her descriptions of the city contain religious imagery, and Flanner seems at times to imply that in the modern metropolis the skyscraper has replaced the temple, and the city—perceived as omnipotent— has become the object of modern man's awe and adoration. There is, for example, a reference to "a new spiritual faith" in the following description of Times Square:

Money-colored lights dappled walls of surrounding buildings—lights shining like coined planets, like constellations of gold-pieces strung on invisible wires. Erect on the roofs angling the Square and bright in lively legends of electricity, a bull, a cat and two peacocks, all their parts gleaming, shone like emblems of a new spiritual faith placed visibily this time in the heavens close above the faces of credulous humanity.

While Flanner seems principally concerned with man's quest for spiritual meaning in the modern metropolis, Damon Runyon seems to have been far more interested in his quest for booze, broads, gossip, and cheesecake along "the Great White Way." Himself a sportswriter for a newspaper, Runyon's subjects were Broadway gossip columnists, who during the twenties were establishing themselves as prominent figures on the New York scene, hoods, gamblers, and chorus Judys, almost all of whom turned out to be surprisingly tenderhearted. And he has immortalized Lindy's Restaurant. A gathering place for celebrities located at 1626 Broadway, Lindy's—called Mindy's by Runyon—had a nation-wide reputation for its incomparable cheesecake as well as for its famous patrons.

Stories like "Leopard's Spots" and "Big Boy Blues" are set in Lindy's, usually late at night or in the wee hours of the morning. Sitting in the restaurant reading the sports page of the morning paper, Runyon meets up with a variety of Broadway types such as "West Side Willie," a former ticket speculator who was

known far and wide for his skill in manipulating with tickets to theatres and prize fights and hockey games and one thing and another that everyone wants but are unable to get unless they see Willie and pay his ice, which is a way of saying his premiums.

Runyon also writes about some of the city's best-known speakeasies. He calls the 21 Club—located on Fifty-second Street between Fifth and Sixth avenues, a block renowned for its speakeasies—No. 23, and in "The Big Umbrella" describes it as

a very high-class trap which is patronized only by the better element of rumpots in New York. . . . This No. 23 is a spot where wealthy characters assemble on an afternoon and evening to sit around tables or stand at the bar guzzling old-fashioneds, and Scotches, and other delicacies of this nature, and there are always many swell-looking Judys present, so it is generally a scene of great gaiety. . . .

There the narrator recognizes the doorman, whom he had known years ago when he wasn't "working in a joint as classy as No. 23 " but in "a bust-out joint in West Forty-third, a bust-out joint being a joint where they will cheat your eyeballs out at cards, and dice, and similar devices."

Runyon calls Sherman Billingsley's Stork Club, located first on Fifty-eighth Street and later on Fifty-first, the Pigeon or Canary Club. Described in "Broadway Incident" as "a very high-class gaff where the food department is really above par," in "Neat Strip" it is said to be "patronized only by very high-class rumpots."

Whether he is writing about the Stork Club or the Polo Grounds, about Lindy's or Bryant Park, about 21 or Italian Harlem, Runyon's is a vernacular history of "the big town" during the postwar years. The same can be said about the New York stories of Ring Lardner.

Unlike Runyon, Lardner is not generally thought of in connection with New York. Some of his stories are, however, set there, and some of his characters—the hustlers, the prizefighters, the theatrical agents, the Tin Pan Alley songwriters—are reminiscent of Runyon's. His tone, however, is ironic rather than sentimental. Lardner writes about stupidity, cupidity, vanity, and phoniness, and his hard-bitten characters rarely if ever prove to be tenderhearted.

Many of Lardner's New York stories are about Midwesterners who have come East. In "Dinner" a naive young visitor to the city describes her impressions of New York and of its mayor, Jimmy Walker, whom she has seen in a parade. In "One Hit, One Error, One Left From Lose With a Smile," the narrator comes to New York to play baseball with the Brooklyn Dodgers in Ebbetts Field[14] but is soon fired by Casey Stengel.

A particularly vivid description of the city appears in "Some Like Them Cold," in which another young man in search of fame—this time an aspiring songwriter—records his impressions of the city in the letters he writes to a girl friend back in Chicago. In his first letter he writes that his "whole future is in the big town" and that New York "is the only spot"

for a man that expects to make my liveing in the song writeing game as here is the Mecca for that line of work and no matter how good a man may be they don't get no recognition unless they live in New York.

He explains that he is living in a hotel on "47th St. right off old Broadway and handy to everything," where he is paying twenty-one dollars a week for a room and bath and preparing to fight the "battle of Broadway."

His next letter is less enthusiastic as he describes the city in the midst of a heat-wave and speculates that New Yorkers are immoral "because they think they are all ready in H—— and can not go no worse place no matter how they behave themselves." The letter continues,

Honest girlie I certainly envy you being where there is a breeze off the old Lake and Chi may be dirty but I never heard of anybody dying because they was dirty but four people died here yesterday on acct. of the heat and I seen two different women flop right on Broadway and they had to be taken away in the ambulance and it could not of been because they was dressed too warm because it would be impossible for the women here to leave off any more clothes.

He explains that he hasn't yet won "the battle of Broadway" because "all the heads of the big music publishers" are on vacation.

In still another letter he describes New York as "a great old town" and wonders how he "ever stood for a burg like Chi which is just a hick town along side of this besides being dirty etc. and a man is a sucker to stay there all their life." He explains that he has taken a job playing in an orchestra but is still working on his songs. The last letter states that he and the girl he is marrying will be moving to Atlantic City, where he will play in a cabaret.

The Big Town: How I and The Mrs. Go To New York To See Life And Get Katie A Husband is about the comic misadventures of a Midwestern couple who come East with a newly acquired inheritance and the determination to marry off Katie, the narrator's sister-in-law.

A Mr. Griffin, whom they meet on the train on their way to New York, recommends that they take rooms at a place called the Baldwin, "where you can get a room for twelve dollars a day for the three of you; and you're walking distance from the theaters . . . or anywheres you want to go." He claims to have learned from experience that if you stay "near the center of things; you'll more than make up the difference in cab fares."

The narrator follows his advice but soon discovers that it is impossible to live cheaply in New York. Dismayed by the high rates at the Baldwin— he winds up paying fifteen dollars a day instead of twelve—as well as by the aloofness of the desk clerks and the discovery that Griffin is courting his wife, not his sister-in-law, the narrator decides to seek quarters elsewhere, and what follows is a lively description of apartment hunting in New York.

The women, who want to live "in a new building and on some good street where the real people lives," decide upon Riverside Drive. When the narrator complains about the high cost of renting there, his wife speaks of friends back in Chicago who have "a dandy apartment on Sheridan Road, six rooms and brand new. It costs them seventy-five dollars a month. And Sheridan Road is Chicago's Riverside Drive." To this, her husband retorts that "Chicago's Riverside Drive is Canal Street" and explains, "If you find a six room furnished apartment for a hundred dollars in New York City today, we'll be on Pell Street in Chinatown."

Eventually they do find an apartment on Riverside Drive, "almost across the street from Grant's Tomb,"[15] for which they pay four thousand dollars a year. Here they meet another possible husband for Katie, but when things don't work out, they vacation on Long Island, and later take rooms at the Graham, a family hotel on Sixty-seventh Street.

When Katie finally marries a comedian who "made a name for himself at the Winter Garden"[16] and is now at the Follies,[17] her sister and brother-in-law, disillusioned by the phonies and the hustlers they have met in New York—to say nothing of the high cost of living—are happy to return home to South Bend:

The town's good enough for me and it suits the Mrs., too, though they didn't neither one of us appreciate it till we'd give New York a try. If I was running the South Bend Booster's Club, I'd make everybody spend a year on the Gay White Way. They'd be so tickled when they got to South Bend that you'd never hear them razz the old burg again.

Ring Lardner called New York "the big town," and with good reason. It was, above all, a big and prosperous city during the decade after World War I. High living in the Jazz Age and the frenetic quality of life in the city of skyscrapers emerge as dominant themes in the New York literature of this period. But the immigrant fiction of the twenties attests to the fact that this prosperity was not shared by all New Yorkers. Particularly noteworthy in this regard are *Christ in Concrete* by Pietro DiDonato and *The Fortunate Pilgrim* by Mario Puzo, two books that depict the hardships of impoverished Italian-American families living in New York during this decade of prosperity.

The characters in *Christ in Concrete* are not dining, dancing, and drinking in the city's exclusive nightclubs and speakeasies; they are breaking their backs, and some are sacrificing their very lives, in the process of building a steel and concrete city second to none.

Di Donato writes about an impoverished Italian immigrant family living in a tenement and of the backbreaking and dangerous work of fathers and sons in the construction industry. A brutal and searing picture of a people betrayed not only by their employers but also by the church and the state, the book does not describe specific New York streets but is rich in its depiction of the quality of life found in the city's slums.

Geremio's widow, Annunziata, and her many children live in

a twelve-family house. There were two families on each floor with the flats running in box-car fashion from front to rear and with one toilet between them. Each flat had its distinctive powerful odor.

The hallway of the tenement is

gaseous in its internationality of latrines, dank with walls that never knew day, acrid in corners where vermin, dogs, cats and children relieved themselves; the defeated air rubbery with greasy cooking and cut with cheap strong disinfectant.

Following the death of Geremio on the job, his young son Paul must take on the burden of supporting his family, and like his father he becomes a bricklayer. For the frail youth, as for many of the older men, the work is exhausting and brutalizing; he sustains many painful injuries, but he does not give up, for his is a battle against hunger, "against an enemy inherited." In freezing cold and intolerable heat he responds like a machine to the boss's cry, "Lay brick! Lay brick! Lay brick!"

Di Donato, who was himself a bricklayer, describes the work in detail, particularly the work and risks involved in the construction of New York's skyscrapers. "Big steel was downtown," where metal skeletons "shot up fifty floors to the sky" and there was always danger of falling or being pushed from a swinging scaffold forty or fifty floors above the street. Or of a derrick cable snapping and sending a girder crashing the scaffold to earth. . . . danger was ever present with falling planks and beams and bolts and white-hot molten steel from acetylene torch and breaking cable and unexpected drop of hoist. . . .

The grimness of the novel is relieved only by the lively and colorful scenes depicting the wedding of Uncle Louis. Soon after it takes place, Paul's godfather, Nazone, is killed on the job, and in 1929 Paul finds himself laid off from work, a victim of the Depression:

The building boom lay back—and disappeared. Builders stopped giving out plans to contractors, building owners lost their holdings, building-loan corporations liquidated, the active world of Job shrunk and overnight men were wandering in the streets trowel on hip and lunch beneath the arm in futile search of wall.

With Paul out of work, the family suffers anguish anew; there is hunger and privation. While still mourning Nazone, Paul must endure two other losses: the death of his mother and the loss of the deep faith that previously had always sustained him under the most adverse circumstances.

The ending of Puzo's *The Fortunate Pilgrim* is not quite so grim. The Angeluzzi-Corbo family, having weathered much poverty, privation, and personal tragedy before and during the harsh years of the Depression, is at last able to move from Tenth Avenue to Long Island, along with many of their neighbors who had lived "along the western wall of the city" and were finally able to grasp "the American dream in their calloused hands." Money was made during the prosperous postwar years; it "rolled over the tenements like a flood," and the tenement dwellers were at last able to buy homes in Babylon, West Islip, Massapequa.

But it is the life on Tenth Avenue, between Thirtieth and Thirty-first streets, where during the twenties all those "sitting on the sidewalks . . . were relatives and friends," that leaves a lasting impression on the reader. Children, "busy as ants," play on the pavement, and each and every tenement is "a village square . . . [with] its group of women, all in black sitting on stools and boxes. . . ." Puzo describes the bakery "near the corner of Thirtieth Street, its festooned lemon-ice stand surrounded by children"; the neighborhood grocery store, "its window filled with yellow logs of provolone . . . and prosciutto hams"; and the barber shop "closed for business but open for card playing."

Women and children and storekeepers—all are pilgrims in "a land of stone and steel." They live amidst "the thunder of trains in the railroad yards across the street" and the filth of the slum. Summer brings the most hardship, for then they must endure "the smell of burning stone, melting street tar, gasoline, and manure from horse-drawn wagons hawking vegetables and fruits."

Here on Tenth Avenue are husbands and fathers who "crumbled under the glories of the new land. . . . who became insane and had to be committed, as if in leaving their homeland they had torn a vital root from their minds." Here are frail children sent out to work: sons who become gangsters, daughters who are denied the luxury of going to school. There is hunger and poverty, sickness and death, but what emerges most strongly is the sense that these pilgrims are survivors, that theirs is a thirst for life that will triumph over the city itself. A description of a group of women returning from the funeral of young Vincenzo Angeluzzi best expresses this thought. Their eyes flashing fire and their bodies radiating energy, the mourners

sucked greedily on rigid paper cups of chilling lemon ice and took great bites of smoking hot pizzas, dripping brown invincible teeth deep into the lava of hot tomato sauce and running rivers of cheese to the hidden yeasty dough. Ready to murder anyone who stood in the way of so much as a crust of bread for themselves or their children, implacable enemies of death. They were alive. The stones of the city, steel and glass, the blue-slate sidewalks, the cobblestoned streets, would all turn to dust and they would be alive.

In Puzo's novel, the city emerges as an antagonist against which the Angeluzzi-Corbo family and others like them must struggle for their very survival. This is, of course, a major theme in the fiction of the twenties. More than a backdrop for novels and stories, New York, with its dominant images of steel and concrete, is frequently portrayed as a tremendous and oftentimes invincible force in the fiction of the postwar period.

7

THE HARLEM RENAISSANCE

Harlem's place in the fiction of the nineteen twenties is a significant one, for during this decade it emerged as a thriving artistic and intellectual community, an entertainment center of worldwide fame, and, in the eyes of some, a black Mecca.

Founded by the Dutch in 1636 and called Neiu Haarlem, or new land, Harlem was in the early years of the nineteenth century an isolated rural village. The construction of the Harlem Railroad in the eighteen thirties transformed it into a growing suburb, however, and after the extension of the elevated railroad, it became a fashionable residential neighborhood with rows of fine brownstones, handsome apartment houses, and escalating property values.

The Harlem Opera House was erected in 1889, and a department store was built on 125th Street in 1890. With its many theatres and fine restaurants, Harlem was at this time an attractive and affluent area inhabited largely by German and Irish and after the great immigration waves of the eighties and nineties, by Jews and Italians as well.

The transformation of Harlem from an upper middle-class neighborhood to a slum was rapid. Escalating property values had resulted in a real-estate boom, but many apartments remained tenantless. A realtor named Philip A. Payton was able to persuade landlords to rent to blacks rather than face financial ruin, and many residents of the Tenderloin and San Juan Hill—a black enclave west of Columbus Circle—who could afford the high rentals seized the opportunity to move into a "good" neighborhood at last.

By 1910 many of the city's prominent blacks were living in Harlem, and by the twenties practically all black institutions in the city had moved their headquarters there. Whites had left in large numbers, and Harlem was —for a brief yet glorious period—viewed by some as a black heaven. Yet even during those good years, Harlem had a large population of poor blacks who had emigrated from the South during World War I. Poverty did not first set in during the Depression, but it became more visible during the thirties, and few could deny that the neighborhood had begun to deteriorate.

During the twenties, when Harlem was at the height of its fame, talented blacks from all over the country flocked to this important artistic and intellectual center, and out of their new sense of community pride and power emerged what is known as the Harlem renaissance. Countee Cullen, Claude McKay, Rudolph Fisher, Wallace Thurman, Langston Hughes, and scores of other gifted black writers found stimulation in an environment where theatre and opera flourished, where literary salons were commonplace, and where one could hear lectures by such prominent figures as W. E. B. DuBois and Franz Boas.

It is ironic that at the same time that many of the Harlem renaissance writers were determined to portray blacks in realistic terms and to destroy old stereotypes, whites were creating new ones, which other black authors appeared to confirm. Viewed by many as primitive, carefree, and uninhibited, Harlem's blacks were of great interest to white visitors who flocked to uptown cabarets to listen to their jazz, to watch them dance; in short, to observe and sometimes even to partake in what they viewed as exotic and colorful in Harlem life.

More than any other novel of the period, *Home to Harlem* by Claude McKay depicts Harlem as sensuous and primitive. Its protagonist, Jake, who has been living in England, longs to return to Harlem to listen to its "sugared laughter," "honey-like talk," and perpetual strains of ragtime and blues. Arriving home, he notices the changes that have occurred in his absence. Harlem has become a "little thicker, little darker and noisier and smellier," but the flavor of the place remains the same:

The niggers done plowed through Hundred and Thirtieth Street. Heading straight for One Hundred and Twenty-fifth. Spades beyond Eighth Avenue. Going, going, going Harlem! Going up! Nevah befoh I seed so many dicky shines in sich swell motorcars. Plenty moh nigger shops. Seventh Avenue done gone high-brown. O Lawdy! Harlem bigger, Harlem better . . . and sweeter.

Of particular interest is McKay's account of changes in the Harlem entertainment scene.[1] Connor's, at its peak from 1914 to 1916, "was losing ground," while Edmond's was "still in the running." As for the other cabarets,

Barron's was still Barron's, depending on its downtown white trade. Leroy's, the big common rendezvous shop for everybody. . . .

Goldgraben's on Lenox Avenue was leading all the Negro cabarets a cruel dance. The big-spirited Jew had brought his cabaret up from the basement and established it in a hall blazing with lights, overlooking Lenox Avenue. . . .

But the Congo remained in spite of formidable opposition. . . . The Congo was a real throbbing little Africa in New York. It was an amusement place entirely for the unwashed of the Black Belt. . . .

Elsewhere McKay describes the Congo, where no whites were allowed, as "thick, dark-colourful, and fascinating," and he writes about Sheba's Palace, a cabaret catering to Harlem's "longshoremen, kitchen-workers, laundresses, and W. C. tenders," as well as about the more respectable Casino, patronized by the neighborhood's "upper class of servitors—bell-boys, butlers . . . waitresses and maids of all sorts."

Whether McKay is writing about the Congo or Uncle Doc's saloon, Aunt Hattie's "chitterling joint" or the legendary Madame Walker's Ambrozine Palace of Beauty,[2] his emphasis is on the good times to be found in Harlem—on what. he calls its "contagious fever"—and he explains how those "wearied of the pleasures of the big white world, wanted something new—the primitive joy of Harlem." Here in cabarets or in apartment speakeasies known as "buffet flats" were "none of the well-patterned, well-made emotions of the respectable world." Here one could lose oneself in a "warm wriggle" and experience "simple, raw emotions."

As if to underscore the differences between Harlem's vital and passionate population and the austere and respectable whites who once lived there, McKay describes a quaint all-white enclave on 130th Street between Lenox and Fifth avenues, which "preserved the most Arcadian atmosphere" in the entire city." Here

desperate, frightened, blanch-faced, the ancient sepulchral Respectability held on. And giving them moral courage, the Presbyterian church frowned on the corner like a fortress against the invasion. . . . But groups of loud-laughing and acting black swains and their sweethearts had started in using the block for their afternoon promenade. That was the limit: the desecrating of that atmosphere by black love in the very shadow of the gray, gaunt Protestant church! The Ancient Respectability was getting ready to flee. . . .[3]

Seemingly contemptuous of other black neighborhoods in the city that lacked the vitality and excitement of Harlem, McKay has written a richly descriptive novel about the country's most famous black enclave. But it also presents a limited and somewhat distorted portrait of a neighborhood that was far more than a primitive and exotic entertainment center. In the nineteen twenties Harlem had a substantial number of working-class residents, many of whom rarely if ever, frequented cabarets, speakeasies, and gambling joints, and it was a thriving intellectual center that attracted black writers and artists from all over the country. For a more realistic portrait of Harlem during the twenties let us turn to Rudolph Fisher's *The Walls of Jericho.*

In *The Walls of Jericho,* a novel about Linda Young, a domestic, and her relationships with employers and suitors alike, Fisher, himself a Harlem resident,[4] uses an effective combination of realism and satire to write about ordinary blacks, educated and avant-garde blacks, and white philanthropists. He also does an excellent job of describing particular Harlem locales.

The novel opens with a description of Fifth Avenue, which at 110th Street "leaves its aristocracy behind":

Here are bargain-stores, babble, and kids, dinginess, odors, thick speech. Fallen from splendor and doubtless ashamed, the Avenue burrows into the ground—plunges beneath a park which hides it from One Hundred Sixteenth to One Hundred Twenty Fifth Streets. Here it emerges moving uncertainly northward a few more blocks; and now—irony of ironies—finds itself in Negro Harlem.

You can see the Avenue change expression—blankness, horror, conviction. You can almost see it wag its head in self-commiseration. Not just because this is Harlem—there are proud streets in Harlem. . . . Fifth Avenue's shame lies in having missed these . . . sections, in having poked its head out into the dark kingdom's backwoods.

Later on in the book, Fisher describes Seventh Avenue, which he calls "the most versatile of thoroughfares," explaining that it is

Harlem's Broadway during the week and its Fifth Avenue on Sunday; remains for six days a walk for deliberate shoppers, a lane for tumultuous traffic, the avenue of a thousand enterprises and the scene of a thousand hairbreadth escapes; remains for six nights a carnival, bright with lights of theatres and night clubs, alive with darting cabs, with couples moving from house party to cabaret, with loiterers idling and ogling on the curb, with music wafted from mysterious sources, with gay talk and loud Afric laughter. Then comes a Sunday, and for a few hours Seventh Avenue becomes a highway to heaven; reflects that air of quiet, satisfied self-righteousness peculiar to chronic churchgoers.

Fisher also writes about Washington Heights, and in particular about Court Avenue, the "most exclusive of the residential streets adjacent to Negro Harlem." It "is a straight, thin spinster of a street which even in

July is cold." With its gaunt, gray buildings, scrawny maples, and "air of arched eyebrows," this "snob of a street" is soon to be overtaken by "the swiftly spreading Negro colony."

One of the residents of Court Avenue, Miss Agatha Cramp, is the object of some of Fisher's sharpest satire. Meant to represent the white philanthropist who is well-meaning in her intentions but prejudiced in her attitudes, Miss Cramp is appalled to learn that a light-skinned Negro with whom she has been speaking at the G.I.A. (General Improvement Association) Ball has just taken a house on her block. In addition to the "professional uplifters" like Miss Cramp, there are other "fay" types who flock to Harlem, some for fun, some for profit. Among them are Noel Dunn, "the Nordic editor of an anti-Nordic journal," and his wife, who are impressed by the " 'wealth of material' to be found in Negro Harlem. . . . Everything in Harlem, to the Dunns, was simply marvelous." White philanthropists, profiteers, and pleasure-seekers are all distrusted by Fisher, and one of his characters goes so far as to say that men who came to Harlem "socially" more often than once "had but one motive, the pursuit of Harlem women."

While a large share of Fisher's satire is directed at whites, blacks are not exempt from his barbs. Many blacks attending the G.I.A. Ball are shown to be shallow and hypocritical, and Fisher is particularly ironic in his treatment of "dictys." Satire of dictys, or high-toned blacks, is commonplace in Harlem renaissance fiction, but is nowhere more effective than in Countee Cullen's novel, *One Way to Heaven*.

In *One Way to Heaven* Cullen, like Fisher, interweaves the story of a domestic worker with that of her employer. Probably the most interesting episodes involving Mattie Johnson, a simple and affable housemaid, are those set in Mount Hebron African Methodist Church, said to be "the largest Negro Church in New York City." Having been adopted by a Harlem minister's family when he was eleven years old, Cullen was familiar with the social as well as with the spiritual importance of Harlem church life, and he depicts this in a realistic and convincing way. Still, the most compelling aspect of *One Way to Heaven* is the ironic portrait of the beautiful and affluent Constancia Brandon, "Harlem's most charming hostess."

Cullen describes the Brandons' "fourteen-room house in what was called by less-moneyed, and perhaps slightly envious, Harlemites Strivers' Row" and goes on to discuss Constancia's soirees, which are attended by artists, authors, and performers. Reluctant to create the impression that she "was built along strictly frivolous lines," he explains that Constancia belonged

to sixteen lodges which she never attended, but in which she was never unfinancial, and at whose yearly women's meetings she was always called upon to speak. She was a teacher in the Episcopalian Sunday school, because it convened in the morning and so left her free for her afternoon visits and her Sunday-evening at-homes. She was a member of the Board of the National Negro Uplift Society and a director of the Diminutive Harlem Theatre Group. . . . Added to this, she belonged to two bridge clubs, one sorority, a circulating library, and she gave one hour a week in demonstrating household duties at the Harlem Home for Fallen Girls.

There is also an ironic portrait of Mrs. Vanderbilt-Jones, a dowager from Brooklyn, where for many years wealthy black families had lived in a highly respectable and prestigious black community. Impressed by what she has heard about Sugar Hill, Harlem's most stylish residential area—located west of Eighth Avenue, from 138th to 155th streets—she informs Constancia that she is bored by Brooklyn and plans to buy one of the "lovely" houses on Sugar Hill, where "all the white people are moving out, bless them, and only the best colored people are moving in—doctors, lawyers and teachers."

Cullen depicts Sugar Hill and Strivers' Row—where during the twenties residents payed rents as high as eighty dollars a month—as "another" Harlem when he describes the arrival of spring in New York. In Mattie's neighborhood, spring is greeted boisterously as people lean out of windows gossiping with their neighbors and "drinking in the sun" or gather on street corners in loud, raucous groups telling stories and jokes.

The rites of spring observed by such personages as Constancia Brandon are different from those observed by Mattie and her neighbors on Fifth Avenue.

They too go out to meet the spring, but, being people of circumstance, doctors, lawyers, teachers, owners of houses, payers of direct taxes, their method is genteel and studied. . . . Their ways were not raucous; they who bear the yoke of gentility must bear it as to the manner born. They dance a minuet with spring, and take no step out of season.

The "two" Harlems are a theme that dominates the fiction of the Harlem renaissance, and invariably Strivers' Row and its inhabitants are depicted as affluent, snobbish, and pretentious. A case in point is *Nigger Heaven* by Carl Van Vechten.

Although Van Vechten was white, he is, as we have already seen, closely identified with the Harlem renaissance. Here he writes about 139th Street, where "the richer social set" owned "the splendid row of houses" designed by Stanford White. The tan brick houses had been built in the early years of the century when Harlem was a German section. Now they had been taken over by rich Negroes; a few ... of international fame, but most of them lawyers, physicians, real-estate operators, or opulent proprieters of beauty parlours.[5]

Van Vechten also comments on the relationship between the prosperous residents of Strivers' Row and the young Harlem intellectuals and how

it had become ... quite the thing for these more affluent folk to take up with the young intellectuals since their work had begun to appear in the Atlantic Monthly, Vanity Fair, the American Mercury, and the New Republic.... Times had changed indeed when brains, rather than money, a lighter colour, or straight hair was the password to social favour. The limits of the Blue Vein circle were being extended.

Although he writes at length about its wealthiest and most socially prominent denizens, Van Vechten believes that Harlem is not "the mecca of the New Negro"; he realizes that the problems of the Negro race are far from being solved and that whites are ruthless in their exploitation of the area. He is contemptuous of the naive out-of-towner who describes Harlem as

magnificent, a dream come true.... A Negro city almost as large as Rome! We couldn't have counted on that a few years ago. You have everything here: shops and theatres and churches and libraries. ...

Other—less naive—characters express more cynical views. One, contemptuous of the whites who frequent the Harlem cabarets, doubts if the blacks really "have" Harlem and claims that "in one or two places they've actually tried to do a little jim-crowing!" Another speculates that Manhattan may become a Negro island if blacks from all over the country keep flocking to Harlem "to take advantage of the opportunities promised by the new metropolis" and whites continue fleeing from their homes and neighborhoods as blacks move in.

Its title derived from the name given to the Negro section in a segregated theatre—usually the topmost balcony—the book implies that Harlem itself is the topmost tier of New York, from which the blacks watch the whites seated below in their comfortable orchestra seats. Yet despite its frequently bitter tone, *Nigger Heaven* contains a vivid picture of Harlem during the nineteen twenties. Van Vechten writes not only about the wealthy and the intellectual classes but also about the poor Harlemites, most of whom must earn their living outside "the walled black city ... in an alien world." He describes the white tourists and the distrust felt for the West Indians in the Harlem community, as well as particular streets, theatres, and cabarets.

Satire of those whites who flocked to Harlem for good times, philan-
thropic causes, or in the case of authors and intellectuals, in search of
material for books and articles, is commonplace enough in the works of
Van Vechten, Cullen, Fisher, and other writers of the period, but it is in
the fiction of Langston Hughes that the Negrophile figures most
prominently.

The Ways of White Folks contains several stories set in New York City,
among them "Slave on the Block" and "Rejuvenation Through Joy," both
about wealthy whites who have a passion for blacks and their culture.

"Slave on the Block" is about an artistic white couple, Michael and
Anne Carraway, who

went in for the Art of Negroes—the dancing that had such a jungle life
about it, the songs that were so simple and fervent, the poetry that was so
direct, so real. . . . They owned all the Robeson records and all the Bessie
Smith. And they had a manuscript of Countee Cullen's. They saw all the
plays with or about Negroes, read all the books, and adored the Hall
Johnson Singers. They had met Doctor Du Bois, and longed to meet Carl
Van Vechten. Of course they knew Harlem like their own backyard, that
is, all the speakeasies and night clubs and dance halls, from the Cotton
Club and the ritzy joints where Negroes couldn't go themselves, down to
places like the Hot Dime, where white folks couldn't get in—unless they
knew the man. (And tipped heavily.)[6]

They hire Luther, a young black, who works a bit in their tiny garden
and does a few chores around the house, but spends most of his time
posing for Anne, who is doing a portrait of a slave, or going off with the
black cook to do the Lindy Hop at the Savoy.[7] They continue to
"employ" Luther even though he drinks their liquor, offends their guests,
and speaks of them in a derogatory way until Michael's mother comes for
a visit and threatens to leave if Luther is not dismissed.

"Rejuvenation Through Joy" is also about those whites who have
created—or embraced—myths and stereotypes about blacks. In this case, a
Mr. Eugene Lesche becomes rich when he offers rich, bored whites a
chance to find happiness through "Things Negro." After a series of
successful lectures on the Negroes, who, he claimed, "were the happiest
people on earth," Lesche has a large enough following to establish a
happiness colony in Westchester. The decor is primitive, and his staff includes tap dancers, blues singers, and "the famous Happy Lane *(a primitif
de luxe),* direct from the Moon Club in Harlem, with the finest band in
America." The cost of staying at the happiness colony is prohibitive but
paid gladly by

old residents of Park Avenue or the better section of Germantown, ladies
who had already tried everything looking toward happiness—now they

wanted to try Joy, especially since it involved so new and novel a course as Lesche proposed—including the gaiety of Harlem Negroes, of which most of them knew nothing except through the rather remote chatter of the younger set who had probably been to the Cotton Club.

Hughes's famous Simple stories deal more with the black community than with white interest in it and are set in Harlem some years later. An excellent treatment of intrablack relations in Harlem during the renaissance period, however, is Wallace Thurman's *The Blacker the Berry*.

The Blacker the Berry is about Harlem's blacks, educated and uneducated, light-skinned and dark, and about their conflicts and prejudices. When the protagonist, Emma Lou, comes to New York after having completed three years of college in California, she discovers that prejudice against dark-skinned Negroes is rampant, even in Harlem.

Emma Lou's search for a job is a long and difficult one. She finds out that there are "three or four employment agencies to every block in business Harlem," but many refuse to give her a referral. And when she is given a referral, she is often denied employment by companies that have a policy against hiring dark-skinned blacks. Among them is Angus and Brown, "an old Harlem real estate firm" on 139th Street that in the early years of the century had handled properties in San Juan Hill, but had later

led the way in buying real estate in what was to be Negro Harlem. They had been fighters, unscrupulous and canny. They had revealed a perverse delight in seeing white people rush pell-mell from the neighborhood in which they obtained homes for their colored clients. . . . and, when the white tenants had been slow in moving, had personally dispossessed them, and, in addition, had helped their incoming Negro tenants fight fistic battles in the streets and hallways, and legal battles in court.

Emma Lou's long period of unemployment gives her ample opportunity to become familiar with Harlem, especially with Seventh Avenue, which "was so active and alive." Less taken with 125th Street, with "its line of monotonously regular fire-escape decorated tenement buildings," Emma Lou   .

thanked whoever might be responsible for the architectural difference of the Y.M.C.A., for the streaming bit of Seventh Avenue near by, and for the arresting corner of the newly constructed Teachers' College building, which dominated the hill three bocks away, and cast its shadows on the verdure of the terraced park beneath.

Other Harlem streets are described when Emma Lou goes apartment hunting. She had been told that all the 'dictys' lived between Seventh and Edgecombe Avenues on 136th, 137th, 138th and 139th Streets . . . [and] in the imposing apartment houses on Edgecombe, Bradhurst and St. Nicholas Avenues. 'Dictys' were Harlem's high-toned people, folk listed in the local social register, as it were.[8]

After encountering prejudice because of her dark skin, Emma Lou finally finds an apartment on 138th Street, between Edgecombe and Eighth avenues, but she continues to meet with discrimination even in Harlem's churches. She discovers for example that the Episcopal church "was dedicated primarily to the salvation of light-skinned Negroes,"[9] but is finally made to feel welcome at St. Marks A. M. E. Church on St. Nicholas Avenue, "one of the largest and most high-toned churches in Harlem."[10]

Things are no different in the clubs and cabarets of Harlem, or even at the famed Lafayette Theatre. Located on Seventh Avenue, near 131st Street, the Lafayette was known for its Darktown Follies, which did much to establish Harlem as New York's most exciting entertainment center. Here light-skinned performers proclaim that "Black cats must go," and the orchestra plays "Bye, Bye Blackbird."

Thurman writes at length about the special midnight performance on Friday nights, which lasted "until four or four-thirty the next morning, according to the stamina of the actors." Following a movie, there was a revue that began with a number by the "Sable Steppers":

This was followed by the usual song and dance team, a blues singer, a lady Charleston dancer, and two black faced comedians. Each would have his turn, then begin all over again, aided frequently by the energetic and noisy chorus, which somehow managed to appear upon the stage almost naked in the first scene, and kept getting more and more naked as the evening progressed.

Every bit as boisterous as the performers, the audience also contributed to the raucous atmosphere. There were loud arguments over seats, whistling and calling to friends, hawkers going "up and down the aisle shouting, 'Ice-cream, peanuts, chewing gum or candy.'" All in all, it "was a most chaotic and confusing scene."

Still another "chaotic and confusing scene" is depicted in Part IV, "Rent Party," which describes a unique method employed by Harlemites to pay their rent during the real-estate crisis of the early twenties when apartments were scarce and rent high. All willing to pay the modest admission fee were welcome, and food and drink were available for a price at these rowdy and sometimes violent parties. Thurman writes at length about the deafening noise, the suffocating heat, the boisterous crowd. Drunk, shooting craps, dancing with violent movements, arguing with one another, the revelers terrify Emma Lou, whose "pilgrimage to the proletariat's parlor social" turns into a nightmare.

Although *The Blacker the Berry* is primarily about prejudice within the black community, it contains the by-now familiar satirical portrait of the Negrophile. For a time Emma Lou is employed as a domestic by Campbell Kitchen, who "along with Carl Van Vechten was one of the leading spirits in this 'Explore Harlem; Know the Negro' crusade."

Nella Larson also writes about the "Explore Harlem; Know the Negro" crusade, but like Thurman, she focuses primarily on intrablack relationships, and the theme of Harlem discovery and exploration pertains largely to light-skinned blacks who are alienated from their race and have come to Harlem in search of their roots.

In *Quicksand* Helga Crane, a sensitive and intelligent mulatto raised in the South by a white family, comes to live in Harlem, which she perceives as a fascinating world set quite apart from the rest of the city:

But, while the continuously gorgeous panorama of Harlem fascinated her, thrilled her, the sober mad rush of white New York failed entirely to stir her. Like thousands of other Harlem dwellers, she patronized its shops, its theaters, its art galleries, and its restaurants, and read its papers, without considering herself a part of the monster. And she was satisfied, unenvious. For her this Harlem was enough. Of that white world, so distant, so near, she asked only indifference.... Her existence was bounded by Central Park, Fifth Avenue, St. Nicholas Park, and One Hundred and Forty-fifth street. Not at all a narrow life, as Negroes live it, as Helga Crane knew it. Everything was there, vice and goodness, sadness and gayety, ignorance and wisdom, ugliness and beauty, poverty and richness. And it seemed to her that somehow of goodness, gayety, wisdom, and beauty always there was a little more than of vice, sadness, ignorance, and ugliness.

In *Passing* Clare Bellow, who has passed as a white and is married to a white man, is also drawn to Harlem. Fascinated by what it represents, she comes from Chicago to visit Irene Redfield, who is married to an affluent black doctor and is socially prominent in the Harlem community.[11] The novel, which depicts Harlem "society," contains some interesting descriptions of the city's black elite and of the community itself, but it, like *Quicksand,* does not idealize Harlem. Whether Larson is writing about an elegant tea given by one of Harlem's finest hostesses, about a dance sponsored by the National Welfare League that is attended by many famous and important white people, about Harlem's cabarets, which are "gay, grotesque, and a little weird," or about Lenox Avenue, her portrait is always a realistic one.

True to Larson's depiction, Harlem during the twenties was both an exciting and vital community with large numbers of affluent and intellectual residents and a playground of worldwide fame, but it was decidedly not a mecca for Helga Crane, who could not find a place for herself in the community, or for Clare Bellow, who met a violent death there. On the eve of the Great Depression, it was not without poverty, squalor, and vice, which would become increasingly visible during the next decade.

8

THE GREAT DEPRESSION

The roaring twenties came to an abrupt end with the crash of the stock market in the fall of 1929. A decade of expansion and inflation, of spending and good times, it was followed by the Great Depression, in which incomes fell, unemployment was widespread, stores and offices were left vacant, and personal fortunes were lost. New York's streets became lined with apple sellers; breadlines were seen all over the city; and shantytowns—the best-known of them in Central Park—sprang up at various locations.

Despite the Depression, two enormous architectural projects were completed in New York during the thirties. The Empire State Building—102 stories, 1,250 feet high, and at that time the tallest edifice in the world—was opened in 1931, its construction having been begun two years earlier, just prior to the stock-market crash. Work on Rockefeller Center did not get underway until 1930. By the end of 1932, the thirty-one story building that houses the Radio City Music Hall was complete. The following year several more structures, including the RCA Building, were opened in the projected three-block center.

Transportation facilities in New York greatly expanded during the thirties, encouraging migration to the outer boroughs and the suburbs, and two airports—Floyd Bennett and La Guardia, which opened as North Beach Airport in 1939—were built. The year 1939 also marked the opening of the World's Fair, which did much to boost the morale of New Yorkers, who were just emerging from the Depression and would soon find themselves involved in World War II.

Despite the repeal of prohibition in 1933, gangsterism, which had gained a strong foothold in New York during the bootlegging twenties, flourished, and the resignation of Mayor Walker in September 1932, a short time before repeal, was in part a result of his connections with racketeers. His successor was Fiorella La Guardia. Affectionately known as the Little Flower, he gained the respect and admiration of New Yorkers and served for three consecutive terms (1933-1945), fighting vigorously against organized crime and taking measures to rebuild a city devastated by the effects of the Depression.

The mood of the literature of the 1930s is for the most part grim. The glitter and glamour, the expansion and promise of New York so prominent in the fiction of the twenties are rarely present, and the focus of literature is increasingly political as many authors turned from self-absorption to social and political involvement, some of them viewing Communism as the only solution to America's problems during this decade of crisis.

Among the leftist authors of the thirties was Albert Halper, whose *Union Square* not only depicts the activities of a group of Communists during the Depression years but also is, as the title suggests, the story of a New York neighborhood.

Union Square—so named because it was the place of union for Bowery Lane (which later became known as Fourth Avenue) and Bloomingdale Road (as once the northern extension of Broadway was called), and not because of the labor union spokesmen who often gathered there to speak—had a long association with left-wing causes. An assembling point for radicals prior to World War I and in 1927 the scene of clashes between the police and those protesting against the Sacco-Vanzetti executions, it was during the 1930s the meeting ground for Communist orators and their sympathizers and the site of many demonstrations and riots.

Long ago exclusively residential, the area surrounding Union Square had become commercialized and was during the thirties, an amusement center and shopping area. Its streets filled with hawkers, beggars, vendors, and crowds of bargain hunters and pleasure-seekers, the area had a Coney Island atmosphere, but beneath its tawdry glitter there was evidence of the anguish and privation wrought by the Depression, whose victims were reduced to peddling their wares on the street, begging for pennies, or if in slightly better circumstances, shopping for bargains or filling the long empty hours, once spent at work, in movie or vaudeville houses where they could escape temporarily from their troubles.

One of the major attractions of Union Square was Klein's,[1] for many years the city's largest department store specializing in low-priced women's fashions. Crowds gathered outside waiting for the doors to open at nine thirty, when they pushed "forward in a powerful surge, grabbing at the dresses on the racks, searching and clawing for bargains. It was cash down here, 'on the Square,' each women held her money in her fist."

On the thronged streets outside of Klein's, there was a carnival atmosphere. Old women were selling pretzels, carted about in battered baby carriages; barkers were shouting bargain prices, and there were

young men and boys who peddled songs printed on big, square sheets of paper, songs that told you all about the silver lining and how to chase the blues away. . . . [and] the high-pressure boys, the lads who spat and hawked their wares at you, offering, for your consideration, socks, bars of candy, twenty-five-cent neckties, . . . shoelaces, needles for the lady of the house, and little Japanese toys to tickle the kiddies' fancy. But the cleverest lads of all were the fellows who sold worthless watches out of small, black leather bags, one eye out for passing suckers, the other on the policeman down the street.

The noise was terrific, everything was bedlam. Folks crossed the street against the traffic and were shouted at by our vigilant police. . . .

Many of the movie theatres opened at ten in the morning, and crowds gathered outside to take advantage of the "early bird" matinees. There was vaudeville at the Fourteenth Street Academy of Music, "a towering building specializing in feature pictures accompanied by eight big-time acts of vaudeville continuous from morn till midnight, matinee 25¢, evenings 50¢," and barkers, attired in new costumes each day, stood outside the nearby Irving Place burlesque theatre, hustling customers. For lonely men there were taxi-dancers, "mere kids with painted faces [who] stood around in long, three-dollar sweat-shop dresses, giving the lads a dreamy, Greta Garbo glance."

With music blaring from the dance halls and record shops, with blazing lights flashing " 'The Flavor Lasts,' 'Save Now, 4%,' and 'Klein's, on the Square,' " Union Square was a noisy and colorful if tawdry place in which to forget one's cares, but a short distance away were streets where the signs of the Depression were all too obvious. There, "in 15-20-30-cent flop-houses," defeated men lay on vermin-infested mattresses "spattered with years of tobacco stain, nasal excretion, and vomit," and in nearby slums, those only slightly better off lined up to receive handouts. Clutching their bundles, they hurried "down side streets, each man or woman going his own way, hoping they wouldn't meet any of their neighbors." And on winter nights, women and children driven out of their tenement apartments by the freezing cold foraged for fire-wood on "the rear platforms of furniture companies, factories, [and] dry goods stores."

Convinced that our economic system had spawned this kind of degradation and poverty, Halper expresses contempt for his capitalistic characters and for politicians who "faced the problem frankly, but when they were through talking, you found they had promised nothing definite." Although he is generally more sympathetic to Communists than to capitalists, Halper is nonetheless scornful of those whose commitment to the cause is more aesthetic or social than ideological, and he describes at length how during the thirties the East Side was becoming "Russia-conscious." He writes of the Acme Theater's Russian programs, the unprecedented demand for the *Daily Worker* and the *Moscow News,* the crowds frequenting the Russian cafés along Second Avenue, and the patrons of Russian specialty shops, most of them "arty-looking couples who lived in small 'studio' apartments below Fourteenth Street . . . [who] had recently swung over from free love to communism."

His admiration reserved for the hardworking comrades seeking a better world for their fellow men, Halper does not idealize all Communist party workers, but he does believe in their cause, and many of the novel's most powerful scenes take place in Union Square when the Communists are making speeches, when demonstrations are taking place and protesters are clashing with the police. Toward the end of the book, Halper devotes many pages to depicting a melee reminiscent of the confrontation that took place on March 6, 1930, between some thirty-five thousand demonstrators and the police, which resulted in more than a hundred injuries and thirteen arrests.

Another work less strident in tone but also about the author's flirtation with Communism during the thirties is Edmund Wilson's "The Princess with the Golden Hair." Here, as in Halper's novel, Union Square figures prominently.

The narrator describes his experiences as an aspiring young author in New York and explains that he took an apartment "just below Fourteenth Street" because the Greenwich Village rents "had gone up to join the uptown rents." Spending many an evening strolling along Fourteenth Street, he comes to relish the photographs of "big-hipped cat-faced women," which were

shown as lures out in front of the Fourteenth Street burlesque show; the announcements of moving-picture palaces bejeweled with paste-bright lights; the little music shops that sold big brass-band instruments and Slavic and Balkan records and had radios that blared into the street; the Field's restaurant window with the white-aproned girl, blue-livid under a mercury tube, making pancakes on a hot metal slab.

It is on Fourteenth Street that he buys Communist newspapers, develops leftist sympathies, and meets Anna, his "proletarian girlfriend," who works as a dime-a-dance girl in the Tango Casino, described by Wilson as "the jazziest and the toughest" of the downtown dance halls.

Although there are some fine descriptions of Greenwich Village in springtime, of Washington Square, which Wilson perceives as "a landing that led to the basement [of New York]," and of "Madison Avenue in the respectable lower East Seventies," with its spacious streets, fine restaurants, and "trim ladies walking dachshunds and Scotties," the most memorable passages are those depicting the narrator's trip to Brooklyn to see Anna.

Disappointed when the train "finally emerged from the tunnel in a raw landscape of tracks and garages, gas tanks, one-story factories and bleak little cheap brick houses in which the factory workers evidently lived," he is pleasantly surprised when he reaches Anna's neighborhood, which seems "inexplicably attractive":

It was Twelfth Street just off King's [sic] Highway, not far from Coney Island and Brighton Beach; and there was space and ocean air and light, and what seemed to me—it was what most astonished me—an atmosphere of freedom and leisure quite unknown on the other side. The great thing here was that there were so few high buildings—the tallest were apartment houses that ran only to six or eight stories, and there were not very many of these; and for the rest, one found little brick shops—delicatessen stores, beauty parlors, drugstores, billiard rooms, kosher butchers, and newsstands with Italian and Jewish papers—that had been relatively newly built and that looked absolutely toylike.

The streets were lined with young trees, and the semiattached houses, although small, seemed "independent dwellings," each with its own backyard and garage, as well as

its little privet hedge on the street, its latticed shades in the windows, its arched doorway with a diadem of bricks that rayed out around the top, and its little flight of steps in front with an ornamental patterned stone bowl in which nasturtiums or geraniums grew.

Brooklyn figures prominently in the New York literature of the 1930s, but few of the areas depicted by authors like Daniel Fuchs, Alfred Kazin, and Thomas Wolfe are as middle class or as attractive as Twelfth Street and Kings Highway. Perhaps the grimmest portrait of Brooklyn during the Depression years is to be found in Wolfe's *You Can't Go Home Again.*

Although Wolfe is generally thought of as writing about the twenties, portions of his last novel are set after the stock-market crash, when George Webber lives in a basement apartment in the Cobble Hill section of Brooklyn.[2] Determined to write realistic fiction, George seeks out the neighborhood's most desolate streets and their inhabitants. His subjects the "Armenians, Italians, Spaniards, Irishmen, and Jews" who live in "the shacks, tenements and slums in all the raw, rusty streets and alleys in

South Brooklyn," Wolfe describes the sights and smells of this "huge and rusty jungle," particularly the smells coming from the old Gowanus Canal, which "gives to South Brooklyn its own distinctive atmosphere."

The most depressing scenes of all are not, however, set in Brooklyn, but just across the bridge in a comfort station near City Hall, which on freezing nights becomes home to the city's homeless. Along with the drunks and the bums "that one sees everywhere . . . in good times as well as bad" are victims of the Depression, the

flotsam of the general ruin of the time—honest, decent, middle-aged men with faces seamed by toil and want, and young men, many of them mere boys in their teens with thick unkempt hair. These were the wanderers from town to town, the riders of freight trains, the thumbers of rides on highways, the uprooted, unwanted male population of America. They drifted across the land and gathered in the big cities when winter came, hungry, defeated, empty, hopeless, restless. . . .

After witnessing homelessness and despair not unlike that described in Robert Nathan's *One More Spring,* a novel about Depression victims who find refuge in the bowl of the drained Central Park reservoir, George feels bitter as he gazes about at the symbols of the city's wealth and power:

The Woolworth Building was not fifty yards away, and a little farther down were the silvery spires and needles of Wall Street, great fortresses of stone and steel that housed enormous banks. The blind injustice of this contrast seemed the most brutal part of the whole experience, for . . . only a few blocks away from this abyss of human wretchedness and misery, blazed the pinnacles of power where a large portion of the entire world's wealth was locked in mighty vaults.

Another of Wolfe's works depicting Brooklyn during the Depression is his short story "Only The Dead Know Brooklyn," which on the surface appears to be little more than an amusing anecdote about the narrator's encounter on a subway platform with an eccentric character who is determined to explore every part of the borough. It contains few descriptions of Brooklyn locales and is of relatively little importance to the present study, but mention should be made of two of its features: the use of Brooklyn dialect and the hint of urban themes such as anonymity, impersonality, and transience, which later would become so prominent in postwar American fiction.

A far more-detailed portrait of Brooklyn can be found in the novels of Daniel Fuchs. *Summer in Williamsburg* and *Homage to Blenholt* are richly descriptive of Williamsburg's Jewish community, and *Low Company* contains a memorable portrait of the Coney Island section during the Depression. Yet although Fuchs's characters are trapped in impoverished areas of the city, although their lives are grim and tawdry, although the sensitive aesthetes recoil from their environs and those with criminal connections are the only ones who—sometimes—make it big, most appear to be victims of more than the Depression, perhaps of life itself.

The author, who himself grew up in Williamsburg, describes his childhood impressions of the neighborhood in the introduction to *Three Novels by Daniel Fuchs,* explaining how he used to associate certain sections with a hangman's noose. Although he claims not to understand why this was so, it is obvious to the reader that many of Fuchs's protagonists feel that Williamsburg is a place of entrapment and death. Balkan, the protagonist of *Homage to Benholt,* who sees himself as the Tamburlaine of Williamsburg, tells his girl friend Ruth, "There's no greatness here, nothing high and strong. . . . Everything is small and mean and dirty." In *Summer in Williamsburg* similar sentiments are expressed by Harry, who writes a letter urging his brother Philip to escape before winding up "worn, poor, and dead before you die."

Philip, however, cannot dismiss Williamsburg so easily. He understands that as part of the process of self-discovery, he "must make a laboratory out of Williamsburg . . . a dictionary of Williamsburg"; and this is precisely what Fuchs himself appears to have done in his two Williamsburg novels.

In *Summer in Williamsburg* Fuchs describes a neighborhood that in warm weather "lived in the open, on fire-escapes, on roofs, in lots, and on the sidewalks." The streets were thronged with pot menders and umbrella fixers, junk dealers, old-clothes men, sandwich-board men, and hot-corn men. The betting parlors, movie houses, and delicatessens, the Wallabout Market,[3] the burlesque shows on Throop Street, and the social hall on Ripple Street were other Williamsburg "institutions" that added color and vitality to the neighborhood.

Local gangs comprised another—and clearly undesirable—Williamsburg institution. Distinguishing between the Irish, Jewish, and Italian gangs of Williamsburg, Fuchs explains that the Irish would "fight most for the fun of it; with the Jews it was often a case of self-defense. But the Italians went out definitely to hurt and maim." He goes on to write about the Maujers, the Hoopers, and the Havemeyer Streeters, a Jewish gang comprised of "newcomers from the East Side" who boasted that they had caused "the Italian migration to Bensonhurst and Bay Ridge."

Despite the claim of the Havemeyer Streeters, the Italian section of Williamsburg remained well populated. Here could be found cafés decorated with murals and calendars depicting "ladies with big overflowing breasts" and grocery stores "where green, odd-shaped cheeses hung from strings, cans of olive oil bore peculiar labels and pictures, and the vegetables appeared fascinatingly foreign." To the young Jewish boys of Williamsburg, Metropolitan Avenue and other streets like it in the Italian section seemed "a strange country altogether."

While Fuchs is best known for his Williamsburg fiction, *Low Company,* which is set in Neptune Beach (Coney Island), should not be overlooked, for it is a realistic portrait not only of the crowded beaches and the dazzling boardwalk attractions but also of a depressed residential area where

nothing was solid, neither the pavements nor the foundations of the buildings. As the sands gave, the sidewalks broke and the houses on their pole foundations never stopped settling.... Ramshackle ugly bungalows these were, for the most part, wooden in construction, once covered gayly with gray and green stucco or imitation brick surface, now hideous with time and neglect.

In summer the stucco houses were crowded with several families who shared kitchen and bathroom facilities with the landlord. The husbands commuted each day to work, and in the evenings when they arrived home "after the terrific jams ... on the Sea Beach, West End or Brighton expresses," everyone spilled onto "the porches and streets." The women sat together, fanning themselves as they discussed "the misfortunes and disasters in their families—operations, deaths, business losses and scandal" and the sacrifices they had made "to come to Neptune for the sake of their children."

In sharp contrast to all of this was Lundy's,[4] called Pundy's by Fuchs. Located "on the other side of Neptune," it "was an elaborate sea-food establishment, the lights were dim and the waiters wore heavily starched monkey jackets." Fuchs describes the "splendors of the place," which are the more striking for being set against the background of "sandy lots and garbage dumps ... [and] queerly curved narrow streets ... lined by the poorest wooden frame bungalows." But Fuchs's interest is primarily in the lower middle class—the year-round residents, the season renters, and the daily visitors—whose tastes and pocketbooks are more compatible with boardwalk fare than with Lundy's seafood specialties, and in this respect, he is similar to Norman Rosten, author of *Under the Boardwalk,* a novel about a young boy whose family owns a boardinghouse in Coney Island and whose responsibilities include hawking locker space in the basement to would-be bathers.

Rosten's novel opens with a description of Coney Island at the height of the summer season:

Come to Coney! The posters called, and everybody listened. And they came. On summer weekends a thousand people a minute spilled from the subway and trolley terminals down Surf Avenue, some to the beach, some to the pools, sailors and girls waiting for evening, and the mystery of the place brocaded with lights and real stars. . . .

From the avenue right at the corner I could hear the early morning barkers trying out their voices: hurry hurry a nickel a nickel hurry a frank a root beer a nickel hurry potato chips fresh all fresh (fresh last week) and corn hot fresh (really warm and soggy) try a ride it's a dime take the little girl along she'll love to be kissed hurry hurry. . . .

It was all starting up again, that long humid day of a million people, and nobody seemed to mind the lies and the sweat, or notice the rundown houses and streets full of the poor. . . .

Across the horizon, the empty Ferris wheel towered, turning on its trial run. . . . At night, a thousand, maybe ten thousand electric bulbs framed the wheel, and on a clear night, when the lights turned, it was as if the nearby stars were turning along with them, you couldn't be sure.

Rosten writes not only of the boardwalk but also of the dark and cool area beneath it, where the dank odor "rose up from the sand and seemed to come from a subterranean source." Here in this "place of halflight" the boy peers up "through the thin spacings between the boards in search of ladies who left their underwear home, an Indian stalking his prey." In a landscape of "corrugated metal and wire fence, entrances to locker houses, frayed billboards, rotting wood, and decayed boats alive with cats and mongrel dogs," he listens to "the rustle of water where the gondola glided through the Tunnel of Love" and watches men and women loitering in the shadows, "some holding hands, some clinging to each other, a man pressing a girl against the concrete pillar, a girl combing a man's hair, others watching, silent, waiting."

Young boys watching lovers under the boardwalk or functioning in some other situation as observers and commentators on the scene around them are commonplace in many Brooklyn novels set in the thirties. In *Teitlebaum's Widow* by Wallace Markfield, Simon Sloan, who is growing up in the Brighton Beach area, relates his impressions of Brighton Fifth Street, Brighton Beach Avenue, Ocean Parkway, Shore Boulevard, and Coney Island Avenue, of the Knishe Queen, the Parkway Baths, Luna Park, and the Brighton Theatre, where there was still vaudeville during the thirties. Markfield also writes about the Brighton Savings Bank, the nearby Hebrew National deli, and the exclusive Manhattan Beach residential area adjacent to Brighton Beach. While Markfield's novel is of some interest, it does not approach the excellence of Alfred Kazin's *A Walker in the City,* which although generally regarded as nonfiction, contains many elements of the *bildungsroman,* and like Norman Podhoretz's *Making It,* is about the intellectual development of a sensitive Jewish youth from Brownsville who is finally able to take what Podhoretz describes as "one of the longest journies in the world . . . the journey from Brooklyn to Manhattan."

Located in East Brooklyn, its boundaries Ralph Avenue, Junius Street, and Liberty and Hegeman avenues, Brownsville had been for many years a sparsely populated rural village, but a large influx of immigrants from Eastern Europe—many of whom had first settled on the Lower East Side— had transformed it into one of the borough's most densely populated Jewish areas. The spirit of this neighborhood is captured by Kazin in a lyrical memoir that depicts both the Brownsville he knew as a youth and its transformation into a slum in the years following World War II when the Jewish community dispersed and the population became predominantly black and Puerto Rican.

Kazin writes about Rockaway, Stone, Dumont, and Blake avenues, about the "ratty little wooden tenements" and the people sitting on the stoops, but his finest descriptions are of Pitkin Avenue, Brownsville's "show street," which was named for John R. Pitkin, a wealthy Connecticut merchant who founded the village of East New York, and of Belmont Avenue and its noisy outdoor market, where pushcarts clogged the streets and the aroma of pickles and herrings from open barrels permeated the air. More than anything else, however, the hearty and shrewd market women dominated the scene: "The street was their native element; they seemed to hold it together with their hands, mouths, fists, and knees. . . ." In hot summer or freezing winter, when they were bundled in six sweaters and wearing long aprons over their overcoats, they cried and cajoled, *"Vayber! Vayber! . . . Oh you lovelies! . . . See how cheap and good! Just come over! Just taste! Just a little look!"*

If Belmont Avenue was Brownsville's Orchard Street, then Pitkin Avenue between Stone and Ralph avenues was its Broadway. Lined with shops, banks, restaurants, and cafeterias, which at one time employed some one thousand people, and boasting Loew's Pitkin Theater, with a seating capacity of thirty-six hundred, the fourteen-block stretch was one of Brooklyn's main shopping and entertainment centers. Its streets were perpetually filled with shoppers, strollers, and loungers, and during the thirties it was a meeting place for Communists and Socialists, who stood on bank corners and "raged at each other." Bank corners were also the gathering points for those employed in the building trades, and Pitkin Avenue on the corner of Stone was where bosses and contractors talked shop and socialized. Kazin makes specific mention of the Municipal Bank on the corner of Stone Avenue, "where every Saturday morning about eleven my father and his fellow house painters gathered in one circle, carpenters and plasterers and bricklayers in theirs." "Business discussions concluded, they would gossip for hours "until it was time to go home for the great Sabbath midday meal."

There were, of course, many Sabbath observers who on Saturday mornings attended the synagogues that could be found on almost every block—sometimes there were two or three on a block—in this predominantly Jewish neighborhood.[5] Kazin writes about the old Dugschitz synagogue, which had probably been a farmhouse at one time, with its scarred wooden pews, gilt-brocaded prayer shawls, and "ancient prayer books and commentaries which . . . looked as if they had come down to us from Moses and the Prophets, with the reverent kiss of each generation in its margins."

There are also descriptions of the movie house on Bristol Street, "whose very lounge looked and smelled . . . like an oriental temple," of lots beyond Betsy Head Park,[6] where children played baseball after "first shooing away the goats," of trucks lumbering along streets to deliver heavy crates of seltzer, "the poor Jew's dinner wine," and of the local Jewish National delicatessen.

Almost from the start of the book, Kazin writes of Brownsville as being somehow apart from the rest of New York, explaining that it was "the eternity of the subway ride" to and from Manhattan that first gave him this feeling. There are descriptions of many stops on the IRT line including Hoyt Street, which was "enlivened by Abraham and Straus's windows of ladies' wear"; Bergen Street, where nobody ever entered or exited from the train; and Franklin Avenue, "where the Jews began." But these were "middle-class Jews, *alrightniks,*" a breed apart from the poorer Jews who got off at such stops as Saratoga, Junius, Pennsylvania, and New Lots, "where the city goes back to the marsh, and even the subway ends."

The sense of Brownsville as "the margin of the city" was reinforced by the car barns where trains and trolleys were locked up for the night, the "raw patches of unused city land . . . filled with 'monument works,'" and the proximity to Canarsie, an undeveloped area of lots, marshes, junkyards, truck farms, and refuse dumps.

Feeling that he is "of the city, but somehow not in it," the young Kazin perceives New York as "a foreign city." Even the nearby "American district" to the north seems to him a distant land, and he feels privileged to walk down the quiet tree-lined streets and gaze at the dignified brownstone houses with their neat awnings and window boxes.

A school trip to the Botanic Garden and the Brooklyn Museum[7] provides another glimpse into what the young Kazin thinks of as the *Beyond,* but the *Beyond* that most attracts him is Manhattan, which he seeks to know not only in its present state but as it was in the past, imagining, for example, Castle Garden as it had been when his parents "first stepped out on the shores of New York" and "Park Row of a winter afternoon in the 1880's."

Particular emphasis is placed on crossing the boundary from Brooklyn to Manhattan, and Kazin writes at length about Brooklyn Bridge, where the El trains shot "blue-white sparks against the black, black tracks sweeping in from Chinatown and Oliver Streets under the black tar roofs and fire escapes and empty window boxes along the grimy black tenements." There are descriptions, too, of the clanging trolleys, the blazing electric signs, and the arcade where vendors sold hot dogs, popcorn, and newspapers. Indeed, the many references to crossing Brooklyn Bridge and the epigraph from Walt Whitman's "Crossing Brooklyn Ferry" suggest that Kazin, like Whitman, saw the journey from Brooklyn to Manhattan as a symbolic one, one which entailed spiritual growth and even transcendence.

A book about crossing borders between neighborhoods, about bridges between boroughs, about Kazin's struggle to become an American artist yet remain a Jewish son, *A Walker in the City* is above all a brilliant portrait of Brownsville. While Brownsville during the depression years is depicted in other novels including Gerald Green's *To Brooklyn With Love,* Isidore Rosen's *Will of Iron,* and Arthur Granit's *The Time of the Peaches,* Kazin's portrait of the neighborhood remains unequaled in American literature.

Although the Bronx does not figure as prominently as Brooklyn does in New York fiction set in the thirties, it is the background for several novels, among them Thomas Bell's *All Brides Are Beautiful* and Jerome Weidman's *Tiffany Street.*

The importance of the Bronx locale in Bell's novel, which is about the struggles of Peter and Susan Cummings, a newly married couple trying to make ends meet during the Depression years, is underscored by the opening paragraph, which discusses the borough's location, population, climate, and other "vital statistics":

The Bronx may be identified as one of New York City's five boroughs which is on the mainland of the North American continent, the others being distributed over three islands off its coast. It has a population of one and a half millions; it is cold in winter, tropically hot in summer, and on a Jewish holiday indistinguishable from a city stricken with a completely successful general strike. A zoo, a cocktail, and a derisory cheer have been named after it. Most of its employed residents earn—receive—twenty-five dollars or less per week and pay an average monthly rent of ten dollars per room. The customary price of a glass of beer is ten cents, of admission to a picture theater twenty-five cents, of a woman two dollars.

Almost immediately after this introduction, Bell launches into a comparison of the East and West Bronx, explaining that Walton Avenue [in the West Bronx] "as a residential district is to Union Avenue [in the East Bronx] as a salary of thirty-five dollars a week is to wages of twenty-five dollars a week." The West Bronx—with its tall, new apartment houses—was at this time inhabited by the moderately well-to-do, while apartments in the East Bronx—most of them railroad flats—were inhabited by less affluent German and Irish families and by blacks. The streets of the East Bronx were "cluttered with ashcans scrawled with house and street numbers," and even the "old, dingy, and slow buses" that ran there were inferior to the "new and powerful" ones that traversed the stately streets of the West Bronx.

The section of the Bronx depicted in most detail by Bell is the High Bridge area. There are many descriptions of High Bridge itself, the oldest of New York's great bridges. Under construction from 1837 to 1848, and a part of the Croton Aqueduct system, it was built to carry a water main across the Harlem River. Although in the early nineteen twenties some renovations were made, the massive stone arches remained, and to Bell's characters the bridge looked "older than Rome."

About a quarter of a mile north of High Bridge is the 181st Street Bridge, which on the Washington Heights side leads to High Bridge Park. Unemployed and with time on his hands, Peter often walks across the bridge and notices that in the park and on 181st Street itself "there were too many men about with nothing to do." He has plenty of time, too, to stroll along the streets of the Bronx. Ogden Avenue, with its butcher shops, beauty parlors, cafeterias, bakeries, saloons, drugstores, its "backyard tenors," and "hucksters . . . offering to buy old clothes, old gold, old typewriters, and old sewing machines," is only one of the many Bronx streets described by Bell. He writes of Boscobel and University streets, of Castle Hill, Shakespeare, and Sedgewick avenues, of Prospect Avenue, which below 163rd Street "suddenly blazed with picture theaters, stores, cafeterias, photograph studios, and 'Dress Suits & Evening Gowns to Hire' shops," and of the Grand Concourse, the Park Avenue of the Bronx, where affluent families lived in modern elevator apartment houses that lined the 180-foot-wide thoroughfare stretching for four and a half miles through the West Bronx.

His focus invariably fixed on the contrasts between the haves and have-nots, Bell has written a painfully realistic novel about the hardships endured by a young middle-class couple during the Depression. Peter's long and frustrating search for employment and his growing leftist sympathies are depicted in scenes set on Sixth Avenue, with its "lines of [employment] agencies . . . and the dispirited, shuffling throngs before them," and in Union Square, where there is a gathering of Communists on May Day. There are even scenes set in Brooklyn's Bushwick Terminal area, where Peter finally finds a job. But *All Brides Are Beautiful* is above all a Bronx novel, which, like *Tiffany Street,* portrays a borough often neglected in the fiction about New York City.

Although parts of *Tiffany Street* take place in the sixties and deal with the efforts of Benny Kramer, a successful New York lawyer, to help his son avoid the Vietnam draft, its most compelling sections are flashbacks to the thirties, when Benny's family moved from East Fourth Street[8] to the residential section of the Bronx that Benny calls "uptown." The adjustment is difficult, particularly for Mrs. Kramer, who feels like "Pocahontas on Ebury Street in London." Even Benny, who realizes that "socially he is a cut above East Fourth Street," sometimes wishes that he were "smelling the sharp, oil-rich odor of the East River." He perceives Tiffany Street as "too quiet" and misses the noise of the old neighborhood, but it is his mother who suffers the most:

On East Fourth Street my mother had been on intimate terms with all our neighbors. On Tiffany Street she did not know the names of our neighbors. Neither did I. The Tiffany Street tenements were smaller than the monstrous gray stone buildings in which I had been raised on East Fourth Street. The toilets were indoors. We even had a bathtub. The sidewalks were cleaner. But they were deserted. People did not sit out on the stoops in the evening eating Indian nuts and gossiping. . . .
   All of her years in America my mother had dreamed of "improving" herself. . . . Now she had done it. And what did she have? In her own Yiddish words: "A great big fat empty day with nothing to do except cook for Papa and stare out at the trees."
   But it was the trees that eased her fears and enabled her to turn her back on what I see now was disappointment. A street with trees on it was what America was all about, and she had finally made it to a street with trees.

In this saga of Benny's rise to success through hard work and determination, Weidman describes many Bronx locales, such as Fox Street, Mosholu Parkway, and Intervale Avenue. A particularly vivid description is of Loew's 180th Street, where Benny and his girl friend Hanna eat Gabilla knishes in the balcony.
   Indeed, New York's gastronomical delights are treated at great length by Weidman, who writes about pastrami sandwiches from Lou G. Siegal's Thirty-ninth Street restaurant and lunch at Shane's. Located on Twenty-third Street, Shane's was "one of those restaurants . . . mentioned regularly in the newspapers, usually in the Broadway columns, in connection with the activities of famous people." Most nostalgic of all are Weidman's

descriptions of meals at the Automat,[9] where Benny is "fascinated by the little windows out of which popped foods I had never heard of" and by the girl who "spilled out the nickels" in the "huge, white, blindingly white chamber."

Among the descriptions of Manhattan locations, those of Seventh Avenue are particularly memorable. The author of *I Can Get It For You Wholesale,* the best-known of the garment-center novels, Weidman writes about "the huge garment-center trucks" that brought traffic almost to a standstill and the loft buildings in the area, most of which

had very distinctive odors. Not necessarily unpleasant. In fact, as you moved up the avenue from 34th Street (dresses) to 37th (frocks) toward Times Square (gowns), in the buildings around 39th Street, where the more expensive gowns were manufactured, the smell was not unlike that of the perfume shop in Macy's. The models were higher priced. The things with which they sprayed themselves came from distant countries.[10]

Deserted on Sundays, Seventh Avenue is compared by Weidman to "the north bank of the river Styx."

Weidman's emphasis—whether he is writing about the Kramers' move from East Fourth Street to Tiffany Street or comparing the city as it was in the thirties to New York in the sixties—is on change, and invariably he is nostalgic about "the good old days," when "everything was simpler. . . . Simpler and better."

That "everything was simpler. . . . Simpler and better" in her youth is hardly the impression one gets when reading Louise Meriwether's auto-biographical novel *Daddy Was A Number Runner.* Set in Harlem during the Depression, it is about the Coffin family, whose patriarch, unemployed yet too proud to accept relief or allow his wife to clean other people's apartments, becomes a number runner to support his family.

Respected in his community and middle class in his outlook, Mr. Coffin's decision to become involved with the Mafia, which he knew "controlled everything in Harlem—the numbers, the whores, and the pimps who brought them white trade," was not an easy one, and the fruits of his illegal labors are not many. The Coffins live in an apartment that has "greasy walls lumpy with layers of paint over cracked plaster." There are leaks and bedbugs, and the linoleum "was worn so thin you couldn't even see its pattern and there was a jagged hole in the floor near the pipe almost big enough to get your foot through."

Not far from their apartment on Fifth Avenue and 118th Street is Francie Coffin's junior high school, P.S. 81, "one of the worst girls' schools in Harlem, second only to P.S. 136 uptown." Many of Francie's classmates belong to "the Ebonetters . . . the sister gang to the Ebony Earls, the roughest street fighters this side of Mt. Morris Park." Meriwether writes about gang wars, describing how the Earls jumped the Jewish boys "who attended the synagogue on 116th Street or mugged any white man caught alone in Harlem after the sun went down," and about the Harlem riots protesting the conviction of the Scottsboro boys and the fatal beating of a Puerto Rican youth caught shoplifting by the police.

Both Harlem's commerce and its religious institutions are depicted by Meriwether, who describes the Kress's on 125th Street, the Miles and National shoe stores half a block away, and the "open-air market on Park Avenue under the el" where hundreds of pushcarts sold "everything from pickled herrings to cotton bloomers,"[11] as well as the renowned Abyssinian Baptist Church,[12] the Mount Olivet Sunday School on 120th Street, and Father Divine's,[13] where during the Depression a chicken dinner could be purchased for fifteen cents.

There were good times to be had in Harlem during the Depression years, but they were few and far between. Francie went to the Jewel and Regun theatres and to the Apollo, where for ten cents she "sat upstairs in the buzzard's roost" to see the show and the movie, and there was the celebration in Harlem streets when Joe Louis won the world heavyweight boxing championship in 1937. But Harlem—which she thinks of as "nothing but one big garbage heap"—is, above all, a place from which Francie dreams of escaping. Still, her thoughts of other worlds are fraught with anxiety. When she finds herself in the nearby Puerto Rican community, where people were "babbling away in Spanish, just like it was high noon instead of midnight," she is depressed at being in "another world and not knowing what anybody was talking about."

On another occasion Francie, standing on her roof and looking "across Central Park at the lights twinkling in the skyscrapers," experiences a not dissimilar feeling:

That was another world too, all those lights way over there and this spooky park standing between us. But what good would those lights do me anyway? I bet they didn't even allow colored in those big buildings.

Yet, like her namesake in *A Tree Grows In Brooklyn,* Francie continues to dream of the world beyond, wishing that she were "way down Fifth Avenue on the other side of the skyscrapers" instead of in Harlem, which to her is a "black valley" trapped between the bell tower of Mount Morris Park and the Empire State Building. She fantasizes that she is traveling "down Fifth Avenue, past Central Park, and the Empire State Building and up into the moonlight" with the young man of her dreams, and on the last page of the book she tells her brother, "Mother says we're gonna move off of Fifth Avenue one of these days." His cynical reply, repeated by Francie, is the last word of the novel.

While many New York novels set in the thirties depict the unemployment and poverty so widespread during the Depression years, some of those that we have discussed touch upon the Depression only tangentially, if at all, and a number of these novels still remain to be considered. One such book is *Miss Lonelyhearts* by Nathanael West, who grew up in New York and during the Depression worked as night manager for the Kenmore Hotel, on Twenty-third Street, and later at the Sutton Hotel, at 330 East 56th Street, where he provided lodgings to such literary figures as his brother-in-law S. J. Perelman, Erskine Caldwell, Edmund Wilson, Lillian Hellman, and Dashiell Hammett at little or no charge. It seems apparent that the sordid and depressing people he saw at these hotels and the record number of suicides committed from the Sutton's sundeck, which he called "Suicide Leap," had a major influence on his writing.

Yet while West's characters are desperate and entrapped, their anguish —even more so than that of Daniel Fuchs's characters—appears to be unrelated to the specific social and economic ills brought about by the Depression. Rarely depicting identifiable New York locales but consistently conveying a sense of urban despair, West, anticipating authors like Saul Bellow, suggests that city life itself is one cause of the angst experienced by modern man.

Employed as an advice-to-the-lovelorn columnist for the *New York Post-Dispatch,* Miss Lonelyhearts becomes obsessed with the suffering of his correspondents, imagines himself a Christ figure, and is shot to death while attempting to "save" Peter Doyle, a miserable and bitter cripple. While Peter Doyle, like so many of West's other characters, appears to be a victim of unjust and capricious life itself, the city is frequently depicted as both a cause and a reflection of the anguish suffered by its inhabitants, who feel alienated and threatened in an impersonal metropolis of skyscrapers.

New York is, in fact, portrayed as nothing less than a wasteland, as can be seen in West's description of this unnamed park, where

there were no signs of spring. The decay that covered the surface of the mottled ground was not the kind in which life generates. Last year ... May had failed to quicken these soiled fields. It had taken all the brutality of July to torture a few green spikes through the exhausted earth.

The sky, to Miss Lonelyhearts, "looked as if it had been rubbed with a soiled eraser," and at one point he is distressed by the "skyscraper that menaced the little park from all sides" and by the "tons of forced rock and tortured steel." His spirits are raised only when he goes off to the country for a few days, but the respite is temporary. Back in the Bronx slums, he is once again sickened by urban scenes of human misery and pain.

On the surface, John O'Hara's *Butterfield 8*—its title derived from a telephone exchange serving the fashionable East Side—appears to be a far less dismal novel than *Miss Lonelyhearts*, but while its dominant settings are the city's glamorous night spots, it also is a novel about despair and emptiness as it traces the history of Gloria Wandrous, a call girl making the rounds of midtown Manhattan's speakeasies, nightclubs, and hotels.

Written while O'Hara was living in a brownstone in the East Fifties, *Butterfield 8* is in some measure a reflection of the author's own life style. As described in Finis Far's *O'Hara, A Biography*, O'Hara was able "to recognize the faces of scores of cops and doormen between 42nd Street and 59th" and was known by employees of "speakeasies and the Algonquin and Sardi's."[14] That he drew on these experiences when he wrote *Butterfield 8* is particularly evident in the following passage about the "evolution" of the speakeasy:

From serving furtive drinks of bad liquor disguised as demi-tasse the speakeasy had progressed to whole town houses, with uniformed pages and cigarette girls, a string orchestra and a four or five-piece Negro band for dancing, free hors d'oeuvres, four and five bartenders, silver-plated keys and other souvenir-admittance tokens to regular patrons, expensive entertainment, Cordon Bleu chefs, engraved announcements in pretty good taste, intricate accounting systems and business machinery—all a very good, and because of the competition, necessary front for the picturesque and deadly business of supplying liquor at huge financial profit—powerful radio stations, powerful speedboats and other craft not unlike the British "Q" ships, powerful weapons against highjackers, powerful connections in the right places.

O'Hara goes so far, in fact, to compile a list of the New York speakeasies where Gloria was known. Among the places he mentions are

The Dizzy Club, the Hotsy-Totsy, Tommy Guinan's Chez Florence, the Type & Print Club, the Basque's, Michel's, Tony's East Fifty-third Street, Tony's West Forty-ninth Street, Forty-two West Forty-nine, the Aquarium, Mario's, the Clamhouse, the Bandbox, the West Forty-fourth Street Club, McDermott's, the Sligo Slasher's, the News-writers', Billy Duffy's, Jack Delaney's, Sam Schwartz's, the Richmond, Frank and Jack's, Frankie & Johnny's, Felix's, Louis', Phyllis's, Twenty-one West Fifty-third, [and] Marlborough House. . . .[15]

Far from being an exhaustive list, the above represents only a small sampling of the twenty thousand speakeasies that O'Hara contends could be found "near to and far from Times Square"[16] at this time.

In addition to writing about speakeasies, O'Hara describes many New York restaurants and hotels and does not neglect to mention Radio City, which was then under construction, and Walter Winchell, gossip columnist for the *New York Mirror*, who in the nineteen thirties was as much a New York institution as Radio City.

Mary McCarthy, like O'Hara, was a resident of the fashionable East Side, and while some of the locales depicted in *The Group* are similar to O'Hara's, her subjects are Vassar graduates who frequent theatres, museums, and tearooms far more often than speakeasies.

The novel opens with Kay's wedding in St. George's Church. Sometimes referred to as J. P. Morgan's church because the elder J. P. Morgan was its senior warden, St. George's, erected in 1847, overlooks Stuyvesant Square, which McCarthy depicts as one of New York's loveliest areas. She describes the reaction of the wedding guests, among then native New Yorkers who lived "in tiresome Georgian houses full of waste space in the Eighties or Park Avenue apartment buildings" and now, finally, "in the throes of discovering New York,"

delighted in such out-of-the-way corners as this, with its greenery and Quaker meeting-house in red brick, polished brass, and white trim next to the wine-purple Episcopal church—on Sundays, they walked with their beaux across Brooklyn Bridge and poked into the sleepy Heights section of Brooklyn; they explored residential Murray Hill and quaint Macdougal Alley and Patchin Place and Washington Mews with all the artists' studios. . . .[17]

While the newly married Kay rents an apartment in the East Fifties, other members of "the group" live in different sections of the city, and McCarthy depicts several other New York neighborhoods as well. More memorable, however, than these descriptions are McCarthy's discussions of such cultural attractions as Carnegie Hall, the newly founded Whitney Museum (1931), the Museum of Modern Art (1929), and the Little Carnegie Playhouse on West Fifty-seventh Street, "where they showed foreign movies and you could get free demi-tasses and play ping-pong in the lounge." McCarthy also writes about Greenwich Village restaurants and tearooms, including Alice McCollister's on West Eighth Street and the Jumble Shop on nearby Macdougal Street, where there were "lots of artists and writers . . . and Filipino waiters." Still in existence today, although recently renamed Shakespeare's, the Jumble Shop is the only tearoom to survive from the Village's bohemian period, when West Eighth Street, lined with bookstores and antique shops, restaurants and tearooms and art galleries, was known as the Main Street of Greenwich Village.

Like Thomas Wolfe, McCarthy writes about "Gray's cut-rate theatre place in the bowels of the earth underneath the New York Times building," and there are several interesting discussions about the development of the city, including one about Robert Moses who, during this period, was "transforming the whole face of New York with his wonderful new parkways and playgrounds." Kay and her husband, Harald, speak of Jones Beach as "an inspiring example . . . of planning on a large scale for leisure" and discuss the role of private enterprise in the development of New York, referring in particular to Radio City as "an example of civic planning, undertaken by enlightened capitalists" and to the Museum of Modern Art, also backed by Rockefeller. Kay believed that

New York . . . was experiencing a new Renaissance, with the new Medicis competing with public ownership to create a modern Florence. You could see it even in Macy's, where . . . the store [was being made] into something more than a business, something closer to a civic center or permanent fair-grounds, with educational exhibits, like the old Crystal Palace. . . . the smart new renovated tenements in the Fifties and Eighties, along the East River . . . were still another example of intelligent planning by capital! . . . when you thought that they had just been eyesores, probably full of vermin and unsanitary hall toilets, till the Astor interest fixed them up! And other landlords were following their example, turning old blocks of barracky tenements into compact apartment buildings. . . .

While McCarthy describes the transformation of run-down Upper East Side tenements into elegant apartment buildings during the thirties and sets many of her scenes in the part of the city that she knew so well, in *Marjorie Morningstar*, Herman Wouk, also drawing on his own experiences as a Manhattan resident, depicts the Upper West Side; in particular, the fine apartment buildings that lined Central Park West during the same decade.

Like his protagonist, Wouk moved with his family from the Bronx to this prestigious neighborhood, and in both *City Boy*, which is set on Homer Avenue, "a brick cliff very much like the other brick cliffs that stood wall to wall for many blocks" in a borough described by the author as a "town of stone," and in *Marjorie Morningstar*, he depicts the Bronx as a depressed area filled with old, run-down apartment houses. Clearly the journey from the Bronx to the Upper West Side has significant social implications for him.

Marjorie, a beautiful but spoiled Hunter College student who dreams of becoming an actress but winds up a contented surburban matron, feels that in their move from the Bronx "to the El Dorado on Central Park West her parents had done much . . . to make up for their immigrant origin."[18]

Equally snobbish in outlook, her mother, who believes that "the good families" live on the West Side and that it is here that Marjorie "has the best chance of meeting somebody worthwhile," disapproves of one of Marjorie's boyfriends on the grounds that "Bronx Park East is a long way from Central Park West." Her attitude, according to Wouk, is not an unusual one, for

snobbishness . . . is a relative thing. The older and wealthier Jewish families, who lived on the upper East Side, would have been distressed had the West Side boys dated their daughters. And those families doubtless caused the well-to-do Christian families to wonder what was becoming of Park Avenue and Fifth Avenue.

When Marjorie's father suffers business reversals, the family must move to a small back apartment on West End Avenue. Whereas the view from Marjorie's bedroom in the El Dorado had been of Central Park, now it is "the usual New York one: window shades, bedrooms, and dirty bricks." The lobby, however, is quite respectable: there are "marble pillars, plenty of gilding, and Persian rugs in good repair." They are still "far away from the Bronx" and considerably better off than Marjorie's friend Marsha, who lives in

a brownstone house midway between Central Park West and Columbus Avenue. Marjorie had walked past it dozens of times, never imagining that anybody who lived in such a house could have any connection with her life. The block was lined with them. Most of them were cheap boarding-houses. The shabby people who came in and out of them looked like small-towners down on their luck and stranded in New York. In the windows the usual sights were fat dusty cats, unhealthy geraniums, and wrinkled old ladies peeking through grimy curtains.

Her reduced circumstances do not deter Marjorie's pursuit of a romantic, exciting husband and a successful theatrical career, but at the end of the novel she is a contented suburban housewife married to an affluent if somewhat dull lawyer. Her youthful dreams dashed, she is none-theless, a fairy-tale princess in the fiction of the Depression decade. For every Marjorie Morningstar written about in New York novels set in the thirties there are many less fortunate protagonists. Affluent neighborhoods figure far less prominently in the fiction than do poverty-stricken ones, and spoiled girls are not exactly the mainstay of the literature of this period. Social, political, and economic concerns are often at the center of these novels, some of which depict the conversion of a disillusioned protagonist from capitalistic to Communist beliefs. Sometimes a battleground in which ideologically disparate groups clash and often an emblem of despair, the city in the fiction of the thirties is—with few exceptions—rarely depicted as the brilliant, carefree place it is portrayed as being in the literature of the twenties.

9

WORLD WAR II AND ITS AFTERMATH

Having barely recovered from the Depression, America found herself involved in World War II, and it is not surprising that war novels like Norman Mailer's *The Naked and the Dead*, Irwin Shaw's *The Young Lions*, Herman Wouk's *The Caine Mutiny*, and James Jones's *From Here to Eternity* should dominate the literary scene in the immediate postwar years. Clearly these books—most of which depict particular campaigns in Europe and in the Pacific—are not New York City novels, but there is a considerable amount of fiction set in New York during the forties that deals explicitly or implicitly with World War II and its impact. Servicemen hanging around in the seedy bars on Forty-second Street or in Brooklyn's Navy Yard area, soldiers readjusting to civilian life, holocaust survivors carving out a new existence for themselves in various New York neighborhoods—these are not uncommon subjects in the fiction of the postwar years.

Although obviously not affected in the same way as the major European cities were, New York's involvement in the war was far from inconsiderable, with the harbor shipping out half of all the American troops and one-third of all the supplies that were sent overseas. Food rationing, black-marketing, dimouts, and air-raid drills were the order of the day. Columbia University was a center for atomic research and the New York Public Library the place where the Japanese navy code was broken through the use of an outdated Mexico City directory. Streets were thronged with uniformed men and women waiting to be shipped out or on leave from nearby army camps like Fort Dix.

New York emerged from World War II a far different city. The huge demand for factory workers during the period of expanded production had brought about major demographic changes in the city. While poor blacks and Puerto Ricans came to New York in large numbers, middle-class whites left for the suburbs. When after the war the economy again contracted, there were larger welfare rolls and higher crime rates. Certain neighborhoods deteriorated quickly, and the contrasts between neighborhoods became even more apparent, with "good" and "bad" neighborhoods sometimes being separated by no more than a few hundred yards. As can be expected, themes dealing with urban despair, alienation, and violence, which would come to dominate the New York fiction of the next several decades, began to emerge.

Despite the impact of the war and its aftermath on New York life, there were many authors who depicted the city as curiously untouched by the catastrophic events that had taken place in Europe and the Pacific. If and when they dealt with the effects of the war, it was in terms of the overall prosperity created by the wartime economy. Indeed, it is one of the ironies of history that the war catapulted the nation out of the Depression and that the war years, characterized by high wages and big spending, were a time of great, if short-lived, prosperity, when New York hotel rooms were always booked and restaurants always crowded.

One author whose comments on New York during the war years are of particular interest is John P. Marquand. Generally associated with Boston rather than New York, Marquand came to live on Beekman Place after winning the Pulitzer Prize in 1937. *So Little Time* and, to a lesser degree, *Point of No Return* appear to have been based on his experience as a resident of the fashionable East Side.

Both novels are about successful and affluent men who are experiencing marital and career problems during what seems to be a mid-life crisis. In *So Little Time,* Jeffrey and Madge Wilson have a duplex apartment on the Upper East Side, and the book opens with a description of the view of brownstone rooftops, bulky apartment houses, and the "pointed top of the Chrysler Building"[1] that can be seen from their window.

This is indeed an appropriate beginning for a book that is as much about New York during the war years as it is about the problems of its protagonists: it is about the city's hotels, shops, churches, and clubs, its streets, squares, and libraries, its publishing houses and its apartments. Both Marquand's interest in the city and his amazement that despite the war in Europe things continued as before are made clear when Jeffrey expresses his surprise that New York,

in October of 1940, could look as it always had, beautiful and indifferent, or how there could be new model cars, or how there could still be antiques and silver and flowers and saddles and bridles and tweeds for sale on Madison Avenue.

A similar sentiment is expressed elsewhere in the novel when Jeffrey, worried about the probable fall of France, wonders as he walks west along Fifty-ninth Street "whether everyone else shared his feeling of suspense." Ominous thoughts of the war recede only when he reaches the Plaza—a place he has "always liked . . . if only because it was one of the few surviving buildings in New York which had been with him always" —and he feels even better when he arrives at the Fifty-ninth Street entrance to the Park, where

General Sherman was all in gold with his gold angel walking at his horse's head, and the nude lady on top of the marble fountain was basking in the sun, and three Victorias with spavined horses stood in the sunlight, and the balloon men and the peanut men were out.[2]

Always interested in the changes taking place in the city, Marquand describes Jeffrey's visit to an apartment on upper Fifth Avenue, a neighborhood he realizes is out of date: "He had never noticed before how dingy the baroque façades of the private houses had grown. He had never noticed how many of them were unoccupied, how many were for sale or to let." Remembering the area as it had been depicted in a story by Richard Harding Davis, he reflects that

the Park had scarcely changed, except for the additions to the Art Museum, which had been too large before, and except for the monument to the 27th Division. But opposite, the houses and the apartments looked as dusty and as technically dated as the works of Davis.

Jeffrey sees New York "changing faster than he had ever known it, although it had always been a restless city; and what was more, there was a continual hint of more change to come." While he laments certain changes, claiming, for example, that contemporary New York has "too much of everything," Jeffrey still regards it as "the greatest city in the world," and Marquand depicts with seeming relish its many facets. He writes about the Bulldog Club, "one of those organizations of reporters and editors . . . [reputed to have] been founded either by Horace Greeley of the *Tribune* or Bennett of the *Herald*," about the Hotel Lexington, on Lexington Avenue and Forty-eighth Street, about St. Bartholomew's Church, "which resembled a model in the Metropolitan Museum now that so many high buildings rose around it," and about St. Patrick's Cathedral, which in 1858 when construction on it began was considered to be in the "country."

There are flashbacks to Jeffrey's younger days when he courted Madge and waited for her in the parlor of an old Murray Hill brownstone, "which had now practically vanished along with the brownstone stoops of New

York," and when they met on the steps of the then recently constructed New York Public Library building at Fifth Avenue and Forty-second Street.[3] There are also glimpses of various New York neighborhoods in years past as Jeffrey recalls apartments in Greenwich Village, on West Eighteenth Street, and on the Upper West Side, where they lived until Jeffrey was earning twenty thousand dollars a year and he and Madge could move to the Upper East Side.

Nostalgic about the city's past, Jeffrey thinks of such tunes as "In Old New York, in Old New York" and "Tell me what street compares with Mott Street in July" and reminisces about Newspaper Row and the publishing world, which when he came to New York in 1919 was beginning to change, with new companies like the Viking Press and Random House growing up alongside of the more traditional houses like Scribner's, Macmillan, and Harpers.

The descriptions of New York city in *Point of No Return* are less copious than those in *So Little Time*. This is partly because Charles Gray and his wife live in the suburbs and partly because a substantial portion of the novel is set in Clyde, Massachusetts, where Gray was born. Early in the book, however, there is an excellent description of Grand Central Station, with its polished-marble lower level and "the starry vault of the concourse on the upper level."[4] Obviously fascinated by the station and its surroundings, which he also described in *So Little Time*, Marquand goes on to depict the scene immediately outside on Forty-second Street and Vanderbilt Avenue, which to Charles Gray always signals his arrival "home":

Whenever he emerged from the station and set foot on Forty-second Street, he experienced in varying degrees a sense of coming home. Sometimes this feeling was one of deep gratitude and more often only one of boredom, but whenever he arrived there, all those other times he had reached Forty-second Street somehow added themselves together into an imponderable, indivisible sort of sum. His mind was adjusted to the traffic, to the drugstores and the haberdasheries, to the Lincoln Building and the Park Avenue ramp. . . .

It did not matter that he had not been born and raised there, because New York belonged almost exclusively to people who came from other places.[5]

A former GI and now a banker, Charles Gray is particularly interested in New York's financial institutions. Marquand writes at length about various banking establishments, and even the following discussion of a Park Avenue cooperative apartment building "built in 1926 on an unstable foundation of high mortgages" emphasizes financial factors:

Charles could recall as he walked under the green awning off the street through the travertine marble doorway into the travertine marble hall that the Whitakers' equity on the fifteenth floor of the house had cost them originally two hundred thousand dollars. He could also recall a later period when equities in nearly all co-operative apartments had dropped from nothing to a minus quantity, and when tenants had frantically endeavored to avoid their upkeep and mortgage charges by giving away their equities and even paying prospective tenants handsome bonuses for taking them off their hands.

An earlier description of Fifth Avenue is, however, decidedly different in its emphasis, and like similar excerpts from *So Little Time,* makes reference to an earlier author's perceptions of a particular New York locale:

It was always changing, but the spirit of it was still as young, confident, and blatant as when Henry James had written of it long ago. It still conveyed the same message that it had when he had walked along it on that first visit with his father [in 1916]. The motion of it had the same strength and eagerness, so different from the more stately motion of Piccadilly and the Strand.

What is particularly striking about both novels is that while Marquand's characters are acutely aware of the city's changes—not all of them for the good—they repeatedly express gratitude for the privilege of being in New York. As one character explains, "New York has everything. Everything's in New York." In short, Marquand's characters loved New York long before "I Love New York" posters and buttons were the order of the day. This is equally true of Jessie Bourne, Marcia Davenport's protagonist in the now little-known novel *East Side, West Side.*

East Side, West Side, the story of an unhappily married woman's love affair with a general who has just returned home from the war, is also about Jessie Bourne's love affair with the city. Early in the book we learn that she "was a snob in her own way, and that consisted of belonging to the special fraternity of people born upon Manhattan Island who had lived upon it all their lives and would not consider themselves alive if they should have to live anywhere else."

The owner of a cooperative apartment overlooking the East River, Jessie lives in an area that prior to the twenties had been "an unknown wilderness of slaughterhouses, coal docks, and miles of five-story cold-water railroad tenements." Even in the nineteen forties it is a neighborhood where affluent residents live in luxury apartments with East River views yet are in close proximity to grimy tenement buildings, tawdry bars, and cheap stores, many of them directly under the shadow of the Third Avenue El. This striking contrast of neighborhoods, also treated in Ilka Chase's novel *New York 22* and Sidney Kingsley's play *Dead End,* would persist until the El was torn down in 1955 and Third Avenue underwent a renaissance.

Jessie, who before her move "had lived almost her whole life along the central spine of Manhattan Island, that long strip of wealth and smartness bounded by Central Park on the west and Lexington Avenue on the east," has now become fascinated by the dingy streets that are home to "the solid common masses." In this neighborhood, where the men are "artisans, bus drivers, policemen, firemen, tradesmen, hackies" and the women buy cans of kerosene to heat their cold-water flats, existence is "meagre, sometimes uncomfortable and always incredibly circumscribed," but there is self-respect and a style of life different from that found in "the frightful raddled warrens of the downtown slums."

Third Avenue, its tawdry Irish saloons the predominant setting of the stories in John McNulty's *Third Avenue, New York,* is considered by Jessie to be "the boundary of this world and its ugliest, most odious feature because of the Elevated which blighted it and made it a gehenna the whole length of the Island." She imagines how it must be for people to live in "tenements with the hideous trackage almost touching their windows," the glances of passengers invading their privacy, and the crashing sounds of the trains disrupting their conversations and even their thoughts.

Empathizing as she does with her poorer neighbors, Jessie enjoys marketing on Second Avenue, where the housewives speak Hungarian or German or Italian or Yiddish. Yet she also likes to shop at Hoexter's, then located on Third Avenue and Eighty-second Street, where "hundreds of old-fashioned substantial people had dealt for nearly fifty years." For all her interest in the lower class, Jessie is a wealthy woman who patronizes some of the city's finest clubs, restaurants, and shops, not all of which are to her liking. She particularly dislikes the Assembly Club, on Park Avenue and Sixty-fifth Street, which she refers to as "the Holy of Holies" because of its policy of exclusivity that does not permit Jews to join. Nor does she like clubs at the other end of the spectrum like El Morocco—at 307 East 54th Street—"where the last barriers of demarcation between the different elements of metropolitan society had long since gone down. . . . And all that was required for inclusion in the galaxy was money (or access to somebody's money) and to be news."

Although she dislikes certain aspects of New York life and is saddened by others, such as the fate of the Fifth Avenue mansions, Jessie's love of the city—particularly of the East Side—is a dominant theme in the novel. She is especially enthralled with fine shops such as Bergdoff's, located on Fifth Avenue at Fifty-eighth Street on the former site of the mansion of Cornelius Vanderbilt II, and Plummer's, a china shop known today as Plummer-McCutcheon and located on East Fifty-seventh Street, which she thinks of as "one of the legacies from that good gone world."

While several fashionable New York shops are identified and described by Davenport, none assumes the importance of Tiffany's in Truman Capote's *Breakfast at Tiffany's,* which derives its title from the world-famous jewelry store located on Fifth Avenue and Fifty-seventh Street.

Like Marquand and Davenport, Capote uses the East Side as his dominant setting, and the novel, written when he himself lived in Brooklyn Heights, opens with a reference to the East Seventies, where "during the early years of the war" he lived in a brownstone apartment, his first New York residence. Writing about the escapades of his neighbor Holly Golightly, whose surname suggests her light-hearted, childlike nature, Capote describes Joe Bell's bar, "a quiet place compared to most Lexington Avenue Bars . . . [which] boasts neither neon nor television," where he and Holly used to make telephone calls, since "during the war a private telephone was hard to come by." He writes, too, of the antique shops along Third Avenue in the Fifties, of auctions at Parke-Bernet, which is now located at Madison Avenue and East Seventh-sixth Street and remains the headquarters for auction sales of fine furniture, art, jewels, rugs, and other items from estates, and of P. J. Clarke's saloon, on Third Avenue at Fifty-fifth Street, outside of which a group of drunken Australian army officers take turns dancing with Holly "over the cobblestones under the El." And, of course, he writes about Tiffany's, where Holly goes when she feels blue. As she explains, the best way to ward off depression is

to get into a taxi and go to Tiffany's. It calms me down right away, the quietness and the proud look of it; nothing very bad could happen to you there, not with those kind men in their nice suits, and that lovely smell of silver and alligator wallets.

Holly's tastes being rather eclectic, she also enjoys shoplifting Halloween masks from Woolworths, reading in the general reading room of the Forty-second Street Public Library, and riding horseback

across the park and out into Fifth Avenue, stampeding against the noon-day traffic, taxis, buses that screechingly swerved. Past the Duke mansion, the Frick Museum, past the Pierre and the Plaza.[6]

Holly cavorts about many other areas of the city as well, including Chinatown and Spanish Harlem, where she abandons her cat in "the right place ... [with] garbage cans. Rats galore. Plenty of cat-bums to gang [sic] around with." And in a rare serious moment, just before her departure for Brazil, Holly walks across the Brooklyn Bridge and promises that one day she will return to New York with her children

Because yes, they *must* see this, these lights, the river—I love New York, even though it isn't mine, the way something has to be, a tree or a street or a house, something, anyway, that belongs to me because I belong to it.

Breakfast at Tiffany's is a gay and spirited portrait of the city during the war years, but the next novel to be discussed, Louis Simpson's *Riverside Drive,* deals with a grimmer side of life in New York during the forties: the return of the psychologically scarred GI.

Before entering the army, Duncan Bell was a college student living in an apartment "overlooking St. John's Cathedral and Amsterdam Avenue, a perspective of apartment houses and drug, stationery, hardware, and grocery stores."[7] After the war, he is at first unequal to living alone and stays for a time with family in the suburbs; later he moves to a small apartment on West End Avenue, where he is decidedly out of place among his affluent neighbors:

On weekends, when I went down in the elevator wearing sneakers, my old Army pants, and a shirt, the other riders were visibly distressed. I was bringing down the tone of the building and when I re-entered the building, the doorman gave me the fish-eye.

There are descriptions of other apartments, some of them on the East Side, and of Third Avenue, where under the El, Duncan could hear "the whiskey-flavored music of 'Mother Machree' rising from the bars" and smell "steak and sawdust" coming from the restaurants, which he imagined were patronized by "old newspapermen, wrinkled with cynicism." Simpson also writes of the Times Square area, where gigantic electric figures of all types "rocked to and fro, poured, jumped, laughed, puffed smoke, and winked; and colored letters spelled out over and over again what you had to buy," and of an orthodox Jewish neighborhood in Brooklyn, where Duncan's grandmother lived "in a part of America that might of [sic] been Lodz or Warsaw," but the most memorable descriptions are of the Upper West Side, and in particular, of Riverside Drive.

Toward the end of the novel Duncan and his girl friend Mona walk past the Soldiers' and Sailors' Monument, Paul E. Duboy's marble Civil War memorial located on Riverside Drive at West Eighty-ninth Street, and Duncan is relieved to see that some things have remained the same:

Asphalt walks in the cracks of which hot tar was melting; yellow-green grass; the enbankment of bushes; and the West Side Highway, with a strip punctuated by lamps, dividing the two-way traffic—it was all unchanged. Across the river the . . . Palisades, topped with blocks of brown, multiwindowed apartment buildings were the same as they had been when we were adolescent.

Although the view has remained unchanged and the Soldiers' and Sailors' Monument is still standing, along with the George Washington Bridge and other landmarks, although there are still old people reading newspapers, nurses wheeling baby carriages, children riding bicycles, and lovers embracing on the wide and lovely Riverside Drive, it is now the nineteen fifties, and looking about her, Mona comments on how the exodus of the Jews to the suburbs and the influx of Puerto Ricans to the Upper West Side has greatly changed the neighborhood. But Duncan, who has lived through a particularly unsettling and enervating wartime experience, persists in viewing Riverside Drive as a symbol of a permanence and security in an otherwise chaotic world.

Michael Lovett, the protagonist of Norman Mailer's *Barbary Shore,* is another former GI living in New York City during the late forties. Suffering from a memory loss, he comes to live in a seedy Brooklyn Heights rooming house, where he becomes involved in a Communist plot launched by his fellow lodgers. For four dollars a week he rents a "small furnished cubicle." Located on "the top floor beneath a flat roof," it has only one window, which opens "upon laundry lines and back yards to the fire escape of an apartment house next door." The room is dilapidated, the paint and plaster peeling, and soot "drifted up from the dock area below the bluffs to cover the woodwork." The house, however, had once been "a modest mansion," and in the once-affluent neighborhood there still lingers something of the elegant past:

the brownstone houses were not without dignity. The spring air contained a suggestion of wood and meadow, and it was possible to imagine the gardens and the trellised arbors as they must have existed years ago. We were on a street which led toward the bluffs, the docks beyond, and the bay.

There are many descriptions of the waterfront, the most peaceful and attractive part of the neighborhood. On once occasion Lovett looks out across the harbor at

the skyline of New York deepening into the final blue of night. Among the skyscrapers, windows here and there were lit, the charwomen had started their work, and throughout those pinnacles of stone the fires were banked, the offices bare.

The ferryboat to Staten Island had begun its trip. From where I stood the boat looked very small, its deck lights twinkling across the water to form the endless flickering legs of a centipede. An ocean freighter nosed across the harbor seeking anchorage, and in the distance bridges arched the river, supporting in a stream the weight of automobiles.

But the waterfront is sometimes spoiled by bums who "have wandered up from the Bowery to retch . . . whiskey into the water," and the settings of *Barbary Shore* are more often than not depressing. Mailer writes about "a bare little park with concrete paths and a stunted tree" located at the foot of the bridge, where an old man sleeps on a bench and a drunk does "a slow blundering dance around an ash can." And the sound of "the El grinding over the rails" makes Lovett think

of the long ride out to the end of the line, and the Negro slums along the way where children sleeping on the fire escape would turn in their slumber as the train passed, moaning a little in acceptance of its fury even as artillerymen will drowse beside their howitzer while a night mission is fired.

While this is not quite the harsh and lurid landscape Mailer would paint almost fifteen years later in *The American Dream,* New York is clearly depicted as a place of loneliness and despair in *Barbary Shore.* Yet Mailer's urban vision, even in *The American Dream,* is not nearly as depressing or as grotesque as that of Hubert Selby, Jr., in *Last Exit to Brooklyn.*

A Brooklyn-born ex-marine, Selby describes the waterfront slum area in the vicinity of the Brooklyn Army Terminal—located west of the Gowanus Expressway and the Sunset Park community and north of Owls Head Park and Bay Ridge—as a veritable hell. A guide through an inferno depicted in six stories linked by common characters, settings, and motifs, Selby writes above lovelessness and boredom, violence and mutilation in a neighborhood reached by leaving the Gowanus Expressway just before the entrance to the Brooklyn-Battery Tunnel at the sign that says "Last Exit to Brooklyn."

His characters are drunken sailors and cruising prostitutes, transvestites high on drugs and alcohol, and local hoods and thugs who hang around "the Greeks, a beatup all night diner near the Brooklyn Army base," roll "doggies" and seamen, gang-rape, beat, and mutilate a prostitute, leaving her for dead, and crucify a man for having sex with a young boy. While there are scenes set in seedy bars and diners and filthy apartments and factories, the street scenes are particularly menacing. In one of them the local thugs beat up a soldier:

The guys . . . leaped on the doggies back and yanked him down and he fell . . . to the ground. They formed a circle and kicked. He tried to roll over on his stomach and cover his face with his arms, but as he got to his side he was kicked in the groin and stomped on the ear and he screamed, cried, started pleading, then just cried as a foot cracked his mouth . . . and a hard kick in the ribs turned him slightly and he tried to raise himself on one knee and someone took a short step forward and kicked him in the solarplexus and he fell on his side, his knees up, arms folded across his abdomen, gasping for air and the blood in his mouth gurgled as he tried to scream, rolled down his chin then spumed forth as he vomited violently and someone stomped his face into the pool of vomit. . . .

In "Coda," the last story of the collection, other equally depressing scenes are set in a nearby housing project, which is probably the Red Hook project, built in an effort to rehabilitate an area known for many years as Brooklyn's "Hell's Kitchen." Called Landsend by Selby, no doubt to suggest the same finality and despair implied in his book's title, its inhabitants' lives are as grotesque and desperate as those of the prostitutes and bums who hang out in the seedy bars and filthy streets near the army base. Garbage is thrown out the windows, a practice referred to as "airmail"; teen-agers steal money and deposit bottles from younger children on their way to the store; Hispanic and black youths throw rocks at each other and set fires in mailboxes. In one particularly memorable scene a group of housewives watch a baby who has crawled out of a window to a precarious perch on a ledge and are actually disappointed when the baby does not fall and the excitement is over.

Inside the housing project and in the surrounding neighborhood, bitterness, violence, and despair prevail. Only one old woman who mourns her dead husband and a pitiful transvestite who reads "The Raven" to her lover seem capable of feeling tenderness in what Gilbert Sorrentino has described as "a real living hell which exists in our own time, in the city of New York."[8]

Gilbert Sorrentino, like Hubert Selby, has written about Brooklyn, and his novel *Steelwork,* set in the Sunset Park area, also depicts squalor, alienation, and violence. The plot—fragmented as it is—deals with the corruption of neighborhood people by money made available by the war economy, but the real protagonist is the neighborhood itself, which is described over a period of sixteen years, beginning in 1935. Sorrentino writes about the houses on Senator Street, about local bars with names like Flynn's, the Lion's Den, the Melody Room, Carroll's, Papa Joe's, and Lento's, where people guzzle beer

to dull the view of despair, to tranquilize, to lift the spirits, to aid sleep, to wash down the hash and home fries, the macaroni and cheese, the spa-

ghetti with oleo, the stale bread.
To make disappear the cockroaches and mice.

He describes other hangouts like Hellberg's ice-cream parlor and the local poolroom and writes about Irish gangs and drunken sailors, the Strauss Store on Fifth Avenue, and Triangle Park, which was "past the new extension of the Cities Service lot . . . past the new A&P on the old tennis court, past the new Baptist Church."

Most memorable, however, are the descriptions of the neighborhood movie houses and how early Saturday morning the kids would "hustle" for the eleven-cent admission. By eleven thirty, there would be hundreds of them on line, shoving, shouting, excited by the prospect of an afternoon at the movies:

Free bags of candy. . . . Sometimes a free creamsicle, a comic book with the cover ripped off, anything, get em in! A double feature, five cartoons, coming attractions, a Pete Smith specialty, a Robert Benchley short, a travelogue *Wonderous Waves of Waikiki,* some theaters a race, the winning ticket got a bicycle, a pair of roller skates, an Erector set. . . . Bags full of water off the balcony, condoms blown up and floated, the horrendous din of the children, the fights, the scrambling in the aisles, the leaping through the dark, up and down the theater. Howls at the movies shown, hisses. Clap for the bad guys in the serials, magnificent bravado. Smoking in the men's room, smoking in the rows, passing the butt back and forth. . . . Feeling up girls, necking. . . . The few adults insane enough to be in the theater complained to the manager for three hours and then left. Those who couldn't raise the money got in through the fire doors in the alleys with a can opener.

Another segment describes the Alpine Theater, which was built "without a balcony, to discourage fornication and prevent smoking," and the Sunset, "a bucket of blood, filled with junior members of downtown gangs." At the Stanley the picture "ran off the reel every show," while the Electra showed pictures nobody ever heard of. The Dyker, located in a better neighborhood a trolley-car ride away, showed "the 'new' pictures," and the Bay Ridge was "huge and full of corridors and stairways, gold leaf and velvet chains, long fake Persian runners."

Sorrentino's detailed if depressing portrait of West Brooklyn's movie houses during the late thirties and the forties is unique in Brooklyn fiction. The movie theatres represent a microcosm of the neighborhood, an emblem of its violence and despair, and Sorrentino appears to hold out little hope for the area or its inhabitants. Its sketches dating from 1935 to 1951, *Steelwork* ends with a segment that describes the construction of a highway "to connect with the new parkway going through the bay, and then out the length of Long Island." It is significant both that the book's final segment is dated 1939 and that it deals with the construction of a new highway. Sorrentino is no doubt underscoring the fact—evident throughout the book as he moves back and forth in time—that little real change has taken place in the neighborhood and in the lives of its residents, trapped as they are in a depressing and brutalizing neighborhood. Clearly, the newly constructed highway cannot transport them to a better place, for they appear condemned to spend the rest of their miserable lives in a part of the city that Sorrentino perceives as hell.

Another novel set in Brooklyn during and immediately following the war years is Paule Marshall's *Brown Girl, Brownstones,* which relates the history of a West Indian community that developed, flourished, and deteriorated within a brief period of time in the vicinity of Chauncey Street. It opens with a description of the long rows of ivy-covered brownstones "with high massive stone stoops and black iron-grille fences staving off the sun." Although similar in design, each

had something distinctively its own. Some touch that was Gothic, Romanesque, baroque or Greek triumphed amid the Victorian clutter. Here, Ionic columns framed the windows while next door gargoyles scowled up at the sun. There, the cornices were hung with carved foliage while Gorgon heads decorated others.

Marshall goes on to explain how

first, there had been the Dutch-English and Scotch-Irish who had built the houses. There had been tea in the afternoon then and skirts rustling across the parquet floors and mild voices. For a long time it had been only the whites, each generation unraveling a quiet skein of years behind the green shades.
But now in 1939 the last of them were discreetly dying behind those shades or selling the houses and moving away. And as they left, the West Indians slowly edged their way in. Like a dark sea nudging its way onto a white beach and staining the sand, they came.

Like *Daddy Was a Number Runner, Brown Girl, Brownstones* is about a sensitive young girl growing up in one of New York's black ghettos. The protagonist, Selina, who is eleven when the novel opens and a college student at its conclusion, lives with her family on Chauncey Street, not far from Fulton Street. Fulton Park seems to her "the fitting buffer between Chauncey Street's gentility and Fulton Street's raucousness."
Always thronged with shoppers and strollers and noisy with the clangor of the trolley and the rumbling of the subway, on Saturday nights Fulton Street is "a whirling spectrum of neon signs, movie marquees, bright-lit store windows and sweeping yellow streamers of light from behind the

cars." There are the smells of "fish sandwiches and barbecue and hot sauce," the sounds of "hooted laughter and curses," police sirens shrieking, "blues spilling from a bar," and "children crying high among the fire escapes of the tenements."

A chronicler of the changes that occurred in the neighborhood after the proud and upwardly mobile West Indians moved there from the roach-infested "cold-water dumps in South Brooklyn" where they had settled upon arriving in New York in 1920, Marshall writes of their attempts to maintain the area, of the Association of Barbadian Home-owners and Businessmen that struggled to prevent deterioration of the neighborhood as brownstones were converted into rooming houses, and of the eventual exodus of West Indians to Crown Heights when the section became a slum.

Toward the end of the novel Marshall describes ruined Fulton Park, which had become home "to the winos who sat red-eyed and bickering all day, to the dope addicts huddled in their safe worlds and to the young bops clashing under the trees and warming the cold ground with their blood"; Fulton Street, where even at noon one could sense "a hint of the night's certain violence"; and the despoiling of the brownstones "as the roomers' tangled lives spilled out of the open windows," along with "the staccato beat of Spanish voices" and music. Some of the houses are being demolished to make way for a city project, and when Selina sees a wall that "stood perversely amid the rubble, a stoop [that] still imposed its massive grandeur, a carved oak staircase [that] led only to the night sky," they are to her emblems of a gracious past amid the wreckage of the present.

Another black neighborhood once fashionable but now in ruins is the setting of Ann Petry's *The Street*. The story of a young black woman's doomed efforts to better her life and that of her son, *The Street* is set primarily on 116th Street, between Seventh and Eighth avenues. Described on the first page of the novel as a dirty, grimy street littered with "theatre throwaways, announcements of dances and lodge meetings, the heavy waxed paper that loaves of bread had been wrapped in, the thinner waxed paper that had enclosed sandwiches, old envelopes, newspapers ... chicken bones and pork-chop bones," 116th Street is one of many Harlem blocks that show the ravages of the Depression and war years. It is discussed throughout the novel and on the last page is referred to as "that god-damned street."

In the opening scene Lutie Johnson has come to 116th Street in search of an apartment. Having made her way through the debris, she arrives at an old and decrepit building displaying a vacancy sign advertising three reasonably priced rooms with steam heat, parquet floors, and respectable neighbors:

Parquet floors here meant the wood was so old and so discolored no amount of varnish or shellac would conceal the scars and the old scraped places, the years of dragging furniture across the floors, the hammer blows of time and children and drunks and dirty, slovenly women. Steam heat meant a rattling, clanging noise in radiators early in the morning and then a hissing that went on all day.

Respectable tenants in these houses where colored people were allowed to live included anyone who could pay the rent, so some of them would be drunk and loud-mouthed and quarrelsome. . . .

As for "reasonable," Lutie concludes that "in this dark, crowded street" the rent was probably "about twenty-eight dollars, provided it was on the top floor."

The interior of the building and the apartment itself are neither better nor worse than Lutie anticipated, but in desperation she rents the cramped and sunless quarters on what she knows is "a bad street": a street whose children, most of them abandoned by their fathers, wear "doorkeys tied around their necks" and wait with apprehensive looks on their faces for their mothers at the subway stop; a street whose children learn to play crap and pool, to swagger and speak obscenities and steal at an early age. Streets like this, Lutie realizes, are found in every big city where people "set up a line and say black folks stay on this side and white folks on this side."

Harlem's commercial streets seem no less miserable to Lutie than its "residential" blocks. The butcher shops along Eighth Avenue displayed "pigs' feet, hog maw, neck bones, chitterlings, ox tails, tripe—all the parts that didn't cost much because they didn't have much solid meat on them," and the vegetable stands were piled high with wilted produce, for here were "sold the leavings, the sweepings, the impossible unsalable merchandise, the dregs and dross that were reserved especially for Harlem."

It is a far cry from the black Mecca described some twenty years earlier in Harlem renaissance fiction, yet Harlem continues to provide an escape from the alien and threatening downtown world. Petry explains, for example, how Lutie "never really felt human" until she reached Harlem, where she was safe from "the hostility in the eyes of the white women" and the "openly appraising looks of the white men."

Uptown or downtown, in the black ghetto or in the white neighborhoods of Manhattan, Lutie feels the pressures of urban life and begins to speculate that perhaps living in a city the size of New York wasn't good for people, because you had to spend all your time working to pay for the place where you lived and it took all the rest of the hours in the day to keep the place clean and fix food, and there was never any money left over. Certainly it wasn't a good place for children.

A grim urban portrait of Harlem in particular and of New York City in general, *The Street* lacks the richness and depth of such classic black novels as James Baldwin's *Go Tell It on the Mountain* and Ralph Ellison's *Invisible Man,* both of which are set in Harlem at about the same time, yet its picture of the area is more detailed. Whereas Baldwin emphasizes the inner life of a young boy in search of his religious identity rather than the external scene and Ellison frequently depicts Harlem in a surrealistic or symbolic style, Petry, writing in the tradition of social realism, appears committed to depicting the streets of Harlem in accurate, if sometimes tedious, detail.

Another depressing portrait of a declining area is found in Nicholosa Mohr's *El Bronx Remembered,* a collection of short stories and a novella set in the South Bronx, which during the nineteen forties became, in effect, a suburb of Spanish Harlem, or El Barrio, the area bounded by 95th and 125th streets, the East River, and Fifth Avenue. By 1930, the right to immigrate, coupled with cheaper air fares and shorter travel time, had brought forty-five thousand Puerto Ricans to New York. During the war years, unprecedented numbers came to the city in search of work, and it was not long before the South Bronx became an extension of over-crowded Spanish Harlem.

Mohr writes about the harsh and oppressive life there—about the head of a family struggling to make ends meet with the meagre wages he earns as a porter, about a welfare mother who refuses to allow her daughter to have a pet because she cannot afford to feed her own children, about Puerto Ricans of all ages experiencing painful changes as they make the transition from a rural to an urban way of life. To them,

city life was foreign . . . and they had to learn everything, even how to get on a subway and travel. . . . [Many were] terribly frightened at first of the underground trains, traffic, and large crowds of people.

Uncle Claudio, who yearns to return home, speaks for many when he explains that Puerto Ricans lose all their values when they come to New York, where

there are too many people living together with no place to go. In his own home, in Humacao, people take it easy and know how to live. They got respect for each other, and know their place. At home, when he walks down the street, he is Don Claudio. But here, in New York City, he is Don Nobody. . . .

There are references to the numbers racket, locally known as the *bolita,* and to drug dealing and street violence. In "Herman and Alice," a novella about the unusual relationship between a pregnant young girl and a middle-aged homosexual, Herman fears going out into the street because of "robberies and muggings" and wishes to move from the area that is now "worse than ever with all those dope dealers." Yet he remains there, knowing that "when they find out you're Puerto Rican they won't rent to you" in good neighborhoods.

In "Love With Aleluya" several Hispanic boys who attend Morris High School go to the Iglesia Pentecostal de Bronx, Inc., a store-front church on Prospect Avenue, in search more of romance than of religion. Less light-hearted in tone is "Mr. Mendelsohn," the story of an elderly Jew who has lived in the South Bronx for forty-five years. As he explains to the Suarez family, neighbors who have befriended him, things used to be different,

not like today. No sir! The Bronx has changed. Then, it was the country. That's right! Why, look out the window. You see the elevated trains on Westchester Avenue? Well, there were no trains then. That was once a dirt road. They used to bring cows through here. . . . These buildings were among the first apartment houses to go up. Four stories high, and that used to be a big accomplishment in them days. All that was here was mostly little houses, like you still see here and there. Small farms, woodlands . . . like that.

Eventually forced to move away because of ill health and the changing neighborhood, Mr. Mendelsohn misses Prospect Avenue and the Suarezes, whom he regards as family. Both in this story and in "The Wrong Lunch Line," Mohr depicts with sensitivity and insight relationships between Jews and Puerto Ricans in the South Bronx during the transition years of the forties.

It is clear that major demographic changes occurred in New York during the postwar period. Certain neighborhoods, once primarily Jewish, rapidly became black and Puerto Rican, while other sections became Hasidic. Two Brooklyn areas that gained large Hasidic populations in the forties were Williamsburg and Crown Heights, and these are the dominant settings of Chaim Potak's *The Chosen, The Promise,* and *My Name Is Asher Lev.*

There had, of course, been a significant Jewish community in Williamsburg prior to the forties. Jews had begun to settle there in large numbers at about the time of World War I. Until then, the only Jewish residents of the area had been affluent German-Jewish families, but there gradually developed a community of Orthodox Eastern European Jews. By 1930, the area had become primarily a lower- and lower middle-class Jewish area, and the non-Jewish population had declined considerably. Many synagogues and yeshivahs were built as Jews from the Lower East Side, Brownsville, and the Bronx moved here. Soon they were joined by Hasidim fleeing from Nazi persecution, and some years later, by those who had survived concentration camps. To this day Williamsburg has retained a large Hasidic community.

In *The Chosen* Chaim Potok, chronicler of many of the changes that took place in the post-World War II Williamsburg, describes the area in the years before the war, when only a small proportion of the population was Hasidic:

Many of the houses were brownstones, set tightly together, none taller than three or four stories. In these houses lived Jews, Irish, Germans, and some Spanish Civil War refugee families that had fled the new Franco regime before the onset of the Second World War. Most of the stores were run by gentiles, but some were owned by Orthodox Jews, members of the Hasidic sects in the area. They could be seen behind their counters, wearing black skullcaps, full beards, and long earlocks, eking out their meager livelihoods and dreaming of Shabbat and festivals when they could close their stores and turn their attention to their prayers, their rabbi, their God.

In *The Promise,* a sequel to *The Chosen,* Potok explains the way in which in the years following the war, the Hasidic population of Williamsburg increased and multiplied:

They had come from the sulfurous chaos of the concentration camps, remnants, one from a hamlet, two from a village, three from a town, dark, somber figures in long black coats and black hats and long beards, earlocks hanging alongside gaunt faces, eyes brooding, like balls of black flame turned inward upon private visions of the demonic. Here, in Williamsburg, they set about rebuilding their burned-out world. Families had been destroyed; they remarried and created new families. Dynasties had been shattered; elders met and formed new dynasties. . . . And by the fifth year after the war, Lee Avenue, the main street of the neighborhood, was filled with their bookstores and bookbinderies, butcher shops and restaurants, beeswax candle stores, dry-cleaning stores, grocery stores and vegetable stores, appliance stores and hardware stores—the signs in Yiddish and English, the storekeepers bearded and in skullcaps, the gentiles gone now from behind the counters, the Italians and Irish and Germans and the few Spanish Civil War refugee families all gone now too. . . .

In both *The Chosen* and *The Promise* Potok writes at length about Williamsburg's many *shtibblach,* where the individual Hasidic sects gathered to pray, and about other, larger, synagogues where the Orthodox but non-Hasidic Jews prayed. He describes religious ceremonies and customs and garb, and dramatically portrays the conflicts between various Jewish factions in Williamsburg in an attempt to show the excruciatingly difficult choices faced by a young Hasid struggling for fulfillment without severing himself from his family and his heritage.

While the conflict between self-fulfillment and religious obligations is also central to *My Name Is Asher Lev,* the setting of this novel is Crown Heights rather than Williamsburg, and Potok's is a detailed portrait of the Lubavicher Hasidim, whom he refers to as the Ladovers.

In addition to calling this group Ladovers rather than Lubavichers, Potok places their headquarters on the nonexistent Brooklyn Parkway. Despite such minor attempts to disguise the identity of his subjects, there is no doubt that Potok had the Lubavicher headquarters at 770 Eastern Parkway in mind in the following description:

The building was a three-story house of tawny stone, with Gothic windows and a flagstone front porch with a whitestone railing. It contained offices, meeting rooms, a room with about a dozen mimeograph machines, two suites of rooms for the editorial offices of the various Ladover publications, and a small press in the basement. Men came and went all day long. They sat behind desks, met in conference rooms, rushed along corridors, talked frenetically, sometimes quietly, sometimes in loud voices. All the men were bearded and wore dark skullcaps and dark suits with white shirts and dark ties. No women worked inside that building; secretarial work was done by men.

There are also many descriptions of the surrounding area—of Brooklyn (Eastern) Parkway, where "old women sat on the benches . . . sunning themselves and gossiping"; of Kingston Avenue, a busy commercial street; and of President Street, with its rows of brownstone houses. Potok writes, too, of nearby Prospect Park[9] and of the Brooklyn Museum, where young Asher finds the artistic inspiration that will eventually put him into conflict with his family and the entire Ladover community.

Awed by the outside of the huge building, which was set back on a wide expanse of lawn and "dominated the area in which it stood, massive glistening in the sunlight," Asher is particularly impressed by the statues of great men set into niches, just below the roof, along the front of the building. Once inside, he hurries past "the teepees and canoes and Indians on the first floor" and climbs "up the wide marble staircase to the galleries," where he sees his first paintings of the Crucifixion and where begins his long and painful struggle to reconcile the conflicting demands of art and religion.

While Potok's awareness of the plight of the Holocaust survivors is keen and some of his minor characters have narrowly escaped death in Hitler's ovens, his protagonists are not themselves survivors. Many modern American novels do, however, relate the history of concentration-camp internees who, against all odds, survived and came to this country to build a new life. Some of these which are set in the fifties or the sixties will be considered in the next chapter, but *Sophie's Choice,* written by William Styron and set in New York City in 1947, will be discussed here.

The tragic story of a young Polish women forced years before by a sadistic Nazi doctor to decide which of her children is to go to the gas chamber and which to the work camp, *Sophie's Choice* is set for the most part in the Flatbush section of Brooklyn, where Sophie herself, her brilliant but demented lover Nathan and Stingo, an ex-marine and aspiring young novelist, are among the roomers living in Yetta Zimmerman's garishly painted house, which is located directly across the street from Prospect Park's Parade Grounds.

On the opening page of the book, Stingo explains how he, "a lean and lonesome young southerner," found himself unemployed and because rents there were cheap came to live in predominantly Jewish Flatbush. There are several flashbacks describing the McGraw-Hill Book Company, where Stingo had for a time been employed as a junior editor. Styron writes not only about the McGraw-Hill Building—"an architecturally impressive but spiritually enervating green tower on West Forty-Second Street"[10]—but also about the firm's not too impressive publishing ventures, and he describes the University Residence Club on West Eleventh Street, where Stingo lived while still in the employ of McGraw-Hill. Although its name "conjured up an image of Ivy League camaraderie .... [it] was only one cut above a flophouse, differing from Bowery accommodations to the extent of nominal privacy in the form of a locked door."

The best descriptions of New York locales are, however, of Flatbush and of Yetta Zimmerman's rooming house. Situated not far from the Church Avenue station of the BMT, the "large rambling wood and stucco house" built around the time of World War I is distinctive because of its garish pink color and its view of Prospect Park's Parade Grounds. To Stingo, the area seems rural, and it is hard for him to believe that he is in a big city:

Only short blocks away traffic flowed turbulently on Flatbush Avenue, a place intensely urban, cacophonous, cluttered, swarming with jangled souls and nerves; but here the arboreal green and the pollen-hazy light, the infrequent trucks and cars, the casual pace of the few strollers at the park's border all created the effect of an outlying area in a modest Southern city—Richmond, perhaps, or Chattanooga or Columbia.

Coming from Poland to Brooklyn via Auschwitz, Sophie's points of reference are quite different from Stingo's. Entirely unfamiliar with American cities—her only previous urban experience has been in Cracow and Warsaw—she is both frightened and fascinated by Brooklyn, which she thinks of as "a new and unknown kingdom."

Prospect Park becomes Sophie's refuge in this strange and sometimes terrifying metropolis where subway travel with its "grime and . . . noise . . . [and] the claustrophobic nearness of so many human bodies" is her greatest challenge. Here in the park she confides part of her tragic story to Stingo, and still other episodes are unraveled in the Maple Court, one of the "few full-fledged bars" in Flatbush. Despite the heavy concentration of Jews in the neighborhood, its clientele consists largely of "Irish doormen, Scandinavian cabdrivers, German superintendents and WASPs of indeterminate status," and Stingo marvels at the lack of foresight on the part of the first owners, who "failed to realize that they had located their establishment in a neighborhood substantially as devoted to order and propriety as a community of Hardshell Baptists or Mennonites."

Other Brooklyn locales discussed by Styron include Coney Island, Jones Beach, reached by a bus departing "from a dingy terminal on Nostrand Avenue," and Brooklyn College, on Bedford Avenue and Avenue H, where Sophie attends English classes. There are references to local Italian and Chinese restaurants, as well as to Gage and Tollner's,[11] where Stingo takes Leslie Lapidus, the "Princess of Pierrepont Street," for dinner, and there are descriptions of both Stingo's expecations of what a New York Jewish home will be like and of what the Lapidus's Brooklyn Heights residence turns out to be: "A gracefully restored Greek Revival brownstone . . . set back slightly from the street against a little green lawn . . . [which] could have been a glossy magazine advertisement for . . . anything suggesting exquisite and overpriced refinement." After viewing the equally gracious interior of the Lapidus's home and meeting its patrician occupants, Stingo realizes that he knows very little "about the urban world up beyond the Potomac, with its ethnic conundrums and complexities."

The Southerner's preconceptions and misconceptions about the North in general and about New York City in particular is a subject treated at length by Styron, who like Stingo came north to write the Great American Novel and lived for a time in a Brooklyn boardinghouse. This theme is enlarged upon when Stingo's father comes to New York for a visit. Although he never reaches Brooklyn, he does spend several days in Manhattan, which he hates for

what he called its "barbarity," its lack of courtesy, its total bankruptcy in the estimable domain of public manners. The snarling command of the traffic cop, the blaring insult of horns, all the needlessly raised voices of the night-denizens of Manhattan ravaged his nerves, acidified his duodenum, unhelmed his composure and his will.

At one point during his visit, he tells Stingo, "The seventy-two hours I plan to spend in this burg is about all most moral men from civilized parts can stand."

Stingo's father visits such tourist attractions as the Statue of Liberty and the Empire State Building; he dines at Schrafft's, where he is appalled that he has to spend four dollars for two dinners, and "at Horn and Hardart's amazing automat, at Nedicks and Stouffer's and in a fling at what in those days . . . [seemed] haute cuisine—at a midtown Longchamps."[12] Throughout he is preoccupied with the rudeness and violence of New Yorkers and is unable to dismiss from his thoughts the black eye he received from a taxi driver, whom he describes as "part of the bottomless dregs of this loathsome city." Equally unsettling to him is his awareness that the seething violence and hatred in the city's black ghettos will someday soon erupt into open warfare.

Unfortunately many of the old man's fears and predictions regarding the future of New York City have been borne out by recent history, and as will be demonstrated in the next chapter, urban violence and despair have become dominant themes in the fiction set in New York in the fifties, sixties, and seventies.

10

THE CONTEMPORARY SCENE

It is indeed true that even a cursory glance at the New York fiction of the past three decades reveals a dominant mood of bleakness and distress as authors deal with themes of urban despair, anomie, and violence. Replete with descriptions of the city's filth, decay, poverty, and crime, and sometimes even implying that the near or actual derangement of a particular character is induced by the travails of urban life, recent New York fiction rarely depicts the city in a favorable light.

Yet the fact remains that New York, despite the severe urban problems it has in common with all major cities, is a unique metropolis. Home to the United Nations and to countless Europeans, Asians, Africans, Hispanic-Americans, and West Indians, New York is a world city. An internationally famous financial, educational, publishing, industrial, and cultural center, it is a vital and important cosmopolis with a magnificent past and with the resiliency to cope successfully with the problems of the present and the future.

This resiliency has been demonstrated time and again, and if New York history teaches us anything, it is that there is a constant flux—that residential neighborhoods become commercial centers and sometimes become residential districts once again, that affluent neighborhoods deteriorate and are reclaimed, that financial crises pass and the city emerges stronger than before. Yet, sadly, New York's strengths and attributes have for the most part remained unsung in modern fiction. If we are fortunate, however, the fiction of the present decade will reflect such heartening developments as the gentrification of particular neighborhoods and the return of substantial numbers of middle-class suburbanites to the inner city.

The purchase and renovation of brownstones in such deteriorated sections of the city as Brooklyn's Park Slope and Boerum Hill and the revitalization of the Brooklyn Academy of Music, which now houses a repertory theatre and attracts visitors from all over the city; the great interest in rebuilding the South Bronx, reclaiming Times Square, and re-establishing Harlem as the cultural center and tourist attraction it was during the twenties and thirties; the new building activity in midtown Manhattan, including the construction of six new luxury hotels—among them the Grand Hyatt, rebuilt from the shell of the old Commodore Hotel on East Forty-second Street, the Helmsley Palace on Madison Avenue and Fifty-first Street, and the Milford Plaza on West Forty-fifth Street; the wave of construction in the downtown financial district —these are but a few recent developments that augur well for the future of both the city and its fiction.

Although the fiction of the past thirty years has reflected far more of the problems than the promise of New York, certain novels have depicted the city less harshly than others. One such work is *Enemies: A Love Story* by Isaac Bashevis Singer. The first of several novels about Holocaust survivors to be discussed in this chapter, it narrates the story of Herman Broder, who lives with his second wife, Yadwiga, in the Coney Island section of Brooklyn, has a mistress in the Bronx, works on Twenty-third Street in Manhattan, and suddenly discovers that his first wife, believed to have been murdered by the Nazis, is alive and well and living in her uncle's house on East Broadway.

Perhaps the novel's finest descriptions are of Coney Island. Described by Daniel Fuchs some twenty-five or thirty years earlier, the neighborhood had undergone many changes since then and was now inhabited by large numbers of elderly Jewish refugees. Broder and Yadwiga live in an old apartment house a few blocks from the ocean, on a "little street between Mermaid and Neptune avenues," where

many elderly refugee couples who needed fresh air for their health had settled. . . . They prayed in the little synagogue nearby and read the Yiddish papers. On hot days they brought benches and folding chairs out on the street and sat around chatting. . . .

Mermaid Avenue is described as having "an Eastern European flavor," and long after the high holidays have passed,

posters announcing cantors and rabbis and the prices of synagogue pews for the High Holy Days still hung on the walls. From the restaurants and cafeterias came the smells of chicken soup, kasha, chopped liver. The bakeries sold bagels and egg cookies, strudel and onion rolls.

There are also descriptions of the boardwalk and of Stillwell Avenue, with its "carousels, shooting galleries, [and] mediums who would conjure up the dead for fifty cents," of a ferry ride from Sheepshead Bay to Breezy Point—a relatively secluded beach at the tip of Rockaway separated from Manhattan Beach by Rockaway inlet—and of the once exclusive Manhattan Beach Hotel on West End Avenue, which at present has deteriorated into a welfare hotel.

Singer's descriptions of other areas of New York are also noteworthy. He writes of East Broadway and of the bus ride from Union Square that takes him there:

The neighborhood had changed since his arrival in America. Now many Puerto Ricans lived there. Whole blocks of buildings had been torn down. Nevertheless, one still occasionally saw a sign in Yiddish, and, here and there, a synagogue, a yeshiva, a home for the aged. . . . The bus passed kosher restaurants, a Yiddish film theater, a ritual bath, a hall that could be rented for weddings or bar mitzvahs, and a Jewish funeral parlor. Herman saw young boys with earlocks longer than any he had seen in Warsaw, their heads covered by broad-brimmed velvet hats. It was in this section and on the other side of the bridge in Williamsburg that the Hungarian Hasidim, followers of the rabbis of Sacz, Belz, and Bobow, had settled. . . .

A long-time resident of the Upper West Side, Singer writes about West End Avenue and the Bronx, where Broder visits his mistress, Masha, who works in a cafeteria on Tremont Avenue and lives in a dilapidated apartment house not far from there. Together they go to the Bronx Zoo, the reputation of which had "reached them even in Warsaw."[1]

Surprisingly enough, many of Singer's short stories—which we generally think of as being set in a Polish *shtetl* or perhaps in Warsaw—take place in New York City. "A Day in Coney Island" is about a Yiddish author who rents a room in Sea Gate. Several stories are set in cafés and cafeterias on the Lower East Side;[2] the locale of others, including "The Séance," which is set in a Central Park West apartment, is the Upper West Side. Of particular interest is "Sam Palka and David Vishkover," a story describing Brownsville over a period of several decades, beginning in the nineteen thirties when it "was the land of Israel. You couldn't find a Gentile there for your life." About a bittersweet romance between Chana Basha, a beautiful young immigrant girl, and a wealthy but married property owner who conceals his true identity from her, the story opens when the Hopkinson Yiddish Theatre, with its seating capacity of nine hundred, was doing a brisk business in Brownsville and ends when almost all the Jewish residents of Blake Avenue have moved away and the neighborhood has become predominantly black and Puerto Rican.

Despite his awareness of urban problems, Singer's prose lacks the bitter edge found in much modern New York fiction, including Edward Lewis Wallant's *The Pawnbroker*. The protagonist of this novel, Sol Nazerman, is also a concentration-camp survivor. Nazerman, who lost in the Holocaust not only his wife and children but also his capacity to feel, earns his living as a pawnbroker in Harlem.

Still a prisoner after all this time, Nazerman from behind his locked, protective cage in the pawnshop sees despair in the eyes of his customers —prostitutes, drug addicts, and the decent poor who must pawn their treasures to feed their families. He senses the same feeling of desperation on streets lined with "dirt-caked tenements," and there is a vivid description of Harlem life when Nazerman walks down

a motley avenue, past a church that looked like an old theater and promised Redemption in hand-lettering, past a butcher shop whose sign was in Spanish and whose screen door was blanketed with meat-hungry flies, past a dazzling dental office that looked like a big store and advertised a dozen dentists.... Past the Army-Navy store, and the open-air clothing mart, its bins filled with color, its pipe racks decked with house dresses, and the dark women moving chatteringly around and about the clothing like eager birds; past a fried-chicken and fish-and-chips restaurant redolent of frying fat and saloons sending out gusts of beer smell and coarse laughter.

There are a few pleasant sights such as the Harlem River, but Nazerman, who notes "its oil-green opacity and the indecipherable things floating on its filthy surface," knows that the beauty of the scene, with "the tarnished gold light on receding bridges, the multi-shaped industrial buildings, and all the random gleams that bordered the river and made the view somehow reminiscent of a great and ancient European city," is deceptive.

What is real to him, however, is the filth of the city. The subway station, with its "gum-and-spittle scarred steps" and a platform where everything was "the color of grime and everything was mutilated—signs, walls, trash cans, everything," is an abomination to Nazerman. Watching the subway train emerging from the tunnel, "coming from a hundred filthy platforms like the one he was standing on, heading for a hundred more," he thinks that all of New York is "cancered with these dim tunnels whose filth spread to the streets above with the people, spread to the whole world." Even worse than disgust is Nazerman's fear of the trains, which he has come to associate with destruction and death.

The heat imagery that pervades the novel is not only associated with the subway; it is also sustained through repeated references to the heat that melts the asphalt streets, burns the sky "to the pallid blue of scorched metal," and seems "to soften the very stone and brick of the stone buildings." At one point, "the repulsive faces" around him "appeared to melt before his eyes, and Sol imagined them dissolving to dark smudges on the pavement."

While the heat imagery probably relates back to the crematoria he dreams about at night, it also—through the image of melting—prepares the reader for a "thaw" in Nazerman, which occurs after his assistant, Jesus Ortiz, takes the bullet intended for his employer during a hold-up he has helped plan. Reborn after the death of his aptly named assistant, Nazerman is finally able to experience emotion, but the conclusion of the novel can hardly be described as uplifting.

It can be argued, of course, that the urban vision in *The Pawnbroker* is colored by the protagonist's scarring experiences during the Holocaust and that the Harlem setting is more depressing than most. But Wallant's later novel, *The Tenants of Moonbloom,* which is about a rent collector's weekly visits to his desperate and unhappy tenants, depicts an equally unpleasant metropolitan scene.

Norman Moonbloom is not a survivor of the Holocaust, but he, too, is portrayed as a victim as he makes his rounds from the miserable four-family house on Second Avenue to the rubbish-strewn property on Mott Street, with its "dingy grocery shops . . . gutters wedged with paper and orange peels, [and] crowding, crooked, narrow buildings," and thence to Thirteenth Street, where

small, fly-specked luncheonettes alternated with wholesalers who dealt in narrowly specialized items. Here were costumes dusty and dated, there a place that was established in 1907 and specialized in shoe trees; next to a cleaner's was an outlet for doll's eyes—Only to the Trade. The street seemed to be avoided by the Department of Sanitation in memory of a forgotten feud, but the dirt there was not particularly repugnant, seeming to consist mostly of paper. The buildings, above the tawdry shop fronts, were noble in their antique cornices and dark green, scaly paint, and yet, taken all together, the street presented the gritty complexity of a broken rock.

Norman himself lives in the West Seventies in the "best" of the four buildings he manages, but like the others, it is in constant disrepair, and the book is a veritable study of New York's decrepit housing and the mentality of the slumlord—in this case, Norman's brother Irwin—who refuses to hear about leaking roofs, rats, broken toilets, rusty water, faulty wiring, and the like.

Chronically depressed by the misery of his tenants, Norman begins to perceive the city itself as menacing. "The daytime noises of the street were huge and hideous" to him, and he experiences terror in "luncheonettes where people swallowed mouthfuls whole, their eyes bulging, their mouths working painfully." On one occasion he imagines that he sees a "monster from the North Pole looming over the skyscrapers downtown" and on another has "the strange feeling that he was the only person left in the city, or that he was in the wrong city." It is not until the end of the novel that Norman finds inner peace when he decides to spend his own money to repair the apartments and, he believes, the lives of their tenants. Thus, Norman Moonbloom, like Sol Nazerman, is reborn into life.

The theme of rebirth also appears in Bernard Malamud's *The Assistant,* which in several respects is strikingly similar to *The Pawnbroker.* Both Sol Nazerman and Morris Bober are middle-aged Jewish storekeepers in non-Jewish neighborhoods and the frequent targets of anti-Semitic abuse. Both mourn dead children and reluctantly become surrogate fathers to Gentile assistants who are at once their victimizers and saviors. Still another parallel is the use of city settings to reflect the despair of the protagonists.

A Brooklyn-born grocer's son, Malamud has set his novel in an uniden-tified Brooklyn neighborhood inhabited largely by Italians, Poles, and Scandinavians. The Bobers, along with two other Jewish families, "had somehow . . . drifted together here where no other Jews dwelt," and it is their unhappy lot to operate a small grocery on a block of "faded yellow brick houses, two stories squatting on ancient stores." With its nearby freight yard and cemetery, the neighborhood is depicted as a wasteland, which appears as much a reflection as a cause of the characters' despair.

Malamud's use of setting to reflect a character's emotions is apparent when Morris's daughter, Helen, who has just rejected a marriage proposal and feels that she has come to the end of both her youth and her oppor-tunity, finds herself in Sea Gate at the west end of Coney Island. Summer has passed, and everything

was deserted, except here and there an open hamburger joint or pinball machine concession. Gone from the sky was the umbrella of rosy light that glowed over the place in summertime. A few cold stars gleamed down. In the distance a dark Ferris wheel looked like a stopped clock. They stood at the rail of the boardwalk, watching the black, restless sea.

Few such specific locales are identified, but Malamud does write about Sixth Avenue in Manhattan, where a desperate Morris Bober, no longer able to eke out a livelihood in the grocery, joins "a silent knot of men who drifted along . . . stopping at the employment agency doors to read im-passively the list of jobs chalked up on the blackboard signs." For the most part, however, the settings in *The Assistant,* including the Lower East

Side funeral parlor where Morris's funeral takes place and the Queens cemetery where he is buried, are unidentified but decidedly bleak.

Many of Malamud's short stories are also set in the city, but the work most richly descriptive of a particular New York locale is *The Tenants,* a novel that deals with the ambivalent relationship between two writers, one Jewish and one black, who are living in an abandoned "year 1900, faded bulky brick tenement" on Thirty-first Street and Third Avenue, where demolition is the order of the day. The house on the left

had long ago evaporated into a parking lot. . . . and there was a rumor around that the skinny house on the right, ten thin stories from the 1880's (Mark Twain lived there?) with a wrought-iron-banistered stoop and abandoned Italian cellar restaurant, was touched for next. Beyond that an old red-brick public school, three stories high, vintage of 1903, the curled numerals set like a cameo high on the window-smashed façade, also marked for disappearance. In New York who needs an atom bomb? If you walked away from a place they tore it down.

The interior of the house, with its "grimy vestibule" containing mailboxes, "several maimed, hammered in, some torn out," stairs that "stank a mixed stench, dirt, the dirtiest, urine, vomit, emptiness," and doors from which knobs and locks had been picked off, is described in detail, and Malamud writes of the "uninvited guests: bums, wet-pants drunks, faceless junkies" who slept in empty apartments to escape from the cold and

in the morning smashed in a window or two in payment for the night's unrepose—thereafter the wind and rain roamed the unrented flat until somebody boarded the broken glass—ransacking what they could: light fixtures, loose nails, mirrors, closet doors lifted off hinges or left leaning on one; and pissed and shat on the floor instead of the toilet, where it was available. Even some of the bowls were gone, or where unsnatched, their seats removed. . . .

The author describes one apartment in particular that is "desecrated now, the bedroom walls defaced, torn by graffiti, bespattered with beer, wine, varnish, nameless stains, blots" and the roof of the building, where there

was once an attractive small garden. . . . Gone garden, all gone, disassembled, kidnapped, stolen—the potted flowering plants, window boxes of pansies and geraniums, wicker chairs, even the white six-inch picket fence a civilized tenant had imaginatively put up for those . . . who enjoyed a moment's repose this high up in the country.

A novel about racial conflicts and destructive human relationships, *The Tenants* is developed within the larger context of urban violence and destruction, and like the New York novels of Saul Bellow, depicts the urbanite as victim.

As perceived by Bellow, New York is a crowded, noisy, dirty, and frequently terrifying place. Emblematic of the chaos and burdens of modern life, it weighs heavily upon its residents, and more than once Bellow implies that the recovery of a beleaguered protagonist is contingent upon his flight from the city.

Born in Montreal, Bellow lived for a time in Chicago, and did not come to New York until the nineteen forties. First a resident of Greenwich Village and later of the Upper West Side, where he had an apartment on Riverside Drive, he made increasing symbolic use of New York, and by the mid-sixties, it played a major role as Artur Sammler's antagonist in *Mr. Sammler's Planet.*

As early as *The Victim,* published in 1947, Bellow was already suggesting that life in New York was oppressive, even menacing, but this theme was not fully developed until some nine years later in *Seize the Day.* Its protagonist is Tommy Wilhelm, unemployed, divorced, unhappy, and by the end of the novel, penniless, whose woes are due in large measure to the stresses of urban life. On one occasion he explains to his father that everything in New York creates anxiety:

"Like the alternate parking. You have to run out at eight to move your car. And where can you put it? If you forget for a minute they tow you away. Then some fool puts advertising leaflets under your windshield wiper and you have heart failure a block away because you think you've got a ticket. When you do get stung with a ticket, you can't argue. You haven't got a chance in court and the city wants revenue."

Desperately unhappy in this city of "sheer walls, gray spaces, [and] dry lagoons of tar and pebbles," Wilhelm asks himself,

Why did I come here in the first place . . . ? New York is like a gas. The colors are running. My head feels so tight, I don't know what I'm doing.

Later he refers to New York as "the end of the world, with its complexity and machinery, bricks and tubes, wires and stones, holes and heights" and describes New Yorkers as uncommunicative, alienated, and even crazy:

Every other man spoke a language entirely his own. . . . You had to translate and translate, explain and explain, back and forth, and it was the punishment of hell itself not to understand or be understood. . . . You had to talk with yourself in the daytime and reason with yourself at night. Who else was there to talk to in a city like New York?

Pastoral nostalgia is a theme that runs through the novel as Wilhelm remembers the clear country air and compares it to the polluted air in Manhattan, where the sun is "not clear but throbbing through the dust and fumes, a false air of gas visible at eye level as it is spurted from the bursting buses."

Lost in a landscape of pollution, tumult, and despair, Wilhelm is living with his elderly father in the fictional Hotel Gloriana, located on the Upper West Side. Because most of the Gloriana's guests are retired, Wilhelm feels out of place there, as he does in the surrounding neighborhood populated largely by the elderly, who sit on benches in "the tiny railed parks and along the subway gratings from Verdi Square to Columbia University"[3] and fill to overflowing "the shops and cafeterias, the dime stores, the tea-rooms, the bakeries, the beauty parlors, the reading rooms and club rooms."

Wilhelm feels that a kind of garishness characterizes the Upper West Side, and there are descriptions of the carnival atmosphere of Broadway and of the Hotel Ansonia, on the northwest corner of Broadway and Seventy-third Street, which is perhaps the best-known emblem of that garishness. Explaining that it was built by the famed Stanford White,[4] Bellow describes it as resembling "a baroque palace from Prague or Munich enlarged a hundred times, with towers, domes, huge swells and bubbles of metal gone green from exposure, iron fretwork, and festoons."

While several scenes from Bellow's *Herzog* are set on the Upper West Side some years later, the locales described in this vast and sprawling novel include other New York neighborhoods as well, not to mention such places as Chicago and Martha's Vineyard. (It is on Martha's Vineyard that Morris Herzog, professor, author, cuckolded husband, and victim of modern urban life, begins to regain his composure after a harrowing period of emotional unrest.)

Frightened of subway travel and of muggers, Herzog warns his son, "Take care on the subway. And around the neighborhood, too. Don't go down into Morningside Park. There are gangs down there." And he perceives the sights along Upper Broadway as depressing if not actually menacing:

In midstreet, on the benches, old people: on faces, on heads, the strong marks of decay: the big legs of women and blotted eyes of men, sunken mouths and inky nostrils. . . . An escaped balloon was fleeing like a sperm, black and quick into the orange dust of the west. He crossed the street, making a detour to avoid a fog of grilled chicken and sausage. The crowd was traipsing over the broad sidewalk. Moses took a keen interest in the uptown public, its theatrical spirit, its performers—the transvestite homosexuals painted with great originality, the wigged women, the lesbians looking so male you had to wait for them to pass and see them from behind to determine their true sex, hair dyes of every shade.

Everyday New York street scenes fill Herzog with dread. On Thirty-eighth Street and along Park Avenue, he watches the demolition and erection of buildings:

The Avenue was filled with concrete-mixing trucks, smells of wet sand and powdery gray cement. Crashing, stamping pile-driving below, and, higher, structural steel, interminably and hungrily going up into the cooler, more delicate blue. Orange beams hung from the cranes like straws. But down in the street where the buses were spurting the poisonous exhaust of cheap fuel, and the cars were crammed together, it was stifling, grinding, the racket of machinery and the desperately purposeful crowds—horrible! He had to get out to the seashore where he could breathe.

However menacing New York is to Moses Herzog, it is infinitely more so to Artur Sammler, the frail, elderly Holocaust survivor who is the protagonist of *Mr. Sammler's Planet.* An intellectual and genteel man, he perceives the city as a "quivering, riotous, [and] lurid" place where commercialism, crime, and immorality flourish at the expense of the human spirit.

When the novel opens, we learn that for several days Mr. Sammler, in transit on the bus from the Forty-second Street Library to his yellow-brick apartment house on West Ninetieth Street, has observed a pickpocket in operation. A concerned and conscientious citizen, he goes to great pains to notify the police, and for his efforts he discovers to his outrage that the police are not interested in such a crime and that the majority of "outdoor telephones were smashed, crippled. They were urinals, also. New York was getting worse than Naples or Salonika."

Outrage is heaped upon outrage when Mr. Sammler, who has been thinking while walking home that public transportation is "an abomination," is followed into his apartment building by the pickpocket, who in "a corner beside the long blackish carved table, a sort of Renaissance piece, a thing which added to the lobby melancholy, by the buckling canvas of the old wall, by the red-eyed lights of the brass double fixtures," unzips his fly and exposes himself to Mr. Sammler.

In the days following this unsettling episode, Mr. Sammler is unable to shake the sense of squalor and decay that surrounds him. Even the Stuyvesant Square area, where instead of the "new New York of massed apartments" one sees "the older New York of brownstone and marble," is not immune from urban problems. Flowers are covered with "the fallout of soot" and the grass is "burned by animal excrement." He sees "a female bum drunkenly sleeping like a dugong, a sea cow's belly rising, legs swollen purple; a short dress, a mini-rag." A short distance away a wino is "sullenly pissing on newspapers and leaves."

Columbia University also seems to him to be touched by urban blight:

Between the pillars at One hundred-sixteenth Street Sammler looked into the brick quadrangles. . . . He saw growing green. But green in the city had lost its association with peaceful sanctuary. The old-time poetry of parks was banned. Obsolete thickness of shade leading to private meditation. Truth was now slummier and called for litter in the setting—leafy reverie? A thing of the past.

More than anything else, the sights on Broadway and West Ninety-sixth Street make Mr. Sammler realize how demeaned and miserable human life really is:

By a convergence of all minds and all movements the conviction transmitted by this crowd seemed to be that reality was a terrible thing, and that the final truth about mankind was overwhelming and crushing. . . . This poverty of soul, its abstract state, you could see in faces on the street.

Written more than two decades after *The Victim, Mr. Sammler's Planet* offers a far grimmer view of New York than the earlier novel, and its inescapable conclusion is that while there may be hope for Mr. Sammler, there is very little—if any—hope for the city itself.

Another one-time resident of Riverside Drive, J. D. Salinger also writes about the Upper West Side and other New York locales, implying that urban life is at the very least partially responsible for the alienation and despair experienced by his characters.

Even in the early works collected in *Nine Stories,* his characters express their unhappiness with New York life and its pressures. In "Pretty Mouth and Green My Eyes" a husband blames his marital problems on the city:

"What a rat race. Honest to God, I think it's this goddam New York. What I think maybe we'll do, if everything goes along all right, we'll get ourselves a little place in Connecticut may be. Not too far out, necessarily, but far enough that we can lead a normal goddam life."

In "De Daumier-Smith's Blue Period" a young man who has recently returned from a long stay in Paris is involved in an unpleasant experience on the Lexington Avenue bus and prays "for the city to be cleared of people, for the gift of being alone—a-l-o-n-e: which is the one New York prayer that rarely gets lost or delayed in channels, and in no time at all everything I touched turned to solid loneliness."

Much of Salinger's fiction about the Glass family is also set in New York, with the Glasses living for a time at the Hotel Alamac on Broadway and Seventy-first Street and then in an apartment house at 110th Street and Riverside Drive, one block from where Salinger grew up. Later they move, as did the Salingers, to the East Side. While it is evident that some of their problems are attributable to the strains of urban life, this theme is best developed in *Catcher in the Rye,* which is about Holden Caulfield, a sensitive and troubled adolescent who runs away from boarding school and spends a "lost" weekend in New York.

Although he goes home briefly to visit his sister, Phoebe, Holden does not wish to see his parents, so he spends one night at a hotel and another in the Grand Central Station, which he doesn't "feel much like discussing" except for explaining, "It wasn't too nice. Don't ever try it. I mean it. It'll depress you."

Holden finds other New York scenes equally depressing. Walking along Fifth Avenue, where the "scraggy-looking Santa Clauses . . . and the Salvation Army girls, the ones that don't wear any lipstick or anything" are ringing bells, he feels as if he is sinking "down, down, down, and nobody'd ever see me again." As for Broadway, it "was mobbed and messy. Everybody was on their way to the movies—the Paramount or the Astor or the Strand or the Capitol or one of those crazy places."[5] Depressed by the long lines of well-dressed people who actually *want* to go to the movies, Holden can't "get off that goddam Broadway fast enough."

Later he meets Sally, a girl friend, under the famous clock at the Biltmore,[6] where "about a million girls" are "waiting for their dates to show up." The afternoon that he and Sally spend at a matinée and later ice-skating at Rockefeller Center deeply distresses Holden, who tells an uncomprehending Sally how much he hates living in the city:

"Taxicabs and Madison Avenue buses, with the drivers and all always yelling at you to get out at the rear door, and being introduced to phony guys . . . and going up and down in elevators when you just want to go outside, and guys fitting your pants all the time at Brooks. . . ."

After leaving Sally, he goes to see the Christmas show at Radio City and is depressed by "the goddam stage show," in which the Rockettes are "kicking their heads off" and angels are "coming out of . . . everywhere, guys carrying crucifixes and stuff all over the place, and the whole bunch of them—*thousands* of them—singing 'Come All Ye Faithful!' like mad."

Manhattan and its world-famous attractions clearly do not impress the despairing adolescent whose feelings of alienation are exacerbated in the city. There are two places, however, that he does like—the lagoon in Central Park, which to him is emblematic of uncorrupted nature in the midst of a hypocritical society, and the Museum of Natural History,[7] which as a child he used to visit almost every Saturday. Salinger describes many of the exhibits in detail, and Holden explains that he loved "that damn museum" because nothing ever changed there:

Nobody'd move. You could go there a hundred thousand times, and that Eskimo would still be just finished catching those two fish, the birds would still be on their way south, the deers would still be drinking out of that water hole. . . .

Searching for permanence in a perpetually changing world, innocence in a society that he perceives as corrupt, and love in a city he thinks of as cold and uncaring, Holden suffers a breakdown. As it turns out, he is one of many protagonists in contemporary New York fiction who meet with a similar fate.

Another contemporary work in which a young person's breakdown is in part attributable to the pressures of the urban environment is Sylvia Plath's autobiographical novel *The Bell Jar,* which on the first page associates the horror of the execution of convicted spies Julius and Ethel Rosenberg with the misery of life in New York City. Immediately following a reference to the executions being "the worst things in the world," Plath writes:

New York was bad enough. By nine in the morning the fake, country-wet freshness that somehow seeped in overnight evaporated like the tail end of a sweet dream. Mirage-gray at the bottom of their granite canyons, the hot streets wavered in the sun, the car tops sizzled and glittered, and the dry, cindery dust blew into my eyes and down my throat.

The images of hot streets and sizzling car tops relate directly to the Rosenbergs' deaths in the electric chair and are predictive of the shock therapy that Esther Greenwood, Plath's protagonist, is to receive following the time in New York that precipitates her illness.

A college student who has won a writing contest and thereby the opportunity to work during the summer on a glamorous New York fashion magazine, Esther and the other contest winners stay at the Barbizon Hotel, on Lexington Avenue and Sixty-third Street. Closed to men until nearly two decades after the publication of the novel in 1963, it was called the Amazon in *The Bell Jar* and described as a residence hotel for women only, and they are mostly girls my age with wealthy parents who wanted to be sure their daughters would be living where men couldn't get at them and deceive them; and they were all going to posh secretarial schools like Katy Gibbs, where they had to wear hats and stockings and gloves to class, or they had just graduated from places like Katy Gibbs and were secretaries to executives and junior executives and simply hanging around in New York waiting to get married to some career man or other.[8]

The rooms, one single one after another, remind her of a college dorm, and from her window she can see "downtown to where the U.N. balanced itself in the dark, like a weird green Martian honeycomb."[9]

Although she recognizes that there are "thousands of other college girls . . . all over America who wanted nothing more than to be tripping about in those same size-seven patent leather shoes" she had purchased at Bloomingdales, which at its Lexington Avenue and East Fifty-ninth Street location is one of the city's trendiest and most fashionable department stores, Esther is miserable. She describes her anxiety about tipping in New York and her feelings of inferiority in a city where past successes "fizzled to nothing outside the slick marble and plate-glass fronts along Madison Avenue." At times she feels completely cut off from the city, which, she explains, "hung in my window, flat as a poster, glittering and blinking, but it might just as well not have been there at all, for all the good it did me."

Disoriented and depressed as she is, Esther imagines at one point that "New York is dissolving . . . and that dirt that settled on my skin . . . is turning into something pure." It is evident that she is unable to heed the advice of Jay Cee, the editor of *Ladies Day,* who tells her, "Don't let the wicked city get you down." New York has done more than get Esther down: it has exacerbated already existing problems and before long will precipitate a nervous breakdown.

Among other authors who have depicted characters undergoing severe emotional stress while living in contemporary New York are Irvin Faust, Muriel Spark, William Maxwell, and Sue Kaufman.

In *Roar Lion Roar and Other Stories,* Irvin Faust depicts many characters who are emotionally unbalanced and makes New York a symbol of a frightening modernity that is converging on them and causing them to seek escape through withdrawal or fantasy.

The opening story, entitled "Philco Baby," is about a young stock boy who lives in a dark room on West Eighty-eighth Street, visits Coney Island on Sundays, and avoids all contact with people by listening to the radio constantly. Another bizarre character is Googs Korngold, who in "Googs in Lambarene" decides to save the city. Explaining to his friend that there is a mission to be done, "right here in our jungle," he proceeds to camp out in Central Park, where he attempts to administer "emotional first aid, moral bandaging, ethical splinting" to distraught New Yorkers.

Others of Faust's characters imagine themselves to be Adolf Hitler or to be singing a duet with King Kong on top of the Empire State Building. Ishmael Ramos, protagonist of the title story, is in the mental ward of a hospital, having thrown himself into the Hudson River after the Columbia Lions lost to the Princeton Tigers. A Puerto Rican youth from an impoverished background, Ishmael had long dreamed of working at Columbia:

Man, he prayed. With Lady of Fatima on 98th Street and St. Christopher on 123rd and the Protestant saints in St. John's and Moses and the other Jew cats in their church on 110th and even in the big house on the Drive, where he bugged old United States Grant. But most of all he prayed to the big, handsome chick named Alma on the front steps of Low Library.

His prayers answered when he secures a job as janitor at Columbia, Ishmael begins to emulate the students, buying clothes at Kenny's Kampus Korner, having "cokes and Drake's Cakes in the Lion's Den in Ferris Booth, sitting under the great bronze seal like United States Grant," and even attending classes. All of a sudden,

New York it don't bug him no more. Or put him down no more; he could walk down any street with his uniform and shoes and book and he don't feel *frijoles* inside. Columbus Avenue and Manhattan and the whole stupid west side with all the spiks was a drag, streets to be walked over, not *through*, without his heart splitting his chest. Subways, man, overnight they cut out being dragons that was busting his ears and about to stomp him.

With his coed girl friend he goes on a boat ride around Manhattan and is thrilled to learn from the guide that Columbia once stood on the present site of Trinity Church and that it owns property rented to Rockefeller. So complete is Ishmael's identification with Columbia that he believes that he has nothing to live for when its football team is defeated by Princeton.

Another of Faust's stories set near Columbia is "The Madras Rumble." Its protagonist is an Indian named Wilmat Shanker, who is living at International House—a residence and cultural center for foreign students, which was built on Riverside Drive in 1924 with funds donated by John D. Rockefeller—and working in a youth program at St. Mary's, on 133rd Street near Amsterdam Avenue. Faust writes about "the area between Broadway and Amsterdam from 122nd to 135th," which he calls "a social worker's paradise" because of its various ethnic groups, including blacks,

Puerto Ricans, Filipinos, Jews, and Japanese, and describes the neighborhood's "major power centers," among them

Jaime's Bodega; Al's Esso Station; Tim Buzzio's Bowling Alleys; the Claremont Bar; the Canton Palace; the deserted ferry pier at 125th Street, under which a body a month popped up; the north end of Riverside Park, where fourteen babies a year were abandoned (and Lord knows how many conceived).

While his behavior is rather bizarre and he is eventually discovered to be extorting protection money from Chinese laundries, Wilmat Shankar is hardly as deranged as most of Faust's characters and certainly more emotionally intact than the characters appearing in Muriel Spark's *The Hothouse by the East River,* which might well have been entitled *The Madhouse by the East River.*

The Hothouse by the East River is about the Hazlett family. Paul and Elsa Hazlett live in an apartment overlooking the East River in a house soon to be demolished, and from their windows they can see Welfare Island, since renamed Roosevelt Island, which appears as "a mass of leafage," as well as the UN, the Pan Am Building,[10] and across the river, the borough of Queens. Their son has an apartment on East Seventy-sixth Street, and he and his parents and his sister, who lives on East Sixty-fourth Street, as well as the family's therapist and friends, appear at times to be deranged.

Spark focuses on the New York of luxurious East Side apartments, exclusive Madison Avenue stores, experimental off-Broadway theatres, and nightspots called "The Personality Cult" and "The Sensual Experience," as well as more sedate places like the Plaza's Oak Room[11] and the St. Regis Hotel. She writes also of Jimmy Ryan's, known for its jazz and located on West 54th Street, and L'Etoile, no longer in existence as a brasserie in the Sherry Netherland Hotel. More than once she indicates that madness is a state of mind related to urban life:

New York, home of the vivisectors of the mind, and of the mentally vivisected still to be reassembled, of those who live intact, habitually wondering about their states of sanity, and home of those whose minds have been dead, bearing the scars of resurrection: New York heaves outside the consultant's office, agitating all around her. . . .

Elsewhere she describes Manhattan as a "mental clinic . . . where we analyze and dope the savageries of existence," as a "sedative chamber where you don't think at all and you can act as crazily as you like and talk your head off all day, all night." And when in the novel Elsa Hazlett compares her psyche to a skyscraper of glass and steel, the identification between madness and the city is complete.

Not neglectful of the specific problems that drive New Yorkers into insanity, Spark has one of her characters explain,

we . . . have the youth problem, the racist problem, the distribution problem, the political problem, the economic problem, the crime problem, the matrimonial problem, the ecological problem, the divorce problem, the domiciliary problem, the consumer problem, the birth-rate problem, the middle-age problem, the health problem, the sex problem, the incarceration problem, the educational problem, the fiscal problem, the unemployment problem, the physiopsychodynamics problem, the homosexual problem, the traffic problem, the heterosexual problem, the obesity problem, the garbage problem, the gyno-emancipation problem, the rent-controls problem, the identity problem, the bisexual problem, the uxoricidal problem. . . .

When several pages later a waiter in a bar calls New York "a fun city," the irony is painfully sharp.

The characters in William Maxwell's title story in *Over By the River and Other Stories* are also well-to-do New Yorkers living on the Upper East Side. Their money, however, can neither ease their increasing sense of dread and despair nor do away with the fears and nightmares induced by New York life.

The story opens pleasantly enough with a description of the sunrise as viewed from the Carringtons' apartment:

The lights on the bridges went off, and so did the red light in the lantern of the lighthouse at the north end of Welfare Island. Seagulls settled on the water. A newspaper truck went from building to building dropping off heavy bundles of, for the most part, bad news, which little boys carried inside on their shoulders. Doormen smoking a pipe and dressed for a walk in the country came to work after a long subway ride and disappeared into the service entrances. When they reappeared, by way of the front elevator, they had put on with their uniforms a false amiability and were prepared for eight solid hours to make conversation about the weather. With the morning sun on them, the apartment buildings far to the west, on Lexington Avenue, looked like an orange mesa. The pigeons made bubbling noises in their throats as they strutted on windowsills high above the street.

Before long, however, the scenes from the Carringtons' windows begin to acquire a menacing edge. Maxwell describes East End Avenue in the middle of the night, when a young policeman, fearful of the Civil Liberties Union, resists the temptation to arrest a suspicious-looking junkie. Later the junkie scavenges for still edible food in the trash bins of Carl Schurz Park,[12] frightens "the dog-walkers, who supposing—correctly—that he had a switchblade in his pocket and a certain amount of experience in using it, chose a path that detoured around him," and as dawn approaches enters the open window of a ground-floor apartment on East End Avenue and moments later reappears, wheeling a new ten-speed bicycle.

Unpleasant and frightening events occur in profusion: imposters claiming to be from Boys' Town go from door to door selling magazine subscriptions; policemen escort a handcuffed man from a building; a woman commits suicide in the East River; George Carrington thinks "somebody's been murdered" but soon realizes that the woman lying on the "stoop of one of the little houses on East End Avenue facing the park" is not dead but asleep on the stone; on another occasion he hears piercing screams and believes that someone is "being robbed or raped or murdered" but, uncertain about what to say, fails to notify the police.

George's wife, Iris, concerned about her family's increasing anxiety, comes to believe that it's a mistake to raise children in New York, a view also expressed at a cocktail party, where the subject of discussion is how unsafe the city is for children. But the Carringtons stay on in New York, and life in the metropolis proceeds along what to them has become a terrifying course.

New York is depicted as an equally frightening place in Sue Kaufman's *Diary of A Mad Housewife* and *Falling Bodies,* both of which are concerned with the trials and tribulations of two educated and affluent women who are under great stress, owing in part to marital problems and in part to anxieties related to urban life.

Diary of A Mad Housewife opens with a reference to the city's pollution, which is followed by a discussion of the narrator's fear of walking her dog in Central Park during the daylight hours:

> Today I swore I'd make myself go in there, and got as far as the entrance when I saw the man in the middle of the path, standing and loonily smiling up at the trees. He was a very old man with white hair, who was probably just somebody's poor old retired Dad, or a senile bird-watcher hoping, perchance, to spot a purple finch—but I wasn't going to risk it. Not these days. Not me.
> So it was the dirty gutters with torn pages of the *Daily News*. The minute I got back up here I locked this door. . . .

As soon becomes clear, Bettina, this intelligent, articulate woman, is afraid not only of Central Park, but also of elevators, subways, bridges, tunnels, trains, cockroaches, muggers, rapists, and other commonplace aspects of modern urban life, and "ever since that gory murder . . . where some poor Bronx woman was raped and stabbed in the basement of her building and stuffed in the cold furnace with her feet dangling out," she has refused to enter the basement of her apartment building. She is also fearful of allowing her young daughters to wait for the school bus on Central Park West at eight o'clock in the morning. Not all of her fears, however, appear to be as well founded as her terror of walking her dog in Central Park. Finally working up the courage to do so, Bettina encounters a tramp sleeping on a bench, a huge ugly rat, and finally a man with a "wildly evil smile" who undoubtedly means to attack her. Frozen in her tracks, Bettina stands there "dimly wondering was it going to be for money, rape, or the thrill of what the papers called an 'assault.'" She is saved, however, by the timely arrival on the scene of two huge dogs and their master and later reflects that the incident "was the sort of thing that's completely commonplace, the sort of thing you have to expect in a big city like New York with all the crackpots and loonies around." She goes on to explain that the "exhibitionists in the subways, the rapists in the elevators, the muggers in the streets—why, even those telephone perverts who say obscene things—they're all a sign of the times."

Even when rape and murder are not on her mind, Bettina finds the city an uncongenial place. She is ordered off a crowded bus "by a swearing driver who wouldn't break . . . [a] five-dollar bill" and must walk seven blocks before she can find a storekeeper who will give her change. Later that same day a cabdriver is abusive when she politely asks him to wait for her while she stops for her daughter at a friend's house.

Rude taxi drivers are also unnerving to Emma Sohier, the protagonist of *Falling Bodies,* but they are the least of her problems. Having recently witnessed two suicides in which the victims jumped from high buildings, Emma is terrified of walking on the street lest a body fall on or near her. The first time she witnessed a suicide, she "felt it was basically like so many other New York horror stories one was always hearing or reading about, and wouldn't let herself dwell on it," but after it happens again, Emma is unable to shake her terror. She becomes increasingly aware of the indifference and alienation of New Yorkers, and the city streets, filled as they are with anguish and despair, begin to take on a nightmarish quality for her:

The man whipping his collie with its steel leash. The black boy . . . pedaling the heavy, overloaded grocery cart, his arms and legs like burnt matchsticks, his toes bursting from the sneakers pumping the pedals around. The old woman whose grocery bag had burst, and who was gropingly trying to retrieve rolling canned goods and oranges, while people (like herself) walked briskly by. The young nursemaid with the face of Himmler, bending over the weeping little girl in the stroller, softly whispering threats in German. The boy unscrewing hub caps from the car at the curb, the emaciated cat cowering under the car. . . .

The nightmarish quality of the city is brought into sharpest focus during a blackout. Listening to the sounds of sirens, Emma wonders, "What were all those sirens? Police cars? Ambulances? Rescue squads? Fire trucks? Had the blackout touched off a wave of violent lootings and muggings and terrible incidents?" While she is preoccupied with these thoughts, her husband is trapped in an elevator, where he remains sitting on the floor in a fetal position for almost two hours. Later, coming out into "the chaos of Eighth Avenue," he is confronted by a frightening spectacle:

the cars inching along with headlights blazing and horns blaring, the cars hopelessly jammed in an intersection without traffic signals, the people groping along the sidewalks, some lighting their way with flashlights and lanterns, some picking their way along in the glare of the headlights, others just standing around in those strange little clusters, getting some kind of comfort and reassurance out of company.

He then makes the decision to undertake the fifty-four-block walk home: "Nothing—no mugger or errant car or anything else—was going to keep him from it." Clutching a torch and cleaving to buildings, he makes his way through "the strange noises, the confusion, the blanketing darkness."

Invariably present then in both *Diary of A Mad Housewife* and *Falling Bodies* is Kaufman's sense of New York as a dangerous place in which to live. Not only women but also men are fearful of being on the city streets. Emma's husband expects to be mugged during the blackout, and Bettina's husband feels that the Upper West Side is a dangerous area. Explaining that "it's the borderline of the Negro and Puerto Rican neighborhood," he quickly adds, "that's not bigotry.... It's just plain reason, common sense. It's not safe over there, which is a fact everybody in New York knows."

That it is not only dangerous but sometimes even fatal to live in New York is taken as a given fact in much contemporary fiction, ranging from hostage novels like John Godey's *The Taking of Pelham One Two Three* to popular murder mysteries like Judith Rossner's *Looking for Mr. Goodbar,* which deals with the brutal slaying of a young woman living alone in New York. While further examples of these genres can be cited, a discussion of one book of each type seems adequate for our purposes.

Although hardly remarkable for its emphasis on the dangers and violence that threaten New Yorkers even in the most commonplace situations, *The Taking of Pelham One Two Three,* which as its title implies, is about the hijacking of a train, is unique in its discussion of the New

York subway system and its operations. Godey provides statistics on the average length of a subway car, the number of seats it contains, and the number of cars in service, as well as information about the physical features of particular stations, the number of subway escalators in operation, the underground rat population, and the ridership of each division. Early in the novel a motorman comments that a small percentage of "the better class" rode the IRT, which "ran a poor third to the BMT and the IND." Elsewhere Godey writes about the subway riders' "embattled coexistence with the city. Like animals in a jungle, like plants, they adapted, they mutated toward specific defenses and suspicions created to cope with specific threats."

Of particular interest is the author's description of the headquarters of the Municipal Transit Authority in downtown Brooklyn:

370 Jay is a comparatively modern structure surrounded by many older, darker-toned, more graceful, and architecturally complicated buildings that constitute the heart of Kings County's official center: Borough Hall, courthouses, administrative bureaus. Although this area of Brooklyn is not just another Brooklyn joke, nevertheless it is classed as a province of the island across the nearby river, and suffers a loss of stature thereby.

Following a lengthy description of the physical plant is an analysis of transit operations, and Godey explains how dispatchers communicate with motormen by two-way radio and discusses the hierarchy of power, with dispatchers reporting to trainmasters, who in turn report to supervisors.

In the course of the novel, other New York locales are described. Among them are Police Headquarters located in an "old and forbidding building" at 240 Centre Street, the Police Academy on East Twenty-first Street, Gracie Mansion, and the Federal Reserve Building, "an impregnable fortress, a square block of monolithic stone with barred windows on its lower floors," located "at 33 Liberty Street in the center of New York's great financial district." Here at the Federal Reserve Building, the ransom of one million dollars is picked up by policemen, whose route to the hijackers takes them along torturously narrow Nassau Street, and Godey provides the reader with a guided tour of downtown Manhattan as the police roar past John, Fulton, Ann, Beekman, and Spruce streets.

Although his primary focus is on the terror in the subway and the frantic efforts of the Transit Authority, police, politicians, and others to save the lives of the hostages, Godey also describes other frightening aspects of city life. A policeman recalls his days as a plainclothesman in the East Village when he had worn long hair, a poncho, and beads and had "gone down among the Ukranians, the motorcycle freaks, street people, addicts, weirdos, students, radicals, acidheads, teen-age run-aways, and dwindling hippie population of the East Village." There are also descriptions of downtown Brooklyn in the evening when "the lawyers and law-makers and judges and politicians" have deserted "the great dignified buildings the borough had inherited from its past," leaving the neighborhood to "drunks and muggers and the homeless, prey and hunter." Like the rest of the book, such descriptions bespeak of New York City as a landscape of violence, alienation, and unspeakable human waste.

The same can be said of *Looking for Mr. Goodbar.* Its protagonist a lonely young woman who frequents singles bars and finally meets up with her killer in one of them, the novel contains few, if any, pleasant descriptions of the city. St. Mark's Place, where Theresa lives, is "too crowded for her taste, with kids and other strung-out types, and too dirty." While she does not heed the advice of a lover who tells her to move to Queens, where rents are cheaper and there are no junkies hanging out on the streets, Theresa's anxiety about living in the East Village is expressed in her dreams. In one dream she is crawling on the street, unable to find her way home

because the whole street was covered with some kind of dark material that turned it into a tunnel so you couldn't see the sky. And the sidewalks were covered with jive-ass spades with knives, hustling everyone, except they didn't see her because she was on her knees. Just as she was finally getting close to her house a huge red Checker cab chased her right up onto the sidewalk and out of the dream. . . .

In another dream, she imagines that she is in a store on St. Marks Place whose front

had been torn away, maybe by a bomb or some kind of explosion, so you could see the whole street. Except it didn't look like St. Marks Place. There was a river and some dark woods and the BMT subway was running through and there were trapezes in some of the trees.

To avoid having nightmares, Theresa often walks the streets during the night, but little solace is to be found there. At four in the morning she finds herself on Sixth Avenue, deserted except for a few unsavory characters:

Staggering along. Curled up in doorways. One throwing up in a waste-basket. Creeps. So bad even the Statue of Liberty wouldn't let them huddle under her robes. A very young queen, his arm around an elderly dwarf, smiled at her as they passed.

Fourteenth Street, "devoid of its shoppers, its hangers-out, its cheap wares spilling out of large brown cartons on the sidewalk, was unbelievably ugly" at this hour, and on Herald Square she sees "a man, or the body of a man . . . curled against the slats" of a bench and wonders "if he was dead or alive."

Whether she is writing about nearly deserted Herald Square in the early morning hours or the crowded West Village on a weekend evening when it is filled with "old winos and young dopers," panhandlers, bums, and "Saturday nighters from New Jersey" who are fascinated by the Village regulars and the windows of the head shops, Rossner's portrayal of the city streets is a grim one.

As might be expected, the interiors described in *Looking for Mr. Goodbar* are equally depressing. Theresa's apartment is filthy and crawling with roaches. When she picks up a man and goes with him to Greene Street, "which was dark and ugly and littered with garbage," they have to climb

onto a huge cement platform to enter the building, which had a strange, musty smell. Then he used a key to open a grate in front of the elevator doors which then opened vertically . . . bringing to mind guillotines and other unpleasant images.

Finally the elevator opens into the huge, cold, and almost empty room that is to be the scene of their lovemaking.

Among other depressing interiors are the singles bars, emblems of urban alienation. Yet while Rossner treats the loneliness and terror of New York life, she does not approximate the stunning horror to be found in John Retchy's *City of Night* or James Leo Herlihy's *Midnight Cowboy,* both of which deal with one of New York's least-known subcultures—that of the male hustler. While other settings are used, the dominant one is that of Times Square, which is depicted as a scene of human degradation and wretchedness.

Its climactic scene a murder, *Midnight Cowboy* prepares the reader for violence almost from the very beginning when Joe Buck arrives in Times Square determined to strike it rich as a "cowboy," or male prostitute. He soon discovers, however, that rich women willing to pay for sex are not easy to find and joins the ranks of drifters, hustlers, bums, and perverts who hang out, waste time, and try to score in the Times Square area.

For a time Joe moves in with a crippled pickpocket named Ratso Rizzo, who is living in a house slated for demolition on "a largely Puerto Rican block in the West Twenties." As Herlihy explains, such buildings are always to be found in New York and are easily identifiable by the white Xs taped across the windows of each vacated apartment. Whenever he needed a place to sleep, Ratso would search for such a building:

Sometimes he had to break a lock, but more often the door had been left wide open. And occasionally he would even find that the departing tenant had left behind a few sticks of furniture for him. He would move his own meager belongings into the place and use it as his home until the management became aware of his presence, or until the last legitimate tenant had left and the water had been turned off.

Joe finds Ratso's current quarters comfortable, even luxurious, after having lived for a time on the street, where he had quickly learned the skills of survival:

He learned cheap ways to eat: the Automat gave you baked beans or macaroni and cheese for only twenty cents, you could go to the A & P and fill your pockets with raisins and carrots for a quarter, apples could be stolen on Ninth Avenue. . . . [He slept] in trucks or movie theaters, or on benches at Pennsylvania Station or at the Port Authority bus terminal. . . . Carrying soap and a disassembled razor in his pocket and a toothbrush in his sock, he used the public facilities of the cafeterias and saloons.

Like the other street boys, he had learned how to scan "the doorways and theater lobbies and penny arcades in search of a moneymaking opportunity" and how to attract Johns by projecting

just the right degree of interest-disinterest that would make them come up and talk to you: give them the nerve to, and yet not cause them to lose interest. At that point another skill entered into it: what to say, what not to say, when to close the deal, when to hold out for more.

Out hustling one night, Joe picks up a man who takes him to the Hotel Europa, which with its once-magnificent lobby now seedy and partitioned off into small shops sounds strikingly like the Ansonia. For his brief pleasure in the Hotel Europa, the John pays a dear price. Desperate for money to take the dying Ratso to Florida, Joe murders him in a fitting climax to a novel about the alienated, the desperate, and the deviant who hang out in Times Square, where violence is all too often a way of life.

Perceived by Joe Buck as a "cell [that] was shrinking at a nightmare rate," Manhattan is also a scene of despair for John Rechy's protagonist. A "part of the 42nd Street army of punks," the narrator of *City of Night* is, like Joe Buck, a male hustler, sleeping in the balconies of Times Square movie houses, hanging out at Bickford's[13] or the Automat, and always on the lookout for a score.

From the moment of his arrival in the city, he perceives New York as a lonely and menacing place. He lives for a time in a "soul-squashing building" on East Thirty-fourth Street, near the Armory, which has long since moved to West Fourteenth Street. On the corner, "Lexington Avenue rushes determinedly past bars and stores and checker-tabled Italian restaurants, and everywhere gray steel buildings stab the sky." Here, in a building "known as the Casbah for its menagerie of Twilight people," Joe adds

to the shadows in one of those thousands of hallways in New York City in immense apartment houses erected in the large American cities before buildings grew tall and skinny rather than short and fat. They squat self-consciously in the midst of slick skyscrapers waiting sullenly to be bought, torn down, replaced. . . .

In his exploration of New York's homosexual subculture, Rechy writes about Third Avenue, "where figures camped flagrantly in the streets in a parody stagline; the lurid 'Hi' floating into the dark," about "Howard Thomson's restaurant on 8th Street in the near dawn hours [where] they gathered . . . for the one last opportunity before the rising sun expelled them, bringing the Sunday families out for breakfast,"[14] and about "the jungle of Central Park—between the 60s and 70s, on the west side," where on Sunday afternoons homosexuals "prowled," confident that they could "make it, right there, in the tree-secluded areas."

But the dominant setting of *City of Night* is Times Square, which is described as "an electric island floating on a larger island of lonesome parks and lonesome apartment houses and knife-pointed buildings stretching up." Fearful that Manhattan will one day "tear its wharf-lined fringes from the ocean and soar in desperation to the sky," the narrator describes sleazy Forty-second Street, with its

racks of magazines with photographs of almost-naked youngmen . . . [an] army of youngmen like photographs in a strange exhibition: slouched invitingly, or moving back and forth restlessly; pretending to be reading the headlines flashing across the [Times] Tower—but oblivious, really, to the world those headlines represent. . . .

In sum, the life of the male hustler—on Forty-second Street or elsewhere in New York—is portrayed by Rechy as nightmarish, a feeling that is also conveyed by Charles Wright in *The Messenger*.

Wright's protagonist, Charlie, a black writer who earns a meager living as a messenger, which he supplements by working as a male prostitute, lives on Forty-ninth Street, between Sixth and Seventh avenues. The block is a frantic mixed bag of colors. Chinese and French restaurants, the Gray Line sightseeing buses, juke-box bars catering to soldiers and sailors and lesbian prostitutes, parking lots and garages filled with people returning from the theatre. And tourist hotels.

West Forty-ninth Street is the focal point of the novel, and the view from Charlie's window is described at various times of the day. In the morning he sees a solid mass of crawling cars stretching as far as Fifth Avenue, which he likens to "a hem in the great cape of Rockefeller Center," and the young trees planted along the street seem to him to resemble "cheap corsages." On hot, humid summer evenings when "you would expect the neon signs to melt like multi-colored candles," the street is filled with litter and people standing around "like wilted sentries." Charlie also has a view of the dark, deep "open doorway between Pizza House and Tip Top Parking," which is used by winos and others for drinking, urinating, and even for sex.

Although Forty-ninth Street is not without opportunities for sexual encounters, Charlie sometimes goes to Forty-second Street to cruise for Johns. But he is discouraged by the competition from "cheap hustlers" who do "what comes naturally for a meal and a pad to sleep. Cigarettes and coffee money for . . . the next morning. Thirty cents for the waiting-in-line nine a.m. movie." Occasionally he cruises on Wall Street, hoping to run into a "stock or investment queer," and at other times tries his luck on the East Side, where bartenders "will set up Johns for a cut." He laments, however, that the East Side is not what it used to be in the forties and early fifties, when "all you had to do was just walk down Third Avenue. You could even afford to be grand. Turn down tricks."

Whether Wright is describing the Upper East Side, which he calls "the over-developed cage of smart New Yorkers" or Harlem, where he sees "young men, sharp as diamonds in suits they can't afford, leaning against flashy cars that don't belong to them, or stepping smartly as if on their way to a very high-class hell," the legendary San Remo or the White Horse Tavern,[15] his portrait of the city is for the most part a grim one. Charlie feels that he is "being strangled by the sophisticate scum of New York, by those millions of feet making it toward Mr. Greenbacks and what it takes to be a 'smaht' New Yorker." He claims to be saving "nickels, dimes, dollars" so that he can leave this city he calls a "Stone Hades" and "a big-time prostitute."

New York, "which will accept victory or defeat with the same marvelous indifference," is to Wright a place "where a pleasant breeze arrives and leaves as suddenly as if it had breathed on the wrong, maimed city."

Although modern black authors have no monopoly on urban despair, their portraits of New York are often especially bitter as they depict an environment which they perceive to be particularly hostile to blacks. In *Another Country,* for example, James Baldwin writes about Rufus, a talented young black musician, and how his search for fulfillment is thwarted by bigotry. Like Baldwin, a product of Harlem, Rufus remembers

the boys on the stoops, the girls behind the stairs and on the roofs, the white policeman who had taught him how to hate, the stickball games in the streets, the women leaning out of windows and the numbers they played daily . . . the juke box, the teasing, the dancing, the hard-on, the gang fights and gang-bangs . . . his first taste of marijuana, his first snort of horse. Yes: and the boys too far out, jackknifed on the stoops, the boy dead from an overdose on a rooftop in the snow.

Despite its proud past, Harlem has become a miserable prison. On Lenox Avenue

horse carriages had once paraded proudly . . . and ladies and gentlemen, ribboned, beflowered, brocaded, plumed, had stepped down from their carriages to enter these houses which time and folly had so blasted and darkened.

The people who lived in these houses had taken pride in their homes and kept them well. "Now no one cared: this indifference was all that joined this ghetto to the mainland. Now, everything was falling down and the owners didn't care; no one cared."

Indifference and loneliness probably best characterize urban life as depicted by Baldwin. Rufus's friend Vivaldo, a white man, feels "totally estranged from the city in which he had been born" and wonders "if anyone could ever put down roots in this rock." Another white friend, Eric, returns from Europe to find that in New York a

note of despair, of buried despair, was insistently, constantly struck. It stalked all the New York avenues, roamed all the New York streets. . . . He could not escape the feeling that a kind of plague was raging, though it was officially and publicly and privately denied. Even the young seemed blighted—seemed most blighted of all.

In their struggles to survive in the cold and indifferent city, Vivaldo and Eric are at least free from the racially motivated hostility that must be endured by Rufus. Whenever he is not in Harlem, he is acutely aware of his special status as outsider, even in a city where alienation is common-place. Walking in Washington Square with his white girl friend Leona, he is the object of stony stares and hatred: "Villagers . . . looked them over as though where they stood were an auction block or a stud farm."

Later when his relationship with Leona is doomed and he is on the verge of suicide, Rufus's despair is described in relation to the city. He feels crushed, "for the weight of the city was murderous," and it is here in New York, in one of the world's most populous cities, that he feels com-pletely alone, "and dying of it."

Baldwin's theme of the black's uniquely alien status in the city is also presented in *Go Tell It on the Mountain,* whose most memorable scenes depict young John's wanderings in "white" New York, which both fasci-nates and terrifies him, and in many other works, including the short story "This Morning, This Evening, So Soon." Returning by ship from a long stay in Europe, the narrator of the story remembers "how ugly New York summers could be" and comments that to him the Statue of Liberty "had always been an ugly joke." Soon after disembarking, he is assaulted by the noises of the city, which

came from a million things at once, from trucks and tires and clutches and brakes and doors; from machines shuttling and stamping and rolling and cutting and pressing; from the building of tunnels, the checking of gas mains, the laying of wires, the digging of foundations; from the chatter-ing of rivets, the scream of the pile driver, the clanging of great shovels; from the battering down and the raising up of walls; from millions of radios and television sets and jukeboxes. The human voices distinguished themselves from the roar only by their note of strain and hostility.

Reiterating the idea that New York is a hostile city, particularly to blacks, Baldwin has his narrator explain that while he'd been "scared in Alabama," he had almost gone "crazy in New York."

In Baldwin's fiction, New York is a city of stony hostility and estrange-ment for all, yet for blacks it is more: it is a place of raised expectations, dashed hopes, and unending bitterness.

While *Another Country* describes several Harlem locales, it can hardly be described as a Harlem novel in that its primary emphasis is on the black's devastating experiences when he ventures outside the ghetto into "white" New York. The same is not true of Warren Miller's *The Cool World,* which depicts in painful detail the bitter life of a Harlem youth who has been charged with murder. With many scenes sharply reminiscent of those found in Claude Brown's nonfictional *Manchild in the Promised Land,* it is often difficult to remember that Miller's book is fiction.

A first-person account of the seamy side of Harlem life, *The Cool World* is narrated by a youth named Richard, who describes the blighted street where he grew up. There are houses in the middle of the block and stores on the corners—a pharmacy that "do a bisness in cundums an Kwik-Kill rat pellets an stuff like that," a supermarket the people call "the Bank because that where all the money go," and Daddy Beatitudes Church, which was once a small department store.

In addition to the "legitimate" businesses,

the street fulla rackets. Evrybody on the street bisy survivin an doin this & that to get thru the week an get up the rent an the bread for the super market. They some women open up a bisness right in they house for reading fortunes.

The street is cluttered with ordinary litter, and in the space where one of the houses has fallen down there is a junk pile; the other houses are decrepit. After describing the exteriors that look "like they bin washt in dirt," Richard turns to the equally dismal interiors:

The floor all rollin an heavin like the ocean at Coney. In them bildings the floor never strait. It either buckle or it tillty. . . . You cant no more straiten out the floors than you can get rid of the roaches.

Water drippin in the sink all the time. They always a leak in something if it aint the sink it the tub or the toilet.

Because such apartments depress them, Richard and his friends

just as soon stay out in the hall. In the winter time when it cold out side the halls of all these bildings fulla kids. They neck in the halls. Have fights in the halls. Smoke pot in the halls.

Although housing projects are being constructed in Harlem, Richard knows that such efforts are doomed to failure: "People paint they walls an fight the roaches an then it all start over again. Some time they goin to tare down the projeck because evry thing get taren down an it will be same all over again."

Poverty and violence, drug dealing and gang wars, hopelessness and misery: these are the givens of Harlem life, according to Miller. The black ghetto is not, however, the only New York locale to be depicted as hellish, and Miller, at once underscoring the importance of environment and making a negative judgment on the city, has Richard dream of a lion devouring the metropolis:

He come in over Washington Heights and he dont hardly touch it an it fall down. The George Washington Bridge. Alls down in the river. Then he heads down town an the bildings fall they go crashin down knockin into each other. . . . Christman he open his mouth and bite the Crysler Bilding in half an the Empire state an all them sky scrapers. Chomp. An they gone. Chomp.

After the grim social realism of Warren Miller, it is a relief to be able to mention a book like Chester Himes's *Pink Toes*, which, satirizing New York's white liberals and those blacks who curry their favor, depicts Harlem as a vital and exciting neighborhood, and in a more general vein, to move on to consider a number of other contemporary novels that depict the city in a more favorable light than the fiction discussed so far in this chapter.

One of the few modern authors who knows New York's upper class intimately enough to be able to write about it and who often appears to be offering us an updated version of Edith Wharton's work is Louis Auchincloss. Auchincloss may be limited in his scope, but this limitation results in novels that reassure us that there is more to New York than a crime-infested, polluted metropolis whose residents live in constant fear for their lives and sanity. Although far from oblivious to the physical, moral, and social changes that have tarnished the splendor of old New York and its most patrician families, Auchincloss depicts a city less ravaged than usual by the kinds of urban problems that have become a staple in so much contemporary New York fiction.

Born and bred on the fashionable East Side, Auchincloss has written several New York chronicles. While many scenes are set in the past, *The House of Five Talents* centers primarily around the later generations of the affluent Millinder family who, because it is currently the custom for the wealthy to be less ostentatious, live more modestly than their fore-bears, yet graciously, comfortably, and quite insulated from the problems generally associated with life in the inner city. The same is true of the Denison family in *Portrait in Brownstone*, which begins with the Denisons' exodus from Brooklyn to Manhattan at the turn of the century when Aunt Dagmar's husband built for his bride "a French Renaissance mansions with . . . [a] pink façade and big pedimented windows" on Fifty-third Street. In the course of more than half a century there have been many changes, and the elegant houses on Fifty-third Street between Fifth and Sixth Avenues have been torn down to make way for commerce:

Uncle Philip's house at the corner was gone. A jewelry store occupied its site. Uncle Willie's had made way for a parking lot, and her father's was a night club, or perhaps worse. Everything in New York reminded one of the prevalent dust to which, almost immediately, it seemed, one was condemned to return. If one didn't seize that day, a contractor would.

Yet the block remains an affluent one, as are most of the other locales depicted by Auchincloss. Auchincloss's New York is the home of the Metropolitan Opera and fashionable Fifth Avenue shops, galleries, and museums, of smart and expensive restaurants, of the Harvard, Knickerbocker, and Racquet and Tennis clubs.[16]

Not unmindful of urban problems, Auchincloss writes about the decline of the aristocratic Shallcross family in *The World of Profit,* which, although it contains many flashbacks, is not strictly speaking a chronicle. With its many references to fashionable New York clubs, shops, and restaurants, it is reminiscent of many other Auchincloss works, but it differs from them in that segments are set in Queens, the site of the stately Shallcross Manor, which faces Flushing Bay. The surrounding area,

in 1960, although long urbanized, was still saved from the heartlessness of the uniform housing that stretched like a graveyard to the east, by its dedication to transport. From the west of the manor, across the bay, came the muffled but never interrupted roar of traffic along the Grand Central Parkway. On the retinas of thousands upon thousands of motorists' eyes the image of those six columns must have been at least transiently stamped, while to other thousands of daily commuters, seeing it to the right in the morning and to the left in the evening, it may have become confused with other symbols of early Federal distinction: the Lee Mansion overlooking Arlington, Jefferson's rotunda in Charlottesville, even the White House.

In the course of the novel the Shallcrosses decide to sell the property because, as one family member states, their ancestral home "is an anachronism." She goes on to explain,

"The neighborhood is deteriorating. Sneak thieves abound. Young savages copulate on our lawn at night. Look down at that proud double line of great apartment houses moving north up Park Avenue like the Wall of China! That's how the modern elect are meant to live. In glass or concrete towers, with guarded entrances, high over streets where the scum of Puerto Rico eddies dangerously at night!"

The World of Profit is a novel about the gracious past yielding to the demands of the crass present. To Sophie, the Shallcross most attached to things of the past, New York, shunning its patrician past and embracing nondescript modernity, is a depressing place:

Where things in the city were old, they were simply dreary; where they were new, they were simply grim, remorselessly utilitarian, bare of decoration, barren of hope. New York seemed to be moving into a future that was terrifying in its dullness, where every little tassel of imagination and gaiety had been sheared off, leaving nothing but walls and windows, squares and oblongs.

This is indeed a despairing note to be struck by Auchincloss who, while acknowledging the decline of New York's old families, generally makes an effort to depict the still impressive remnants of its past.

If Auchincloss's uniqueness as a contemporary author is based in part on his treatment of New York's upper class, it is also due in part to his familiarity with the practice of law in New York City. Himself a lawyer, Auchincloss has written many novels on the subject. Among them are *Powers of Attorney, The Great World and Timothy Colt,* and *The Partners,* the text of which is preceded by an announcement regarding the change of address of the law firm of Shepard, Putney & Cox. The firm is said to be moving from 65 Wall Street to One New Orange Plaza, and beneath the announcement is the following statement, purportedly from the *Sunday New York Times* real-estate section:

The single note of the past in the great glass cube that Joseph Lazarus, Jr., has constructed on the Battery is its address. A few readers may recall that our city was briefly known as "New Orange" after the Dutch reoccupation of 1673.

Interestingly enough, the "great glass cube" is also the setting for *Powers of Attorney,* which contains twelve chapters, each dealing with a different member of the law firm of Tower and Strong.

The Great World and Timothy Colt is about the problems, personal and professional, that beset a young lawyer who lives with his family in an apartment house near the East River. From his window he can glimpse the river "between the two red multilateral apartment houses across the way." While his own circumstances are relatively modest, Colt, whose professional activities put him in contact with the very rich, has been in clubs where "from the high blue walls between the scarlet curtains former presidents and officers of . . . [the] club looked down on them, Schermerhorns, Livingstons, Jays . . . " and has been to the homes of clients who are among New York's most affluent denizens. On one occasion he visits a

brownstone house on Sixty-fifth Street which wound its discreet way in back through an L-shaped gallery to the "east wing" which was actually another, smaller brownstone facing on Lexington Avenue. . . . It was Timmy's first experience with the lack of ostentation of the very rich. He would never have suspected, behind that sober façade, the parquet floor of the exquisite Adam hall, the stifled luxuriant green of the small conservatory with its plopping fountain, the grey and gold paneled elegance of the French library.

Not all of the Colts' friends and associates live quite so splendidly, however. They attend a party in an "old grey shabby Parisian house in the east fifties now surrounded by shops" and visit people who live at 901 Park Avenue, a building that "had been built in the middle twenties, that easy, spacious architectural era of high ceilings and wasted hall space." All in all though, with its references to East Side townhouses and apartments, art galleries on East Fifty-seventh Street, and some of the city's finest shops, the author depicts a wealthy and fashionable city.

There are, however, several references to the fact that New York "society" has declined. Timothy's mother, for example, is dismayed to discover that marrying the descendent of a rector of Trinity Church means so little in New York and that here "families disappeared as fast as the houses which they had occupied." There is also an amusing reference to the past, when "one behaved. Not like these days when you see girls smoking on Fifth Avenue!"

This theme of the disappearance of old traditions and values is developed further in "The Landmarker," a story included in *Tales of Manhattan*. Its protagonist, Chauncey Lefferts, is an aging bachelor who has spent the best years of his life as an "extra man" at dinner parties given by New York's most prominent hostesses. Recognizing that he has become out of date, he attempts "to recapture the old New York that was dying with him":

He remembered as a young man, before the first war, the exhilaration of riding up Fifth Avenue on the top of an open bus and seeing unfold before him that glorious romp through the Renaissance. He remembered the massive brownstone of the Vanderbilt "twins" at Fifty-first Street, the mellow pink tower of the Gerry château, where the Pierre now stands, and, farther north, the birthday-cake splendor of Senator Clark's. . . .[17]

As part of his effort to recapture the past, Chauncey visits old houses, churches, and shops, and Auchincloss explains that the same person "who had once walked by the Lady Chapel of St. Patrick's Cathedral and Commodore Farragut's statue in Madison Square without turning his head was now happy to pass a morning traveling underground to the center of Brooklyn for a glimpse of the Gothic gates of Greenwood Cemetery."[18] Gazing at "Louis Sullivan's terra-cotta angels with their outstretched arms, high on a cornice over Bleecker Street " or wandering "amid the chaste Greek porticoes of Snug Harbor"[19] or studying "the faded grandeur of Colonnade Row in Lafayette Street," he begins to think of himself as "a sober, four-story brownstone façade, with Gothic arches and an iron grille, such as one might find in Hicks Street over at Brooklyn Heights."

Chauncey becomes passionately interested in the fate of Tinetti's, which, located on the corner of Lafayette and Spring streets, is described by him as having been "the most fashionable department store in the city in 1850." Enamoured of the "great square iron palazzo with a hundred arched windows, like the Sansovino library in Venice," he implores a wealthy friend to take action to save the building, which is then being used as a textile factory. But when he returns to the spot after a lengthy hospital stay, he discovers that the edifice is in the process of being demolished.

Clearly, New York is not what it once was, but Auchincloss's portrait of the city in *Tales of Manhattan* and other representative works is far more favorable than that found in most contemporary fiction.

By no means has all of Auchincloss's fiction been discussed above, and it should be clear from this and from many other similar instances that *Portrait of an American City* does not purport to be an exhaustive study of New York fiction. While no chapter has discussed all the New York fiction of a particular period, this last chapter, perhaps more than the others, has suffered from the omission of important works. The reason is twofold. First, there has been a profusion of New York fiction published in the past three decades, and it simply was not possible to include all of it here. Second, with New York novels appearing in bookstores on what sometimes seems to be a weekly basis, it has proven impossible to keep up with the most recently published ones. Lack of space has, for example, not permitted a discussion of Jimmy Breslin's comic novel *The Gang That Couldn't Shoot Straight.* Set in South Brooklyn, it contains some excellent descriptions of Marshall Street and Columbia Avenue, which Breslin explains is undergoing "reghettoization," in which "a knife comes down the middle of a block and leaves the last of the old minorities [in this case, Italians] on one side of the blade and the new minorities [in this case, Puerto Ricans] on the other side of the blade."

Other regrettable exclusions include the works of Brooklyn-born Jay Neugeboren. Parts of *An Orphan's Tale* are set in the Maimonides Home for Jewish Boys in Brooklyn, and most of the stories in *Corky's Brother* are also set in that borough. With humor and nostalgia, Neugeboren writes about Erasmus Hall High School, nearby Garfield's cafeteria on Flatbush and Church avenues, the Flatbush Boys Club, and downtown movie theatres like the Loew's Metropolitan and the Fox.[20]

Also worthy of mention is Rosellen Brown's *Street Games,* a collection of stories set in Brooklyn on George Street, near Leon, which, with its restored brownstones, communes, impoverished black and Puerto Rican residents, "small factories and broken driveways, and a coffee packing plant that sends out a sharp, bitter very brown smell," is described as "one of those cruel streets, like Park Avenue, that likes to rub your nose in the stick of its differences." Interesting but derivative is Will Oursler's little-known *N.Y., N.Y.,* which, with its interchapters entitled "Signs," "Statistics," and the like, appears to be an updated version of John Dos Passos's *Manhattan Transfer.*

The number of contemporary novels with titles indicating a New York setting is one measure of the continuing importance of New York in modern fiction. Among the many such titles not mentioned previously are Julius Horowitz's *The City,* Pierre Kyria's *Manhattan Blues,* Laurence Barrett's *The Mayor of New York,* Hortense Calisher's *The New Yorkers,* Robert A. Carter's *Manhattan Primitive,* and Gail Parent's *Sheila Levine Is Dead and Living in New York.* More recent additions to New York fiction include Neal Travis's *Manhattan,* Ellen Alexander Conley's *Soho Madonna,* and Vincent Patrick's *The Pope of Greenwich Village.*

Intended to be representative rather than exhaustive, the above list includes only a small fraction of modern fiction that has New York in its title. What matters, however, is not so much the volume of fiction written or the inclusion of New York in a particular novel's title, but rather the way that such fiction depicts the city. It is hoped that the forthcoming years bring a renaissance to the city that will be reflected in novels and short stories that focus more on the promise than on the problems of New York.

Some thirty-three years ago that promise was eloquently expressed by E. B. White in *Here Is New York.* After discussing all the problems that one might have expected to destroy the city and considering the implausibility of its survival and growth to that time, he finally likens it to an old willow tree growing in Manhattan's Turtle Bay section:

It is a battered tree, long suffering and much climbed, held together by strands of wire but beloved of those who know it. In a way it symbolizes the city: life under difficulties, growth against odds, sap-rise in the midst of concrete, and the steady reaching for the sun.[21]

NOTES

1. THE COLONY AND THE EARLY REPUBLIC

1. The customhouse to which Irving refers was razed in 1815.
2. De Herre Straet was the Dutch name for the Broad Way, or Broadway as it is now called; De Herre Graft, which means the great canal, was a wide canal in Dutch times. By 1676, pollution and foul odors had become serious problems, and the canal had to be filled in. Afterward called Brede Street, it is today known as Broad Street.

   Perel Straet, located on the East River, was also called the Strand, A noisy waterfront street named for the mother-of-pearl oyster shells scattered along its edges, it was the business center of New Amsterdam.
3. Browers Straet, the city's first paved street, was later renamed Stone Street. Het Cingle was the Dutch name for Wall Street, which in the 1690s had been built along the line of the short-lived and useless fortification erected in 1653.
4. Three streets in all—Water, Front, and South—were eventually laid out beyond Pearl Street, and West Street was laid out along the Hudson River.
5. Coffeehouses were the centers for news during this period. The Merchants' Coffee House, built in 1740, was a popular gathering place for those plotting the Revolutionary War.
6. Other New York markets included Old Slip, the Fly (also known as the Vly), Coenties, and Peck's Slip, located on the East River, and the Bear and the Crown, which, like the Oswego Market, was closer to the Hudson River.
7. The story of the statue of George III is an interesting one. After the detested Stamp Act was repealed in 1766, funds were appropriated to erect a statue of William Pitt, whose efforts had resulted in the repeal, and one of George III. By the time the statue of the king was dedicated, there had already been clashes between the patriots and the redcoats, and after a public reading of the Declaration of Independence on July 9, 1776, the statue was pulled down by crowds of soldiers and civilians. The head was stuck on a pike in front of the Blue Bell Tavern, and the lead in the rest of the statue was melted down and used for bullets.
8. Fires were common during this period of American history. Houses were densely built; water supplies, short; and fire-fighting techniques, primitive. This particular conflagration, which the British accused the Americans of setting, was said to have originated in the Fighting Cock Tavern.

9. Bloomingdale Road, approximating the course of what is at present Broadway, was one of the two main roads leading into northern Manhattan. The other, the Post Road, also known as the Bowery Lane, extended along the East Side.
10. Hanover Square is one of the few public places in New York City named for British royalty that retained its name after the Revolution. Originally a public common surrounded by wealthy residences and later the home of the *New York Gazette,* the city's first newspaper, it is presently the site of India House, used for many years as a commercial building, before becoming, in 1914, a private businessmen's club.
11. Washington's troops had their encampment on Harlem Heights, which was also the site of an important battle during the Revolution.
12. Located at Broad and Pearl streets, Black Sam's Tavern, also known as the Queen's Head Tavern, was where Washington celebrated after the withdrawal of the British troops.
13. Bounded by Varick, Beach, Hudson, and Laight streets, St. John's Park was laid out in 1803 on land belonging to Trinity Church. There were plans to develop the area and to build elegant row houses around it, but these failed to materialize because the location was considered to be too far north. For twenty years St. John's Chapel stood alone amidst marshes and cow pastures, but with the northward expansion of the city, the area finally became a fashionable residential district.
14. These settlements were not part of New Amsterdam. Until the end of the nineteenth century, New York City consisted only of Manhattan Island.
15. Although there was slavery under the Dutch, it was not until the British takeover that it became a flourishing and profitable institution. In 1709, a slavemarket was established at the foot of Wall Street.
16. In the above quotation Stowman refers to Stuyvesant Manor, the City Common, and Fresh Water Pond. The present day boundaries of Stuyvesant Manor, the farming estate belonging to the Stuyvesant family, would be Third Street on the south, Avenue C on the east, Twenty-third Street on the north, and the Bowery on the west. In the eighteenth century the triangular City Common, also known as the Fields, was at the northern edge of the town and the site of such institutions as the poorhouse and the prison. With New York City's northward expansion, it became a public gathering place, and in 1811 City Hall Park was laid out there. Fresh Water Pond, also called the Collect, which occupied what is now Foley Square, was a favorite spot for ice-skating until it was filled in at the beginning of the nineteenth century.
17. Vilssenger, or Flushing; Newton, which was originally called Middleburgh; and Jamaica were the three principal settlements in Queens during this period.
18. Although William Bradford's *New York Gazette,* founded in 1725, was the city's first newspaper, the *New York Weekly Journal,* established in 1733, was the first to advocate and to practice the principle of freedom of the press.
19. Actually the ordinance, which was in effect until 1760 when oil lamps replaced lanterns, required that lanterns be lit in front of every seventh—not every sixth—house when there was no moon.
20. That New York was a veritable Babel in its early years was attested to by Father Jogues, a Roman Catholic missionary, who as early as 1643 claimed to have heard eighteen different languages spoken there.
     Garden, Princess (Prince's), Duke, and Mill streets are four successive streets located east of Broad Street and south of Wall Street that are found on James Lyne's plan of New York City in 1730.
21. The Town Hall referred to by Cooper is the second City Hall on Broad and Wall streets, which replaced the Stadt Huys in 1703.
22. As it turned out, the church that was rebuilt after the fire was demolished in 1839, and after innumerable delays a new building was completed in 1846.
23. By the time *Satanstoe* was written, Union Square had become a fashionable residential area, and Grammercy Park, once part of Samuel Ruggles's farm, had been laid out.

24. The "new jail," which housed city prisoners, was adjacent to Bridewell and the almshouse, both of which functioned as a prison for minor offenders, as well as work-house, poorhouse, hospital, and insane asylum.

25. The Astor House, which was built by John Jacob Astor, opened in 1836 opposite City Hall Park. It was known for its bar and free lunch, but its popularity began to wane by mid-century as visitors flocked to the newer hotels uptown.

26. Madame Reismer was probably modeled after the notorious Madame Restell, an abortionist who had her establishment on Greenwich Street. She was said to have been connected with the mysterious death of Mary Rogers in 1842, upon which Poe based his story "The Mystery of Marie Roget."

2. THE EMERGING METROPOLIS

1. The house referred to still stands at 7 State Street, between Pearl and Whitehall streets. Built as a private residence in 1793, it eventually became the Mission of Our Lady of the Rosary, a home for Irish immigrant girls. The house, with its curved porch and Ionic columns, is believed to have been designed by John McComb, one of the architects of city hall. As for State Street, bordering on Battery Park and lined with the fine homes of the city's merchant princes, it was New York's most fashionable street until the beginning of the nineteenth century when residents began moving uptown.

2. When the quarters on Wall Street proved inadequate, the new city hall was built on what had been the City Commons. The cost of the building, with its French Renaissance and Georgian influences, was a prohibitive half-million dollars, and in order to reduce expenditures, sandstone was substituted for marble in the rear of the structure.

3. In 1852, Tweed began his political career as alderman of the seventh ward and quickly rose to a position of enormous power, controlling all civic affairs in the state and city. Involved for many years in theft, graft, and blackmail, he was finally indicted in 1871, and justice was served at last when, after a succession of trials, he was convicted and sentenced to prison on Blackwell's Island and later in Ludlow Street jail, where he died in 1878.

4. In *New Year's Day* Wharton refers to the fact that the Fifth Avenue Hotel was often frequented by politicians and Westerners. Indeed, it was the meeting place for politicians and statesmen from all over the country prior to and during the Civil War. The elegant marble hotel, built by Amos R. Eno in 1859, was referred to as "Eno's Folly" in its early days because of its uptown location.

5. James's use of the word "capital" is puzzling since New York City ceased being the federal capital in 1788 and state capital in 1796.

6. The popular Taylor's, located at 365 Broadway, at the corner of Franklin Street, was a large and elegant restaurant. There was a "ladies' saloon" on one floor, where unescorted female shoppers could rest and refresh themselves; downstairs was a dining room for men, where the fare was heartier.

7. Once an attractive residential street, Courtlandt Street was quickly transformed into a commercial area when in 1851 it was widened ten feet between Broadway and Greenwich Street. All the buildings on the south side of the street were demolished, and the usual procedure of business enterprises gradually buying out residents was bypassed. There was a quick influx of dry-goods firms into Courtlandt Street and nearby Dey Street, which was also widened in 1851.

8. Grace Church was famous, among other reasons, for its forty-six medieval stained-glass windows.

9. Delmonico's Restaurant, which catered to an elite clientele, was originally located on Beaver Street. A branch was opened on Madison Square, and later on Fifth Avenue and Forty-fourth Street.

10. The St. Nicholas, located at Broadway and Broome Street, was a luxurious, large hotel, able to accommodate over eight hundred guests; constructed at a cost of one million dollars, it had central heating, which when it opened in 1853 was an unusual feature.

11. The Astor Place Opera House, located on the corner of Astor Place and Clinton Street—which later became Eighth Street—was rebuilt after the riot of 1849, but is no longer extant. The Broadway Theatre, located at 485 Broadway, near Broome Street, underwent numerous changes of name, being known successively as Brougham's Lyceum, Wallack's Lyceum, the Broadway Music Hall, the New York Athenaeum, Mary Provost's Theatre, and finally the Broadway Theatre.

12. Howells, who was born and raised in Ohio, lived for a time in Venice and spent twenty-odd years in Boston and Cambridge before coming to live in New York.

13. This theme is common in the fiction of the period. Some other novels about writers who come to New York in the latter part of the nineteenth century to make a name for themselves in the literary or publishing fields are Bayard Taylor's *John Godfrey's Fortunes,* Henry Harland's *Grandison Mather,* and Brander Matthew's *A Confident Tomorrow.*

14. Life among painters seeking fame and fortune in the city is also a common theme in the literature of this period. One novel treating this theme is Stephen Crane's *The Third Violet,* which is about a group of struggling artists living in dilapidated rooms in an old building in a business section of the city, and is probably based on Crane's own experiences when he lived for a time on East Twenty-third Street with a group of artists.

15. *In Old New York,* Thomas Janvier describes the Greenwich Village of the 1880s as "the distinctly American quarter of New York," explaining that

a sprinkling of French and Italians is found within these limits, together with the few Irish required for political purposes; and in the vicinity of Carmine Street are scattered some of the tents of the children of Ham. But with these exceptions, the population is composed of substantial, well-to-do Americans....This American quarter of New York is a liberal lesson in cleanliness, good citizenship, and self-respect.

16. The "colossal lady on Bedloe's Island" is, of course, the Statue of Liberty, whose torch lit the entrance to New York for the first time on July 4, 1884, and hence was puzzling to the "ghosts of eighteenth-century fashion." As for the elevated railroad, that too was a recent innovation, built in an attempt to alleviate traffic jams on streets filled with horse-drawn streetcars, omnibuses, private carriages, and drays. The first El, built on Greenwich Street and extending for a little more than half a mile, had its first experimental run in 1868, and by 1876, the track covered a distance of some five miles from the Battery to Central Park. By 1880 the Els on the East and West sides of town had been built, extending all the way up to the Harlem River.

17. In Wharton's novel *The Buccaneers,* Mrs. St. George laments the fact that her husband has built their house on Madison Avenue rather than on Fifth. She is especially dismayed when she must give her address to fashionable shopkeepers, who "classed their customers at once, and Madison Avenue stood at best for decent mediocrity," while Fifth Avenue stood for elegance.

18. Although a bid was made to lay horsecar tracks along Fifth Avenue, the move was blocked, and streetcars were banned in favor of the higher, more gaily decorated, and fashionable omnibuses. Drawn by teams of horses, and equipped with sleigh runners instead of wheels when there was snow on the ground, these vehicles offered passengers a better view than the streetcars did and were thought to enhance the appearance of New York's most elegant street.

3. THE GAY NINETIES

1. There is an interesting anecdote about how the vice-ridden Tenderloin district got its name. When Police Captain Alexander Williams was assigned to the Twenty-ninth Precinct, where there was more graft than anywhere else in the city, he said that he'd had nothing but chuck for a long time and now he was going to get some of the tenderloin.

2. Considered part of the Tenderloin, but actually located a few blocks south at Sixth Avenue and Thirtieth Street, the Haymarket was notorious for its gambling, drinking, and prostitution. The boundaries of the Tenderloin were from Thirty-fifth Street on the south to Forty-ninth Street on the north and from Fifth Avenue on the east to Ninth Avenue on the west.

3. Acquired by the city in 1828, Blackwell's Island soon became the site of a prison that achieved great notoriety for its filth, mismanagement, and corruption. During the nineteen thirties, the obsolete buildings were razed, and the prisoners were transferred to new quarters on Riker's Island.

4. Washington Mews was known as Stable Alley until the twentieth century, when its stables, which once housed horses belonging to the wealthy Washington Square residents, were converted into dwellings. With its cobblestone streets and charmingly renovated homes, it is one of New York's quaintest streets.

5. The Astor Library, an Italian Renaissance building that faced Colonnade Row, was completed in several stages: the south wing in 1853; the center wing in 1859; and the north wing in 1881. From 1921 to 1965 the building was the headquarters for HIAS, the Hebrew Immigrant Aid Sheltering Society; it then became the home of the New York Shakespeare Festival.

6. Dreiser, who wrote *Sister Carrie* while living at 6 West 102nd Street, knew the Upper West Side well. His familiarity with that area and with other of New York's neighborhoods is apparent not only in his novels but also in the nonfictional *The Color of A Great City*.

7. The Moorish-designed Casino on Thirty-ninth Street and Broadway, which opened in 1882, was famous for it chorus, which included Lillian Russell, and for the millionaires in its audience, many of whom married the chorus girls. It was known by several names, including "Home of the Casino Girls," "The Gilded Temple of Golden Youth," and "Home of the Seventy Maidens Who Married Millionaires." The Empire, at Broadway and Fortieth Street, was located farther uptown than most theatres were during this period.

8. The elegant Waldorf, completed in 1893, was on Fifth Avenue, between Thirty-third and Thirty-fourth streets. Some years later, a connecting hotel, the Astoria, was built and the whole complex came to be known as the Waldorf-Astoria. In 1929, the old Waldorf-Astoria was demolished to make way for the Empire State Building, and its present location is on Park Avenue, between Forty-ninth and Fiftieth streets. The Hotel Wellington is located on Seventh Avenue and Fifty-fifth Street.

9. Although the Brooklyn Bridge was completed in 1883, the Fulton Ferry continued service until 1903, when the Williamsburg Bridge was opened.

10. The "white light district" in the above quotation refers to the brilliantly lit theatre district, which during the nineties was more commonly known as "the Gay White Way" and after the turn of the century as "the Great White Way."

11. Macdougal Alley, a cul-de-sac located a half block north of Washington Square and running east from Macdougal Street, is one of the city's few alleyways surviving from the last century. Like Washington Mews, it was once lined with carriage houses and stables, which were eventually converted into quaint studios. Entered through an iron gate, it became home for many writers and artists, among them the sculptor Jo Davidson.

12. Like Eugene, Dreiser was for a time a Greenwich Village resident. He lived at 165 West 10th Street, 16 St. Luke's Place, and 118th West 11th Street.

13. In the above passage Dreiser refers to the building of a subway in New York. The city's first subway line was opened in 1904.

4. FROM SHTETL TO SWEATSHOP

1. For many years the offices of the *Jewish Daily Forward* were located at 175 East Broadway, but in 1974 the building was sold to a Chinese-American organization and the *Forward* moved uptown.

2. Many of the cafés on the Lower East Side, like the Odessa on East Broadway, were named after cities in Europe, and each had its own following. The intelligentsia, for example, gathered at the Café Royal on Second Avenue and Twelfth Street. In *The Rise of David Levinsky* Cahan writes about Yampolsky's, where the clientele drank glasses of Russian tea, played chess, and carried on lengthy conversations.

3. The *cheder,* or Hebrew school—this one located in the Grodno Synagogue on Hester Street—is presented in a negative light not only by Ornitz but also by many other writers of the period, who repeatedly described it as dank and gloomy in contrast to the bright and clean public schools.

4. In the above quotation, Bullard refers to a "Raines Law" hotel. Many such "hotels" sprang up in New York when in 1897 the Raines Law was passed prohibiting saloons to sell alcoholic beverages on Sunday. The legislation, however, permitted hotel patrons to have liquor served with their meals, and so many saloons became "hotels," serving a "Raines Law sandwich" with each drink.

5. Tall office buildings began to be seen in New York in the 1870s, and by the 1890s there were "skyscrapers" like the New York *World*'s sixteen-story building on Park Row, opposite City Hall. Legend has it that a visitor getting off the elevator on the newly opened World Building's top floor loudly asked, "Is God in?"

6. By 1880 there were over two hundred Jewish congregations in the United States, and all but a few were Reform. Under the leadership of Rabbi Isaac Wise, the Union of American Hebrew Congregations had been established in 1873; the Hebrew Union College in Cincinnati had been opened in 1875; and it appeared certain that American Judaism would continue in the direction of Reform. With the influx of great numbers of Eastern European Jews, however, many Orthodox synagogues sprang up on the Lower East Side and elsewhere in the city. The oldest Reform synagogue in New York City is Temple Emanu-El, founded in 1845 by German Jews.

5. SKYSCRAPER CITY

1. Bayrd Still, *Mirror for Gotham: New York as Seen by Contemporaries from Dutch Days to the Present* (New York: New York University Press, 1956), p. 257.

2. The "Biggest Store" is probably Siegal-Cooper, established in New York in the 1890s and known as "The Big Store—A City in Itself." The block-long six-story building on Sixth Avenue, between Eighteenth and Nineteenth streets, had as its slogan "Everything Under the Sun" and was even bigger than Macy's.

3. The New York *Herald* was probably the paper that Dulcie bought for the personal column, which appeared on the front page of the classified section. James Bennett, Jr., who ran the paper after his father's death, came under attack from the pulpit and the public when it became known that the column afforded prostitutes a way to advertise their services.

4. Although the store's name and location are different—probably deliberately changed by the author, who had a habit of altering details to avoid positive identification of particular places—it seems probable that O. Henry had in mind William M. Oliffe's drugstore, which was established in 1805. Located at No. 6, The Bowery, it was one of the oldest and best stocked pharmacies in the city, and many uptown residents travelled long distances to have their prescriptions filled there.

5. Opened in 1903, the Williamsburg Bridge, designed by L.L. Buck, was the second to span the East River.

228 / NOTES

6. Reisenweber's Restaurant, located in the Columbus Circle area, was credited with initiating the cover charge on Broadway in 1916.

7. Although Flo's statement about Brooklyn is somewhat exaggerated, it is true that in the early years of the twentieth century the Fulton Street area was a thriving business, entertainment, and municipal center that provided employment for large numbers of the borough's residents.

8. Brooklyn Heights remained an exclusive neighborhood until 1908, when the IRT opened the area to commuters. At that time many well-to-do old families moved out, and their houses were converted into apartments and studios.

9. The "new" Madison Square Garden referred to by Cather is the Stanford White building completed in 1890, the tower of which was copied from the Giralda in Spain and topped with a statue of Diana by Augustus Saint-Gaudens. When *My Mortal Enemy* was published in 1926, it was already the "old" Madison Square Garden since a new building had been erected a year earlier on Eighth Avenue, between Forty-ninth and Fiftieth streets, but because Cather's novel is set in the 1890s the Stanford White building could still be described as "new."

As for Madison Square, it had seen its best days in the 1870s and 1880s when it was a fashionable center lined with fine residences, hotels, and restaurants. By the 1890s it was being invaded by trade, and by the turn of the century many office buildings, including the Metropolitan Life Insurance Company's headquarters on Madison Avenue and 23rd Street, had been established there.

10. Jean de Reszke was the leading tenor of the Metropolitan Opera from 1891 to 1903, and Sarah Bernhardt played Hamlet at the Theatre Sarah Bernhardt, which she herself managed, in 1895.

11. The arch mentioned by Cather is the Washington Arch, which was completed in 1895. Designed by Stanford White, it stands at the foot of Fifth Avenue. Cather also mentions the removal of the Fifth Avenue horsecars from service. Although motor buses were introduced on the Fifth Avenue line at the turn of the century, the horsecars remained in operation until 1907.

12. Built on Fifth Avenue at Ninth Street in 1854, the sedate Brevoort was known for its intellectual and cosmopolitan clientele.

13. Glasgow's acquaintance with London Terrace was through her friend Van Wyck Brooks, who lived in one of the Greek Revival row houses designed by Alexander Jackson Davis. Built in 1845, these houses were demolished in the 1920s and replaced by apartment buildings bearing the same name.

14. The Princeton Club was located at 39 East Thirty-ninth Street and the Columbia Club at 4 West Forty-third Street. The National Arts still stands at 15 Gramercy Park South (its original site), housed in a Victorian mansion that was once the home of Mayor Samuel Tilden, and so also does the Players, its neighbor at No. 16, founded in 1888 by Edwin Booth.

Stuyvesant Square, extending from Fifteenth to Seventeenth streets, between Rutherford and Perlman places, was once part of the farm owned by Peter Stuyvesant. Rutherford Place, on the west side of the square, has long been associated with the Society of Friends, and the Quaker school referred to by Lewis is the Friend's Seminary.

15. Lewis's reference to Newspaper Row is to Park Row and its environs, which from the 1840s until after the turn of the century was where most of the city's newspapers had their offices.

16. Since 1903 the New York Stock Exchange has been located on Broad Street, but until the opening of the New York Curb Exchange on nearby Trinity Place in 1921, some stock transactions were conducted outdoors on the sidewalk. It was not uncommon in the early years of the century to see brokers standing on Broad Street, making buying or selling signals to their colleagues inside the building.

17. The Vanderbilts lived on Fifth Avenue at Fifty-second Street, the Whitneys on Fifth Avenue at Fifty-seventh Street, and the Guggenheims on Fifth Avenue at Sixty-fourth Street. The Frick mansion, now a museum, is located on Fifth Avenue, between Seventieth and Seventy-first streets.

6. THE ROARING TWENTIES

1. Bayrd Still, *Mirror for Gotham: New York as Seen by Contemporaries from Dutch Days to the Present* (New York: New York University Press, 1956), pp. 292-293.

2. Alfred Kazin, "The Writer in the City," *Harpers Magazine,* 237 (1968), p. 122.

3. The Biltmore, where F. Scott and Zelda Fitzgerald spent their honeymoon, until they were asked to leave because of disruptive behavior, was located on Forty-third Street and Vanderbilt Avenue. The newly built Commodore Hotel, also patronized by the Fitzgeralds, was on East Forty-Second Street, adjacent to Grand Central Station and not far from the Yale Club, located at 50 Vanderbilt Avenue.

4. The Coconut Grove was a nightclub in the Park Central Hotel at Seventh Avenue and Fifty-fifth Street.

5. The Ritz referred to by Fitzgerald was in all likelihood the exclusive Ritz-Carlton, located at Madison Avenue and Forty-sixth Street.

6. Fitzgerald's growing disillusionment with New York is probably best depicted in "My Lost City," written in 1932 and published thirteen years later in *The Crack-up.*

7. While it is not feasible to comment on all the places mentioned by Van Vechten in the above passages, some comment is in order about a number of restaurants that were New York institutions in the Gay Nineties, when the theatre district was centered about Longacre Square (later called Times Square).

Shanley's, an elegant and richly appointed "lobster palace," was an overnight sensation and became known far and wide for its after-theatre dinners and good music. Even more opulent than Shanley's was Rector's. Associated with Diamond Jim Brady, it was considered the "in" place to be. At night there were long lines of carriages lined up on Broadway waiting to discharge passengers—many of them luminaries who were seated in the "inner circle." So well-known was Rector's that Paul Potter wrote a play entitled "The Girl from Rector's."

Another famous Broadway restaurant was John Dunston's, better known as Jack's. Its reputation was not based on its elegance or polish, but rather on its lavish portions. Jack's was considered an excellent place to breakfast after a night on the town.

8. Among other meeting places in the Village were the Golden Swan, otherwise known as Hell Hole, the Black Knight, the Purple Purp, Luke O'Connors, Romany Marie's, and the Jumble Shop.

9. The Astor Hotel, which opened in 1904 on Times Square, between Forty-fourth and Forty-fifth streets, was a landmark for over sixty years. A fifty-story office building now occupies the site. The nearby Hotel Algonquin, built in 1902 on West Forty-fourth Street, is still in existence and has retained its decades-old reputation as a hotel for writers and actors.

The Ansonia, located further uptown on Broadway and Seventy-third Street, was, at the turn of the century, one of the city's most opulent hotels. Built in the elegant French Beaux-Arts style, the Ansonia has over the years catered to many stars of the musical world, including Enrico Caruso, Mischa Elman, Enzio Pinza, Igor Stravinsky, and Arturo Toscanini. Designated a New York City landmark in 1972, the Ansonia is at present run-down and neglected.

The Hotel Lafayette on University Place and Ninth Street was, like the Brevoort, a gathering place for intellectuals, both American and European, and was known for its excellent French cuisine. While Huyler's, a restaurant chain established in Manhattan in 1876, was hardly in the class with these famed hotels, it did have a rather fine reputation for its soda-fountain specialties.

10. St. Patrick's, the first major cathedral in America to be built in the Gothic Revival style, was designed by James Renwick. The nave, begun in 1858, was not open for worship until 1877; the cathedral itself was dedicated in 1879. St. Patrick's occupies the entire block on Fifth Avenue between Fiftieth and Fifty-first streets.

11. The Gashouse District was located in the region near the East River between Fourteenth and Twenty-seventh streets. Ever since 1842, when the first gashouse was built on East Twenty-first Street, the threat of leaking gas made the region both an unhealthy and an undesirable one. The city's poor, first the Irish and later the Germans and Jews, lived in tenement houses in this slum area dominated for more than half a century by gangs of young hoodlums.

12. During the 1920s, Second Avenue from Houston Street to Fourteenth Street was called the Yiddish Rialto. Today, there remains little to attest to this flourishing period in Yiddish theatre. All the old playhouses, with the exception of the Eden (once known as the Rialto) on East Twelfth Street, have either been demolished or left vacant.

13. The Heckscher Building, mentioned in the opening paragraph of Flanner's novel, was once the home of the *American Mercury*. At one time the publishing firm of Alfred A. Knopf also had its offices there.

14. The smallest of the city's three major-league ballparks and the home of the Brooklyn Dodgers, Ebbetts Field, on Bedford Avenue and Sullivan Place in Brooklyn, was built in 1912. At present it is the site of an apartment-house complex.

15. Grant's Tomb is located on Riverside Drive near 122nd Street. The sepulcher, designed by J.H. Duncan, was completed in 1897.

16. Located on Broadway, near Forty-ninth Street, the Winter Garden, which opened in 1911, featured vaudeville revues. Among its famed performers was the young Al Jolson, who appeared in its first show and on many subsequent occasions. The Winter Garden was known for its girls, who as early as 1914 shocked New Yorkers when they appeared on stage with bare legs and naked midriffs.

17. The reference is of course, to the Ziegfeld *Follies,* the first of which opened in 1907. Known for its girls and its lavish sets, the *Follies* was the most famous of New York's "leg-shows."

7. THE HARLEM RENAISSANCE

1. An article appearing in the October 23, 1929, edition of the *Amsterdam News* listed eleven "white trade" nightclubs and claimed that there were over five hundred Negro cabarets in Harlem at this time.

2. Known as America's wealthiest black woman, Mme. C.J. Walker was a laundress before she invented the hair-straightening process that made her a millionaire. In 1913 she built a mansion on 136th Street and several years later an estate at Irvington-on-the-Hudson. Her daughter A'Lelia Walker Robinson was Harlem's foremost hostess, and at one time used part of her house as a café—called "The Dark Tower"—where the black intelligentsia could meet to discuss ideas and to make contacts with influential whites.

3. During the early decades of the twentieth century, many beautiful Harlem churches once serving affluent white congregations were sold to black denominations. The church mentioned by McKay appears to have been one of the last remaining white churches in the area.

4. Fisher lived at 2816 Eighth Avenue, in the fashionable Paul Laurence Dunbar apartment-house complex. Named after the black poet, the six buildings were grouped around a central garden and took up an entire city block.

5. Beauty shops were among the few Harlem businesses owned by blacks at this time, and their proprietors were among the area's wealthiest residents.

6. The white-owned Cotton Club, located on Lenox Avenue and 142nd Street, was famous for its "high yaller" chorus line. Its clientele, which included socialites and gangsters, was probably the most exclusive of all the Harlem nightclubs, and bouncers were stationed at the door to keep out blacks. It was not, however, the largest of the "white-trade" clubs in Harlem. That distinction went to Small's Paradise, on 136th Street and Seventh Avenue, which today is owned by former basketball star Wilt Chamberlain.

7. The internationally famous Savoy, located on Lenox Avenue and 140th Street, was the dance hall where the Lindy Hop was said to have originated. Many famous Negro orchestras—including those of Cab Calloway, Louis Armstrong, and Duke Ellington—played here.

8. Most of the Harlem renaissance writers, including Thurman, whose address was 267 West 137th Street, lived in this area.

9. Thurman's reference is to St. Philip's Protestant Episcopal Church, reputed to be the most exclusive Negro church in the city.

10. St. Marks was one of several black churches that owned real estate in Harlem prior to World War I. These churches continued to purchase apartment buildings after the war and by renting to Negroes helped to transform Harlem into a black neighborhood.

11. Larson, like her character Irene Redfield, was married to a Harlem physician. They lived at 236 West 135th Street.

8. THE GREAT DEPRESSION

1. Klein's remained in business on Union Square until 1975, long after Hearn's, Orbach's, Lerner's, and other large stores in the once flourishing retail area had either gone out of business or moved uptown. At present there are plans under way to redevelop the Klein's property, which has been boarded up for some six years, and to revitalize the neighborhood.

2. Wolfe lived for a time in Cobble Hill—on Veranda Place, a mews off Clinton Street, between Congress and Warren.

3. Wallabout Market, at Flushing and Clinton avenues in the Navy Yard area, was a vast wholesale produce market with two-story Dutch-style buildings grouped around a plaza known as Farmer's Square. Its name was probably derived from nearby Wallabout Bay.

4. Lundy's, located opposite Sheepshead Bay on Ocean and Emmons avenues, was for over sixty years Brooklyn's most famous seafood-restaurant. Recently, however, it closed its doors, and at the time of this writing the future of the huge and elaborate dining emporium remained uncertain.

5. During the 1930s there were over seventy Orthodox synagogues in Brownsville. The oldest of these, Beth Hamidrish Hagadal, was organized in 1889 and was located at 337 Sackman Street.

6. Comprised of a playground and an athletic field, Betsy Head Park covers 10.41 acres. The playground, which was dedicated in 1915, is bounded by Blake, Hopkinson, Dumont, and Livonia avenues and Strauss Street.

7. Located on Eastern Parkway and Washington Avenue, the Brooklyn Museum was constructed in four sections between 1897 and 1925 at a cost of $3,300,300. Adjacent to it is the Botanic Gardens, founded in 1910, which occupies fifty acres and is perhaps best known for its lovely Japanese Garden.

8. A more detailed description of the "old" neighborhood can be found in Weidman's novel *Fourth Street East*.

9. Although at the time of this writing only two Automats were left in New York— one on Third Avenue at Forty-second Street and the other on Thirty-third Street and Eighth Avenue—in 1933 there were forty of them. Established in 1912, the Automats served thousands of New Yorkers each day and attracted visitors from all over the world. Today only the Automat on Third Avenue, which was recently restored to its Art Deco splendor, has coin-operated windows, but in the thirties all of them did. Prices were cheap in those days, and cashiers dispensed nickels to customers who could buy a meal for as little as thirty or thirty-five cents.

10. The garment center described by Weidman extends from Thirtieth to Forty-second streets, between Sixth and Ninth avenues. It is a highly congested area, and the traffic is notoriously slow. The curbs are lined with trucks, loading and unloading; racks of garments are wheeled about; and throngs of factory employees fill the streets.

11. In the above quotation, Meriwether is referring to the noisy and colorful municipal market located under the New York Central and New Haven elevated railroad
tracks between 110th and 116th streets.
12. Located at 132 West 138th Street, the Abyssinian Baptist Church, founded in
1908, is the city's oldest and most influential black church. Both Adam Clayton
Powell and his father were preachers there.
13. The fifteen-cent chicken dinner was probably obtained at 152 West 126th
Street, the location of one of several "Kingdoms" of Father Divine, where cheap
meals and lodgings were always available. Believed by thousands to be God in the
flesh, Father Divine was an important and influential Harlem figure during the
1930s.
14. Both Sardi's and the Algonquin, known for their literary and theatrical clientele,
are located on West Forty-fourth Street. Built in 1902, the Algonquin is best remembered for its Round Table, a group of luminaries including Dorothy Parker, James
Thurber, and Robert Benchley who met there for lunch daily, first in the Pergolah
(now Oak) Room and later in the Rose Room. The round table at which they sat
and which gave the group its name can still be seen in the Oak Room.
15. More than a few of the speakeasies listed by O'Hara were controlled by the mob
during the thirties. The Hotsy-Totsy had a particularly bloody history and was the
scene of many murders. On one occasion ten bystanders were killed in order to avoid
their possibly giving testimony regarding a mob-related gun battle that took place
there.

As for speakeasies named Tony's, there were many that went by that name
although only two are mentioned in the quotation.
16. During the 1930s the highest concentration of speakeasies could be found on
West Fifty-second Street, between Fifth and Sixth avenues, where many relocated
after Rockefeller's purchase of the buildings between West Forty-eighth and Fifty-
first streets, the site of the projected Rockefeller Center. Twenty-one was one of
those that moved from West Forty-ninth Street, where it was known as the Grotto,
to 21 West Fifty-second Street, thus acquiring its new name.

One anecdote attesting to the reputation of West Fifty-second Street during the
thirties deals with the owner of a brownstone who put up a sign reading: "This is
not an illicit resort." Later, when the word "not" had been obliterated, he replaced
the sign with one that read, "This is a *private* residence. Do not ring!"
17. While Washington Mews and Macdougal Alley have already been discussed, a
few words about Patchin Place are in order. Directly opposite the Jefferson Market
Courthouse (now a public library) on West Tenth Street and Sixth Avenue, it is a
tree-lined cul-de-sac which with its charming row houses is reminiscent of an old
London street. Such famous authors as Theodore Dreiser, John Masefield, Eugene
O'Neil, and e.e. cummings lived there during Greenwich Village's bohemian years.
18. Located at 300 Central Park West, the El Dorado, a large orange-colored Art
Deco apartment building, was once the home of Sinclair Lewis.

9. WORLD WAR II AND ITS AFTERMATH

1. The seventy-seven-story Chrysler Building on East Forty-second Street was
completed in 1929 and until the opening of the Empire State Building in 1931 was
the tallest structure in the world. Its most distinctive features are its needlelike Art
Deco spire and its automotive motifs.
2. The bronze and gilt equestrian statue of General William Tecumseh Sherman,
which was placed in Grand Army Plaza in 1903, is the work of Augustus Saint-
Gaudens. The "nude lady" referred to in the same quotation is a component of the
nearby Pulitzer Memorial entitled the *Fountain of Abundance*. The work of Karl
Bitter, the bronze female figure holding a basket of fruit stands on a pedestal in the
top basin of the fountain.

3. Following the 1895 merger of the Astor, Tilden, and Lenox libraries, various grants and endowments made possible the construction of the New York City Public Library Building on Fifth Avenue and Forty-second Street, once the site of the Croton Reservoir. Completed in 1911 at a cost of nine million dollars, the library is second in size only to the Library of Congress.

4. Completed in 1913 on the Park Avenue site of Cornelius Vanderbilt's old railroad depot, the Grand Central Terminal is a huge structure extending from Forty-second to Forty-fifth streets. It was designed by Whitney Warren and James A. Wetmore, together with engineers Reed and Stem, and one of its most distinctive architectural features is the vaulted ceiling of its main concourse referred to by Marquand. Supported by 125-foot-high piers, the ceiling is decorated with illuminated constellations of the zodiac, but because of an error in painting, the ecliptic of the zodiac runs the wrong way.

5. The fifty-three story Lincoln Building at 60 East Forty-second Street was built in 1929-30. There are quotes from Lincoln's speeches on the vestibule walls, and a bronze statue of the President dominates the center of the lobby.

6. The Duke mansion at 1 East Seventy-eighth Street was built along Millionaire's Row by the industrialist James B. Duke, who made his fortune in tobacco. In 1958 it was donated by Mrs. Duke to New York University's Institute of Fine Arts. The Frick Museum, formerly the home of Henry C. Frick, the steel magnate, is located at 1 East Seventieth Street on the site of the Lenox Library. The 110-room mansion, designed by Carrère and Hastings and completed in 1914, was opened as a museum in 1935. Nine blocks south at 2 East Sixty-first Street is the sumptuous Pierre Hotel. Completed in 1930, it followed the postwar trend and became a cooperative apartment hotel some years later. Certain rooms continue to be available for transient guests, and restaurants and other facilities are open to the public.

7. Its main entrance on Amsterdam Avenue at 112th Street, the Cathedral of St. John the Divine is the largest Gothic cathedral in the world and dominates the Morningside Heights plateau.

8. Quoted from the book jacket of the first edition of *Last Exit to Brooklyn.*

9. Brooklyn's largest and best-known park, Prospect Park contains more than five hundred acres; it is bounded by Prospect Park West, Prospect Park Southwest, and Ocean, Flatbush, and Parkside avenues. Most of the land was purchased by the city in 1859 from the Litchfield estate, and development, under the direction of James S.T. Stranahan and his commission, was begun in 1866.

10. The old McGraw-Hill Building at 330 West Forty-second Street was built in 1930 with a particularly innovative exterior using horizontal bands of aqua terracotta tile.

11. Gage and Tollner's is a landmark restaurant established in 1879 and still operating at 374 Fulton Street in Brooklyn.

12. Nedick's, one of New York's first fast-food chains, and Longchamps are still in existence, and although greatly diminished in number, an occasional Schrafft's restaurant can still be found in the city. Stouffer's, once occupying the ground floor at 666 Fifth Avenue, closed several years ago, but the Top of the Sixes at the same address is currently under the ownership of Stouffer's.

10. THE CONTEMPORARY SCENE

1. The Bronx Zoo, founded in 1895, is the nation's largest zoo and one of the city's major tourist attractions. Along with the New York Botanical Garden, it is part of 750-acre Bronx Park, located in the central Bronx.

2. Singer, whose association with the *Jewish Daily Forward* began in 1935, was known to frequent the Garden cafeteria on East Broadway at Rutgers Street. Still in existence, it was one of several local restaurants patronized by the Yiddish journalists who worked in the nearby *Forward* offices.

3. Verdi Square, which is located directly north of where Broadway and Amsterdam Avenue cross each other at West Seventy-second Street, is dominated by a large marble statue of the composer standing on a pedestal, flanked by four life-size figures of characters from his operas. Sculpted by Pasquale Civiletti, the monument was erected in 1906.

4. Bellow appears to have made a mistake in stating that the French Beaux-Arts-style hotel, which opened at the turn of the century, was designed by Stanford White. The architect was Henry J. Hardenberg, who also designed the Plaza Hotel.

5. Among the movie houses mentioned by Salinger, the Capitol is particularly noteworthy. When it opened in 1919 on Broadway and 51st Street, it was the largest such building in the world and ushered in the era of motion-picture palaces in New York.

6. The site presently occupied by the Biltmore Hotel was once used as a pasture for Maud S., the famed trotter owned by William H. Vanderbilt, the head of the New York Central Railroad, who enjoyed watching the horse grazing from the window of his office. At the time of this writing the 68-year-old-hotel at 55 East Forty-third Street has closed and is scheduled for demoliton. One of the most famous features of the 900 room hotel is its clock, and most middle-aged New Yorkers are familiar with the saying, "Meet me under the clock at the Biltmore."

7. Officially opened by Rutherford Hayes in 1877, the Museum of Natural History is located on Central Park West from 77th to 81st Streets.

8. The exclusive Katharine Gibbs Secretarial School has its Manhattan headquarters at 200 Park Avenue. There are now branches in Long Island, New Jersey and Connecticut.

9. Designed by an international team of architects, the UN complex, located on the east side of First Avenue, north of Forty-second Street, has been the permanent headquarters of the United Nations since 1952. Its three main buildings are the Secretariat (1950), the General Assembly Building (1952), and the Dag Hammerskjold Library (1963). Along First Avenue, renamed United Nations Plaza, are displayed the flags of the member nations.

10. Built in 1963, the Pan Am Building, designed by Walter Gropius, Emery Roth & Sons, and Pietro Belluschi, met with much opposition. Concern was expressed about added traffic and congestion; the helicopter landing pad on the roof was thought by many to bring unnecessary danger to the area and to interfere with the view of Grand Central Terminal. The Park Avenue building, which until the construction of the World Trade Center provided more office space than any other structure in the world, has recently been sold to the Metropolitan Life Insurance Company for $400 million, said to be the highest price ever paid for a building.

11. While the Plaza has already been discussed, no special mention was earlier made of its famed Oak Room, a favorite luncheon spot for affluent New Yorkers. Legend has it that Frank Lloyd Wright once boasted that he saved the exquisitely panelled Oak Room from a fate worse than death—alteration. The aristocratic St. Regis on Fifth Avenue and 55th Street was built in 1904 and remained in control of the Astor family until the 1960s.

12. Named after the best-known German immigrant of the nineteenth century who held many important public offices and eventually settled in the German community of Yorkville, Carl Schurz Park overlooks the East River and extends from Gracie Square (East Eighty-fourth Street) to East Ninetieth Street. Located opposite Eighty-eighth Street is Gracie Mansion. Built in 1799 as the residence of Archibald Gracie and purchased by the city in 1887, it was used for several years as headquarters for the Museum of the City of New York before becoming the official residence of the mayor.

13. Bickford's is an inexpensive chain restaurant with branches at various New York locations.

14. Howard Thompson's is a thinly disguised reference to the Howard Johnson's on Eighth Street and Sixth Avenue that closed in 1973.

15. An Italian restaurant located on the corner of Bleecker and Macdougal streets, the San Remo was for many years one of the social centers of the Village. Its habitués included James Baldwin, William Styron, James Agee, Allen Ginsberg, Jack Kerouac, and other well-known authors. After 1950, the White Horse Tavern on Hudson and Eleventh Streets became a favorite hangout for such literary figures as Norman Mailer and Dylan Thomas.

16. The Harvard Club, located at 27 West Forty-fourth Street, is one of the city's many university clubs. The exclusive Knickerbocker Club, founded in 1871 by John Jacob Astor III and other affluent New Yorkers, is located in a red-brick Georgian building on Fifth Avenue and Sixty-second Street. The Racquet and Tennis Club, established in 1890, has been housed since 1918 at 370 Park Avenue in a Renaissance Revival building designed by Mekim, Mead, and White. One of the city's finest clubs, its membership once included the Duke of Windsor.

17. Located on "Millionaires' Row," along with the famed mansions of the Vanderbilts, Astors, and other prominent New York families, was the elaborate home of Montana's Senator William A. Clark, on Seventy-seventh Street. A copper tycoon, Clark was reputed to have built one of the most expensive residences in the entire city.

18. The bronze statue of the Civil War naval hero Admiral David Glasgow Farragut, which was unveiled in 1881, is the work of Augustus Saint-Gaudens. Its base was designed by Stanford White. The 478-acre Greenwood Cemetery, located in Brooklyn's Sunset Park area, with its main entrance on Fifth Avenue at Twenty-fifth Street, was opened in 1840. It is the final resting place of many famous New Yorkers, including Boss Tweed.

19. A facility of twenty-six buildings for retired seamen, Sailors' Snug Harbor, located on the northern shore of Staten Island overlooking the Kill Van Kull, was opened in 1833. It remained in operation until 1972, and at present the aging and neglected complex appears slated for a federal takeover.

20. Erasmus Hall High School, located on Flatbush Avenue, near Church Avenue, is still in use, although Garfield's cafeteria has long been gone, its site occupied by a bank. The Fabian Fox Theater on Flatbush Avenue at Nevins Street is also gone, but the Flatbush Boys' Club is still in existence at 2245 Bedford Avenue, and so is Loew's Metropolitan at Fulton and Jay streets.

21. E.B. White. *Here is New York* (New York: Harper & Brothers, 1949), pp. 53-54.

BIBLIOGRAPHY

SELECTED STORIES, SKETCHES, AND NOVELS
DEPICTING NEW YORK CITY

Asch, Sholem. *East River.* 1946.
Auchincloss, Louis. *The Great World and Timothy Colt.* 1956.
———. *The House of Five Talents.* 1960.
———. *The Partners.* 1974.
———. *Portrait in Brownstone.* 1962.
———. *Powers of Attorney.* 1963.
———. *Tales of Manhattan.* 1967.
———. *The World of Profit.* 1968.
Baldwin, James. *Another Country.* 1962.
———. *Go Tell It on the Mountain.* 1953.
———. "This Morning, This Evening, So Soon." In *Atlantic Monthly.* (September 1960).
Barrett, Laurence. *The Mayor of New York.* 1965.
Bell, Thomas. *All Brides Are Beautiful.* 1936.
Bellow, Saul. *Herzog.* 1964.
———. *Mr. Sammler's Planet.* 1965.
———. *Seize the Day.* 1956.
———. *The Victim.* 1947.
Breslin, Jimmy. *The Gang that Couldn't Shoot Straight.* 1969.
Brown, Rosellen. *Street Games.* 1974.
Bullard, Arthur. *Comrade Yetta.* 1913.
Bunner, H.C. *The Midge.* 1886.
———. *Jersey Street and Jersey Lane: Urban and Suburban Sketches.* 1896.
———. *The Story of a New York House.* 1887.
Cahan, Abraham. *The Imported Bridegroom and Other Stories of the New York Ghetto.* 1898.
———. *The Rise of David Levinsky.* 1917.
———. *Yekl: A Tale of the New York Ghetto.* 1896.
Cather, Willa. "Coming, Aphrodite!" In *Youth and the Bright Medusa.* 1920.
———. *My Mortal Enemy.* 1926.
———. *The Song of the Lark.* 1915.

Calisher, Hortense. *The New Yorker.* 1969.
Capote, Truman. *Breakfast at Tiffany's.* 1958.
Carter, Robert. *Manhattan Primitive.* 1971.
Chase, Ilka. *New York 22.* 1951.
Conley, Ellen Alexander. *Soho Madonna.* 1980.
Cooper, Kent. *Anna Zenger: Mother of Freedom.* 1946.
Cooper, James Fenimore. *Home as Found.* 1838.
———. *Homeward Bound.* 1838.
———. *Satanstoe.* 1845.
Crane, Stephen. *George's Mother.* 1896.
———. *Maggie: A Girl of the Streets.* 1892.
———. *The New York City Sketches of Stephen Crane and Related Pieces.* Eds. R.W. Stallman and E.R. Hagemann. 1966.
Crawford, F. Marion. *Katherine Lauderdale.* 1894.
———. *The Ralstons.* 1898.
Cullen, Countee. *One Way to Heaven.* 1932.
Davenport, Marcia. *East Side, West Side.* 1947.
Davis, Dorothy Salisbury. *Men of No Property.* 1956.
Davis, Richard Harding. *Van Bibber and Others.* 1892.
Dell, Floyd. *Love in Greenwich Village.* 1926.
Di Donato, Pietro. *Christ in Concrete.* 1939.
Dos Passos, John. *Manhattan Transfer.* 1925.
Dreiser, Theodore. *The Genius.* 1915.
———. *Sister Carrie.* 1900.
Ellison, Ralph. *Invisible Man.* 1952.
Faust, Irvin. *Roar Lion Roar and Other Stories.* 1965.
Fawcett, Edgar. *A New York Family.* 1891.
Fisher, Rudolph. *The Walls of Jericho.* 1938.
Fitzgerald, F. Scott. *The Beautiful and Damned.* 1922.
———. "The Freshest Boy." In *The Saturday Evening Post* (28 July 1928).
———. *The Great Gatsby.* 1925.
———. "May Day." In *The Smart Set* (July 1920).
———. "My Lost City." From *The Crack-Up.* 1945.
———. "The Rich Boy." In *The Red Book Magazine* (Jan.-Feb. 1926).
———. *This Side of Paradise.* 1920.
Flanner, Janet. *The Cubical City.* 1926.
Ford, Paul Leicester. *The Honorable Peter Stirling.* 1894.
Fuchs, Daniel. *Homage to Blenholt.* 1936.
———. *Low Company.* 1937.
———. *Summer in Williamsburg.* 1934.
Glasgow, Ellen. *Life and Gabriella.* 1916.
Green, Gerald. *To Brooklyn with Love.* 1967.
Godey, John. *The Taking of Pelham One Two Three.* 1973.
Gold, Michael. *Jews Without Money.* 1930.
Granit, Arthur, *The Time of the Peaches.* 1959.
Halper, Albert. *Union Square.* 1933.
Harland, Henry. *Grandison Mather.* 1890.
Henry, O. *The Four Million.* 1906.
———. *Strictly Business: More Stories of the Four Million.* 1911.
———. *The Voice of the City.* 1908.
Herlihy, James Lee. *Midnight Cowboy.* 1965.
Himes, Chester. *Pink Toes.* 1962.
Horowitz, Julius. *The City.* 1953.
Howells, William Dean. *The Coast of Bohemia.* 1893.
———. *A Hazard of New Fortunes.* 1890.
———. *Their Wedding Journey.* 1872.

———. *The World of Chance.* 1893.
Hughes, Langston. *The Ways of White Folks.* 1933.
Huneker, James. *Painted Veils.* 1920.
Irving, Washington. *A History of New York from the Beginning of the World to the End of the Dutch Dynasty.* 1809.
James, Henry. "Crapy Cornelia." In *Harper's Magazine* (Oct. 1909).
———. "The Jolly Corner." In *English Review* (Dec. 1908).
———. *Washington Square.* 1880.
Kaufman, Sue. *Dairy of a Mad Housewife.* 1967.
Kazin, Alfred. *A Walker in the City.* 1951.
Kyria, Pierre. *Manhattan Blues.* 1961.
Lardner, Ring. *The Big Town: How I and the Mrs. Go To New York To See Life And Get Katie A Husband.* 1925.
———. *Round Up: The Stories of Ring Lardner.* 1929.
Larson, Nella. *Passing.* 1929.
———. *Quicksand.* 1928.
Lewis, Sinclair. *The Job: An American Novel.* 1917.
Lewisohn, Ludwig. *The Island Within.* 1928.
Lippard, George. *New York: Its Upper Ten and Lower Million.* 1854.
Mailer, Norman. *The American Dream.* 1965.
———. *Barbary Shore.* 1951.
Malamud, Bernard. *The Assistant.* 1957.
———. *The Tenants.* 1971.
Markfield, Wallace. *Teitlebaum's Widow.* 1970.
Marquand, John P. *Point of No Return.* 1949.
———. *So Little Time.* 1943.
Marshall, Paule. *Brown Girl, Brownstones.* 1959.
Matthews, Brander. *A Confident Tomorrow.* 1899.
———. *Vignettes of Manhattan.* 1894.
———. *Vistas of New York.* 1912.
Maxwell, William. *Over by the River and Other Stories.* 1972.
McCarthy, Mary. *The Group.* 1954.
McKay, Claude. *Home to Harlem.* 1928.
McNulty, John. *Third Avenue, New York.* 1946.
Melville, Herman. "Bartleby the Scrivener." In *Putnam's Monthly Magazine* (Nov.-Dec. 1853).
———. "The Fiddler." In *Harper's Magazine* (Sept. 1854).
———. "Jimmy Rose." In *Harper's New Monthly Magazine* (Nov. 1855).
———. *Pierre: or the Ambiguities.* 1852.
———. "The Two Temples." In *The Complete Short Stories of Herman Melville.* Ed. Jay Leyda, 1949.
Meriwether, Louise. *Daddy Was a Number Runner.* 1970.
Miller, Henry. "The 14th Ward" and "The Tailor Shop." In *Black Spring.* 1936.
———. "The Ghetto (N.Y.)" and "Reunion in Brooklyn." In *The Henry Miller Reader.* Ed. Lawrence Durrell. 1959.
———. *Tropic of Capricorn.* 1939.
Miller, Warren. *The Cool World.* 1959.
Mohr, Nicholosa. *El Bronx Remembered: A Novella and Stories.* 1975.
Nathan, Robert. *One More Spring.* 1933.
Neugeboren, Jay. *Corky's Brother.* 1969.
———. *An Orphan's Tale.* 1976.
O'Hara, John. *Butterfield 8.* 1935.
Ornitz, Samuel. *Haunch, Paunch and Jowl.* 1923.
Oursler, Will. *N.Y., N.Y.* 1974.
Parent, Gail. *Sheila Levine is Dead and Living in New York.* 1972.
Patrick, Vincent. *The Pope of Greenwich Village.* 1980.

Petry, Ann. *The Street.* 1946.
Plath, Sylvia. *The Bell Jar.* 1963.
Poole, Ernest. *The Harbor.* 1915.
Porter, William Sydney. See Henry, O.
Potok, Chaim. *The Chosen.* 1967.
―――. *My Name Is Asher Lev.* 1972.
―――. *The Promise.* 1969.
Puzo, Mario. *The Fortunate Pilgrim.* 1965.
Rechy, John. *City of Night.* 1963.
Rosen, Isidore. *Will of Iron.* 1950.
Rossner, Judith. *Looking for Mr. Goodbar.* 1975.
Rosten, Norman. *Under the Boardwalk.* 1968.
Roth, Henry. *Call It Sleep.* 1934.
Rowson, Susanna. *Charlotte: A Tale of Truth.* 1791.
Runyon, Damon. *Guys and Dolls.* 1932.
―――. *More Guys and Dolls.* Intro. by Clark Kinnaird. 1951.
Salinger, J.D. *The Catcher in the Rye.* 1951.
―――. *Nine Stories.* 1953.
―――. "Raise High the Roof Beam, Carpenters." In *The New Yorker* (Nov. 19, 1955).
―――. "Seymour: An Introduction." In *The New Yorker* (June 6, 1959).
Selby, Hubert, Jr. *Last Exit to Brooklyn.* 1964.
Simpson, Louis. *Riverside Drive.* 1962.
Singer, Isaac Bashevis. *A Crown of Feathers.* 1973.
―――. *Enemies: A Love Story.* 1972.
―――. "The Séance." In *The Séance and Other Stories.* 1968.
―――. "Sam Palka and David Vishkover." In *Passions and Other Stories.* 1975.
Smith, Betty. *Maggie Now.* 1958.
―――. *Tomorrow Will Be Better.* 1948.
―――. *A Tree Grows in Brooklyn.* 1943.
Sorrentino, Gilbert. *Steelwork.* 1970.
Spark, Muriel. *The Hothouse by the East River.* 1973.
Stowman, Knud. *With Cradle and Clock.* 1946.
Styron, William. *Sophie's Choice.* 1979.
Taylor, Bayard. *John Godfrey's Fortunes.* 1865.
Thurman, Wallace. *The Blacker the Berry.* 1929.
Travis, Neal. *Manhattan.* 1979.
Van Vechten, Carl. *Nigger Heaven.* 1926.
―――. *Parties.* 1930.
―――. *Peter Whiffle.* 1922.
Wallant, Edward. *The Pawnbroker.* 1961.
―――. *The Tenants of Moonbloom.* 1963.
Warner, Charles Dudley. *The Golden House.* 1895.
―――. *A Little Journey into the World.* 1889.
―――. *That Fortune.* 1899.
Watson, Virginia. *Manhattan Acres.* 1934.
Weidman, Jerome. *Fourth Street East.* 1970.
―――. *I Can Get It for You Wholesale.* 1937.
―――. *Tiffany Street.* 1974.
West, Nathanael. *Miss Lonelyhearts.* 1933.
Wharton, Edith. *The Age of Innocence.* 1920.
―――. *The Buccaneers.* 1938.
―――. *The Custom of the Country.* 1913.
―――. *The House of Mirth.* 1905.
―――. *Old New York,* 4 vols., 1924.
Wilson, Edmund. "The Princess with the Golden Hair." In *Memoirs of Hecate County.* 1946.

Wolfe, Thomas. *Of Time and the River.* 1935.
———. "Only the Dead Know Brooklyn." In *The New Yorker* (June 15, 1935).
———. *The Web and the Rock.* 1939.
———. *You Can't Go Home Again.* 1940.
Wouk, Herman. *City Boy.* 1948.
———. *Marjorie Morningstar.* 1955.
Zara, Louis. *Blessed Is the Land.* 1954.

ADDITIONAL WORKS CONSULTED

Botkin, B.A., ed. *New York City Folklore.* New York: Random House, 1956.
Brown, Claude. *Manchild in the Promised Land.* New York: Macmillan, 1965.
Brown, Henry Collins. *Brownstone Fronts and Saratoga Trunks.* New York: E.P. Dutton, 1935.
Burnham, Alan, ed. *New York Landmarks.* Middletown, Conn.: Wesleyan University Press, 1963.
Delaney, Edmund T. *New York's Greenwich Village.* Barre, Mass.: Barre Publishers, 1965.
Dreiser, Theodore. *The Color of a Great City.* New York: Boni and Liveright, 1923.
Dunlap, George Arthur. *The City in the American Novel, 1789-1900: A Study of Contemporary Novels Portraying Conditions in New York, Philadelphia, and Boston.* New York: Russell and Russell, 1965.
Edmiston, Susan, and Linda D. Cirino. *Literary New York: A History and Guide.* Boston: Houghton Mifflin, 1976.
Ellis, Edward Robb. *The Epic of New York City.* New York: Coward-McCann, 1966.
Feininger, Andreas. *The Face of New York.* New York: Crown, 1954.
Fifty Years on Fifth, 1907-1957. Publication of the Fifth Avenue Association. New York: Fifth Avenue Association, 1957.
Goldstone, Harmon H. and Martha Dalrymple. *History Preserved—A Guide to New York City Landmarks and Historic Districts.* New York: Simon and Schuster, 1974.
Hapgood, Hutchins. *The Spirit of the Ghetto.* Ed. Moses Rischin. Cambridge: Belknap Press of Harvard University Press, 1967.
Harris, M.A. *A Negro Historical Tour of Manhattan.* New York: Greenwood Publishing, 1968.
Headley, Joel Tyler. *The Great Riots of New York, 1712-1873.* New York: Dover, 1971.
James, Henry. *The American Scene.* New York: Harper & Brothers, 1907.
Janvier, Thomas. *In Old New York.* New York: Harper & Brothers, 1894.
Jenkins, Stephen. *The Greatest Street in the World: Broadway.* New York: G.P. Putnam's Sons, 1911.
Johnson, James Weldon. *Black Manhattan.* New York: Alfred A. Knopf, 1930.
Kazin, Alfred. "The Writer and the City." *Harper's,* Dec. 1968, pp. 110-127.
Kranzler, George. *Williamsburg: A Jewish Community in Transition.* New York: Philipp Feldheim, Inc., 1961.
Landesman, Alter F. *Brownsville: The Birth, Development, and Passing of a Jewish Community in New York.* New York: Bloch Publishing Company, 1971.
Lewis, Emery. *Cue's New York.* New York: Duell, Sloan and Pearce, 1963.
Lockwood, Charles. *Manhattan Moves Uptown.* Boston: Houghton Mifflin, 1976.
Longstreet, Stephen. *City on Two Rivers: Profile of New York Yesterday and Today.* New York: Hawthorn Books, 1975.
Lyman, Susan Elizabeth. *The Story of New York: An Informal History of the City.* New York: Crown, 1964.
McKay, Claude. *Harlem: Negro Metropolis.* New York: E.P. Dutton, 1940.

Marcuse, Maxwell F. *This Was New York: A Nostalgic Picture of Gotham in the Gaslight Era.* New York: Carlton Press, 1965.

Maurice, Arthur Bartlett. *Fifth Avenue.* New York: Dodd, Mead, 1918.

———. *New York in Fiction.* New York: Dodd, Mead, 1901.

———. *The New York of the Novelists.* New York: Dodd Mead, 1916.

Mayer, Grace M. *Once Upon a City.* New York: Macmillan, 1958.

New York City Guide. Guilds' Committee for Federal Writers' Publications, Works Progress Administration. New York: Random House, 1939.

Osofsky, Gilbert. *Harlem: The Making of a Ghetto,* 2nd ed. New York: Harper & Row, 1971.

Riis, Jacob. *How the Other Half Lives—Studies Among the Tenements of New York.* New York: Charles Scribner's Sons, 1890.

Rischin, Moses. *The Promised City—New York's Jews, 1980-1914.* Cambridge: Harvard University Press, 1967.

Slocum, Rosalie and Ann Todd. *Key to New York.* New York: Harper & Brothers, 1939.

Smith, Matthew Hale. *Sunshine and Shadow in New York.* Hartford: J.B. Burr, 1868.

Still, Bayrd. *Mirror for Gotham: New York as Seen by Contemporaries from Dutch Days to the Present.* New York: New York University Press, 1956.

White, E.B. *Here Is New York.* New York: Harper & Brothers, 1949.

Wilson, Earl. *Earl Wilson's New York.* New York: Simon & Schuster, 1964.

Wilson, Rufus Rockwell, and Otile Erickson Wilson. *New York in Literature.* Elmira, New York: The Primavera Press, 1947.

INDEX